MINNESOTA NOTETAKING GUIDE

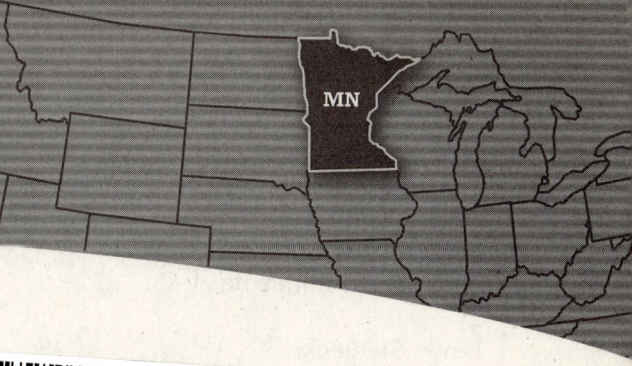

McDougal Littell
Math Course 1

Larson Boswell Kanold Stiff

McDougal Littell
A DIVISION OF HOUGHTON MIFFLIN COMPANY

Minnesota State Reviewers

Cindy Oistad
Hidden Oaks Middle School
Prior Lake, Minnesota

Tanya Siedlecki
Cambridge Middle School
Cambridge, Minnesota

Lynda Skalicky
Isanti Middle School
Isanti, Minnesota

Copyright ©2007 by McDougal Littell, a division of Houghton Mifflin Company.
All rights reserved.

Permission is hereby granted to teachers to reprint or photocopy in classroom quantities the pages or sheets in this work that carry a McDougal Littell copyright notice. These pages are designed to be reproduced by teachers for use in their classes with accompanying McDougal Littell material, provided each copy made shows the copyright notice. Such copies may not be sold and further distribution is expressly prohibited. Except as authorized above, prior written permission must be obtained from McDougal Littell, a division of Houghton Mifflin Company, to reproduce or transmit this work or portions thereof in any other form or by any other electronic or mechanical means, including any information storage or retrieval system, unless expressly permitted by federal copyright laws. Address inquiries to Manager, Rights and Permissions, McDougal Littell, P.O. Box 1667, Evanston, IL 60201.

ISBN 13: 978-0-618-80872-4
ISBN 10: 0-618-80872-8

3 4 5 6 7 8 9 —MJT— 11 10 09 08

A Note to the MINNESOTA STUDENT

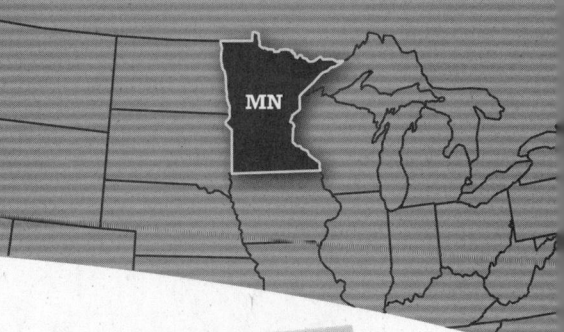

Dear Student,

This **Minnesota Notetaking Guide** contains a lesson-by-lesson framework that allows you to take notes and review the main concepts of each lesson in your math textbook. It has been written so that you will have an organized set of **study notes** providing a place to go for review and to prepare for quizzes and tests.

The Notetaking Guide:

- reinforces the goal of each lesson, reviews vocabulary, and provides a place for you to record key concepts.

- provides extra examples to use as a built-in set of practice problems.

- includes checkpoint questions to help reinforce the material that was taught.

The goal of this Notetaking Guide is to present math in a way that you can understand!

Information on the **Minnesota Mathematics Academic Standards** and the **Minnesota Comprehensive Assessment–Series II (MCA-II)** is covered in the Student Guide and includes:

- an explanation of what the standards mean.

- examples of the types of questions you will encounter on the **MCA-II**.

The **Additional Notetaking Lessons** present supplementary mathematical content. These lessons support state standards and align to the guidelines of the National Council of Teachers of Mathematics.

We wish you success in your math studies as you prepare yourself for a bright future. Think of this as a study guide to help you perform well on the **MCA-II!**

Minnesota Math Course 1
NOTETAKING GUIDE

Table of Contents Preview

This Minnesota Math Course 1 Notetaking Guide includes:

> A Student Guide to
  - Minnesota Mathematics Academic Standards
  - Minnesota Comprehensive Assessments–Series II (MCA-II)

> Lesson-by-Lesson Notetaking Support

> Additional Notetaking Lessons

Student Guide to the *Minnesota Mathematics Academic Standards* and *Minnesota Comprehensive Assessments–Series II (MCA-II)* ix

1 Number Sense and Algebraic Thinking

1.1	Whole Number Operations	1–4
1.2	Whole Number Estimation	5–7
1.3	Powers and Exponents	8–10
1.4	Order of Operations	11–13
1.5	Variables and Expressions	14–15
1.6	Equations and Mental Math	16–18
1.7	A Problem Solving Plan	19–22
	Words to Review	23–24

2 Measurement and Statistics

2.1	Measuring Length	25–28
2.2	Perimeter and Area	29–31
2.3	Scale Drawings	32–34
2.4	Frequency Tables and Line Plots	35–38
2.5	Bar Graphs	39–41
2.6	Coordinates and Line Graphs	42–44
2.7	Circle Graphs	45–47
2.8	Mean, Median, and Mode	48–50
	Words to Review	51–53

3 Decimal Addition and Subtraction

- 3.1 Decimals and Place Value 55–57
- 3.2 Measuring Metric Lengths 58–60
- 3.3 Ordering Decimals 61–63
- 3.4 Rounding Decimals 64–66
- 3.5 Decimal Estimation 67–69
- 3.6 Adding and Subtracting Decimals 70–72
- Words to Review 73

4 Decimal Multiplication and Division

- 4.1 Multiplying Decimals and Whole Numbers 75–77
- 4.2 The Distributive Property 78–80
- 4.3 Multiplying Decimals 81–84
- 4.4 Dividing by Whole Numbers 85–87
- 4.5 Multiplying and Dividing by Powers of Ten 88–90
- 4.6 Dividing by Decimals 91–93
- 4.7 Mass and Capacity 94–95
- 4.8 Changing Metric Units 96–98
- Words to Review 99

5 Number Patterns and Fractions

- 5.1 Prime Factorization 101–103
- 5.2 Greatest Common Factor 104–106
- 5.3 Equivalent Fractions 107–109
- 5.4 Least Common Multiple 110–112
- 5.5 Ordering Fractions 113–115
- 5.6 Mixed Numbers and Improper Fractions 116–118
- 5.7 Changing Decimals to Fractions 119–121
- 5.8 Changing Fractions to Decimals 122–124
- Words to Review 125–126

6 Addition and Subtraction of Fractions

- **6.1** Fraction Estimation 127–129
- **6.2** Fractions with Common Denominators 130–132
- **6.3** Fractions with Different Denominators 133–135
- **6.4** Adding and Subtracting Mixed Numbers 136–139
- **6.5** Subtracting Mixed Numbers by Renaming 140–142
- **6.6** Measures of Time 143–145
- Words to Review 146

7 Multiplication and Division of Fractions

- **7.1** Multiplying Fractions with Whole Numbers 147–149
- **7.2** Multiplying Fractions 150–153
- **7.3** Multiplying Mixed Numbers 154–156
- **7.4** Dividing Fractions 157–159
- **7.5** Dividing Mixed Numbers 160–162
- **7.6** Weight and Capacity in Customary Units 163–165
- **7.7** Changing Customary Units 166–168
- Words to Review 169

8 Ratio, Proportion, and Percent

- **8.1** Ratios 171–173
- **8.2** Rates 174–176
- **8.3** Solving Proportions 177–180
- **8.4** Proportions and Scale Drawings 181–183
- **8.5** Understanding Percent 184–186
- **8.6** Percents, Decimals, and Fractions 187–190
- **8.7** Finding a Percent of a Number 191–193
- Words to Review 194

9 Geometric Figures

9.1	Introduction to Geometry	195–197
9.2	Angles	198–200
9.3	Classifying Angles	201–203
9.4	Classifying Triangles	204–206
9.5	Classifying Quadrilaterals	207–209
9.6	Polygons	210–212
9.7	Congruent and Similar Figures	213–215
9.8	Line Symmetry	216–218
	Words to Review	219–221

10 Geometry and Measurement

10.1	Area of a Parallelogram	223–225
10.2	Area of a Triangle	226–228
10.3	Circumference of a Circle	229–232
10.4	Area of a Circle	233–235
10.5	Solid Figures	236–238
10.6	Surface Area of a Prism	239–241
10.7	Volume of a Prism	242–244
	Words to Review	245–247

11 Integers

11.1	Comparing Integers	249–251
11.2	Adding Integers	252–254
11.3	Subtracting Integers	255–257
11.4	Multiplying Integers	258–259
11.5	Dividing Integers	260–261
11.6	Translations in a Coordinate Plane	262–264
11.7	Reflections and Rotations	265–266
	Words to Review	267–268

12 Equations and Functions

12.1	Writing Expressions and Equations	269–271
12.2	Solving Addition Equations	272–273
12.3	Solving Subtraction Equations	274–275
12.4	Solving Multiplication and Division Equations	276–277
12.5	Functions	278–280
12.6	Graphing Functions	281–284
	Words to Review	285

13 Probability and Statistics

13.1	Introduction to Probability	287–290
13.2	Finding Outcomes	291–295
13.3	Probability of Independent Events	296–298
13.4	Misleading Statistics	299–301
13.5	Stem-and-Leaf Plots	302–304
13.6	Box-and-Whisker Plots	305–307
13.7	Choosing an Appropriate Data Display	308–310
	Words to Review	311–312

Additional Notetaking Lessons

These Additional Lessons have been written to provide enrichment and challenge opportunities and to support state standards.

A	Estimation and Precision of Measurement	A1–A3
B	Metric/Customary Conversions	A4–A6
C	Expressing Place Value Using Exponents	A7–A9
D	Solving Two-Step Equations	A10–A11
E	Slope	A12–A13
F	Coordinate Geometry and Geometric Figures	A14–A17
G	Polygons and Angles	A18–A19
H	Sketching Solids	A20–A22
I	Vertex-Edge Graphs, Circuits, Networks, and Routing	A23–A26
J	Introduction to Recursive Functions for Sequences	A27–A29
K	Histograms	A30–A31
L	Stem-and-Leaf Plots	A32–A34
M	Misleading Data Displays	A35–A37
N	Designing and Conducting an Investigation	A38–A41
O	Experimental vs. Observational Study	A42–A46
P	Inductive and Deductive Reasoning	A47–A49

MINNESOTA STUDENT GUIDE

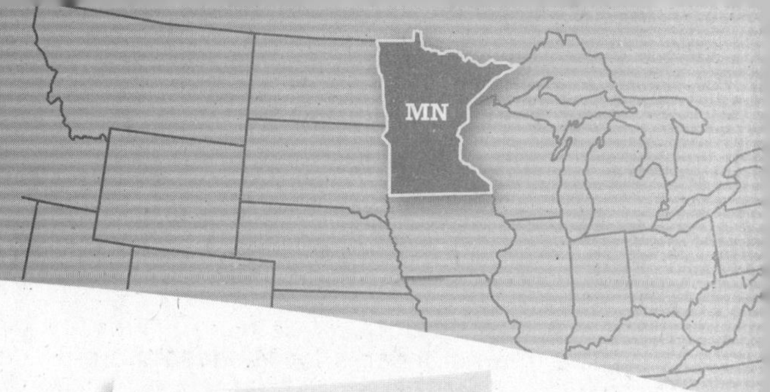

Did you know . . .

. . . that baseball and math standards have some things in common?

. . . and, that your math standards have been written as a commitment to you, the Minnesota student?

So . . .

. . . "What are Math Standards and what do they have in common with baseball?"

Compare the standards to a set of rules that must be followed in a sport event. For example, in a baseball game, the batter must move from first base to second base and then third base before proceeding to the home plate to score a run. Learning this rule enables the team to win the game.

Without the knowledge of how a baseball game is played, the team will not have the fundamental concepts to compete.

Math standards, like the rules in baseball, help you focus on a common foundation of mathematical concepts that you will use in everyday life and later in the workplace.

And . . .

. . . How will learning the Minnesota Mathematics Academic Standards make a difference for you, the student?

It is important to learn material that is closely aligned to the math standards because they are what you will be tested on when it comes time to take your state test.

The standards have been written as a commitment to you, the student, to help you focus on the proper content to achieve both depth and understanding of mathematical knowledge.

How Will You Learn the Minnesota Mathematics Academic Standards?

The math standards for **Minnesota** are divided into the following strands:

I. Mathematical Reasoning
II. Number Sense, Computation, and Operations
III. Patterns, Functions, and Algebra
IV. Data Analysis, Statistics, and Probability
V. Spatial Sense, Geometry, and Measurement

Each strand is divided into sub-strands with descriptive standards and then further broken down into benchmarks. This organization guides your teacher through the mathematical content that needs to be covered to help you be successful on the **MCA-II**.

MCA-II stands for the **Minnesota Comprehensive Assessments–Series II**. It is given in the spring to evaluate your knowledge of the **Minnesota Mathematics Academic Standards**. Your teacher will work with you throughout the year to help you prepare and be successful on this test.

> Minnesota uses a special system to identify the strands, sub-strands, and benchmarks. Here is an example of a particular strand, sub-strand, and benchmark identifier.

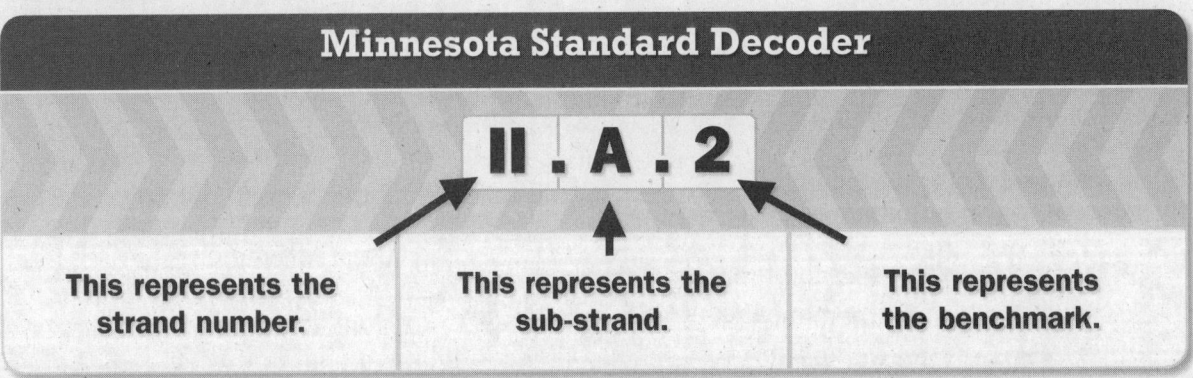

Minnesota Standard Decoder

II . A . 2

This represents the strand number. | This represents the sub-strand. | This represents the benchmark.

So, when you see II.A.2, you know it belongs to:

Strand II: Number Sense, Computation, and Operations

Sub-Strand A: Number Sense

Standard Description: Use positive and negative rational numbers, represented in a variety of ways, to quantify information and to solve real-world and mathematical problems.

Benchmark 2: Use rounding and estimation with integers, decimals, and fractions to solve real-world and mathematical problems

> The information that follows highlights the strands, the sub-strands, the standard descriptions, and the benchmarks, what they mean to you, and examples of what multiple-choice questions might look like on the MCA-II.

II. Number Sense, Computation, and Operations

Sub-Strands (and Standards):

A. Number Sense
Use positive and negative rational numbers, represented in a variety of ways, to quantify information and to solve real-world and mathematical problems.

B. Computation and Operation
Compute fluently and make reasonable estimates with positive and negative rational numbers in real-world and mathematical problems. Understand the meanings of arithmetic operations and factorization, and how they relate to one another. Appropriately use calculators and other technologies to solve problems.

What It Means To You

Understanding numbers is the basis for all math. Studying this standard you will learn how to represent very large or very small numbers, what number system they belong to, and whether a problem needs a rough estimate or an exact answer.

Here is what a question might look like on the MCA-II:

II.A.2 Use rounding and estimation with integers, decimals, and fractions to solve real-world and mathematical problems.

A sports utility vehicle (SUV) and the boat it is towing weigh a total of 7321.5 pounds. After unloading the boat, the vehicle weighs 6208.9 pounds. How much does the boat weigh to the nearest pound?

A. 1112 pounds
B. 1113 pounds
C. 13,530 pounds
D. 13,531 pounds

Solution

Write a verbal model.

Weight of boat = Weight of SUV and boat − Weight of SUV

= 7321.5 − 6208.9

= 1112.6

Since the digit in the tenths place is greater than 5, you round 1112.6 pounds up to 1113 pounds. So, the correct answer is B.

III. Patterns, Functions, and Algebra

Sub-Strands (and Standards):

A. Patterns and Functions
Demonstrate understanding of the rectangular coordinate system.

B. Algebra (Algebraic Thinking)
Apply arithmetic operations in the correct order to simplify and evaluate numeric expressions in real-world and mathematical problems.

What It Means To You

Algebra is the branch of mathematics in which symbols, usually letters, are used to represent numbers and quantities. Studying algebra will help you notice patterns, represent relationships, and analyze how things change.

Here is what a question might look like on the MCA-II:

III.B.1 Apply the correct order of operations including addition, subtraction, multiplication, division and grouping symbols to simplify and evaluate numeric expressions.

Jose weighs $80\frac{1}{2}$ pounds. His older brother, Marco, weighs $32\frac{1}{4}$ pounds more than Jose. Their little brother, Horatio, weighs $\frac{1}{3}$ of Marco's weight. Which expression gives Horatio's weight?

A. $80\frac{1}{2} + 32\frac{1}{4} - \frac{1}{3}$

B. $\left(80\frac{1}{2} + 32\frac{1}{4}\right) \times \frac{1}{3}$

C. $\frac{1}{3} \div \left(80\frac{1}{2} + 32\frac{1}{4}\right)$

D. $\left(80\frac{1}{2} + 32\frac{1}{4}\right) \div \frac{1}{3}$

Solution

You must first find Marco's weight by adding $32\frac{1}{4}$ to Jose's weight. The expression is

$$80\frac{1}{2} + 32\frac{1}{4}$$

To find Horatio's weight, you must multiply Marco's weight by $\frac{1}{3}$. The expression is

$$\left(80\frac{1}{2} + 32\frac{1}{4}\right) \times \frac{1}{3}.$$

The correct answer is B.

Ⓐ　Ⓑ　Ⓒ　Ⓓ

xiv Math Course 1 Notetaking Guide • Student Guide to the Standards

IV. Data Analysis, Statistics, and Probability

Sub-Strands (and Standards):

A. Data and Statistics
Represent data and use various measures associated with data to draw conclusions and identify trends.

B. Probability
Calculate and express probabilities numerically, and apply probability concepts to solve real-world and mathematical problems.

What It Means To You

Data analysis involves processing information to solve problems that come up in work and in life. Probability is the study of the likelihood that a given event will occur. Working within this standard will give you the ability to analyze information, make predictions, and then draw conclusions based on the data.

Here is what a question might look like on the MCA-II:

IV.B.2 Represent all possible outcomes for a probability problem with tables, grids, and tree diagrams to calculate probabilities and draw conclusions from the results.

The spinner below is divided into 4 equal sections. You spin the spinner twice. What is the probability that the sum of the 2 spins is less than 5?

A. $\frac{1}{4}$

B. $\frac{3}{8}$

C. $\frac{1}{2}$

D. 1

Solution

Make a list of all the possible pairs of numbers that you can spin. Then count the number of pairs that have a sum less than 5.

(1, 1) (2, 1) (3, 1) (4, 1)
(1, 2) (2, 2) (3, 2) (4, 2)
(1, 3) (2, 3) (3, 3) (4, 3)
(1, 4) (2, 4) (3, 4) (4, 4)

There are 6 pairs that have a sum less than 5.

The probability is $\frac{6}{16}$ or $\frac{3}{8}$, so the correct answer is B.

Ⓐ **Ⓑ** Ⓒ Ⓓ

V. Spatial Sense, Geometry, and Measurement

Sub-Strands (and Standards):

A. Spatial Sense
Recognize the relationship between different representations of two- and three-dimensional shapes. Understand the effect of various transformations.

B. Geometry
Identify a variety of simple geometric figures by name, calculate various quantities associated with them, and use appropriate tools to draw them.

C. Measurement
Make calculations of time, length, area and volume within standard measuring systems, using good judgment in choice of units.

What It Means To You

Geometry is the study of points, lines, angles, surfaces, and solids. Studying spatial relationships gives us a visual way to understand the properties of geometric shapes. Measurement gives a numerical value to a characteristic of an object, such as the length of a football field. Measurement is important because of all the ways we use it in everyday life.

Here is what questions might look like on the MCA-II:

V.C.1 Solve problems requiring conversion of units within the U.S. customary system, and within the metric system.

Mia uses a square piece of construction paper as a base to make a photo collage of her summer vacation. The side length of the construction paper is 305 mm. What is the area of the construction paper in square centimeters?

A. 61 cm^2
B. 122 cm^2
C. 930.25 cm^2
D. 93025 cm^2

Solution for Question 1

Convert 305 millimeters to centimeters

$305 \text{ mm} \div 10 = 30.5 \text{ cm}$

$A = s^2$ Formula for the area of a square

$= (30.5)^2$ Substitute 30.5 for s.

$= 930.25$ Multiply.

The area of the construction paper is 930.25 square centimeters. The correct answer is C.

Ⓐ   Ⓑ   **Ⓒ**   Ⓓ

A sports bottle holds 372 milliliters of water. If 7 soccer players each have their own bottle, how many liters of water will be needed to fill all the bottles?

A. 2.604 L
B. 26.04 L
C. 260.4 L
D. 2604 L

Solution for Question 2

Convert 372 milliliters to liters.

$372 \text{ mL} \div 1000 = 0.372 \text{ L}$

There are 7 bottles that each holds 0.372 liters of water.

$0.372 \text{ L} \times 7 = 2.604 \text{ L}$

The correct answer is A.

Ⓐ   Ⓑ   Ⓒ   Ⓓ

Whole Number Operations

Goal: Add, subtract, multiply, and divide whole numbers.

Vocabulary Review

Whole number: _____

Sum: _____

Difference: _____

Product: _____

Quotient: _____

EXAMPLE 1 Adding Whole Numbers

To find the sum 867 + 54, you line up the numbers on the _____ place. Next you add the _____, then the _____, then the _____.

```
  1 1
  867
+  54
```

_____ ← _____ + _____ = _____. Regroup the _____ one(s) as _____ ten(s) and _____ one(s).

_____ + _____ + _____ = _____. Regroup _____ ten(s) as _____ hundred(s) and _____ ten(s).

Review: If you need help with place value and regrouping, see pages 737 and 741 of your textbook.

Lesson 1.1 Whole Number Operations | **1**

EXAMPLE 2 Subtracting Whole Numbers

To find the difference of 342 and 58, you line up the numbers on the ⬚ place. Next you subtract the ⬚, then the ⬚, and so on.

```
  342
−  58
─────
  ⬚
```

You need more ones to subtract ⬚, so ⬚.

342 = ⬚ + ⬚ + ⬚.

> Check your answer to a subtraction problem by adding. In Example 2, if you add your answer to 58, you should get 342.

Guided Practice Find the sum or difference.

1. 83 + 49	2. 226 + 75	3. 94 − 56	4. 800 − 136

EXAMPLE 3 Multiplying Whole Numbers

Car Rental It costs $23 to rent a car for one day. How much does it cost to rent a car for 14 days?

Solution You need to find the product 23 × 14.

```
   23
×  14
─────
   ⬚
   ⬚
─────
   ⬚
```

First multiply ⬚ by the ones' digit, ⬚.

Then multiply ⬚ by the tens' digit, ⬚.

Add the partial products.

Answer: It will cost $⬚ to rent a car for 14 days.

EXAMPLE 4 Dividing Whole Numbers

To find the quotient of 481 and 9, you use long division. The dividend is ⬚ and the divisor is ⬚.

```
     ⬚ R ⬚
9)481
   ⬚
  ───
    ⬚
    ⬚
  ───
    ⬚
```

Divide ⬚ by ⬚, because ⬚ is more than 4.

Multiply: ⬚ × ⬚ = ⬚.

Subtract: ⬚ − ⬚ = ⬚. Bring down the ⬚.

Repeat the process.

The remainder is ⬚.

Guided Practice Find the product or quotient.

5. 35 × 28	6. 160 × 18	7. 835 ÷ 7	8. 523 ÷ 13

EXAMPLE 5 **Interpreting Remainders**

Remodeling You plan to retile your bathroom wall. You need a total of 145 tiles. The tiles come in boxes of 8. How many boxes do you need to buy?

Solution

Step 1 You need to divide to find the number times 8 tiles is contained in ▢ tiles.

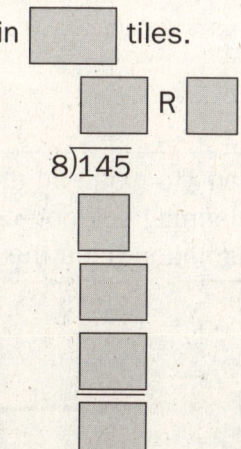

Step 2 Interpret the remainder in the quotient ▢ R ▢.

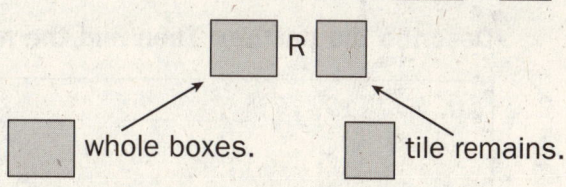

Answer: You cannot complete the bathroom wall without the ▢ remaining tile, so you need to round up to ▢. You need to buy ▢ boxes.

Lesson 1.1 Whole Number Operations

EXAMPLE 6 Finding Patterns

Video Games In your favorite video game, you pass Level 1 after earning 150 points, Level 2 after earning 250 points, Level 3 after earning 350 points, and Level 4 after earning 450 points. Describe the pattern. If this pattern continues, find the number of points needed to pass Levels 5 and 6.

Solution

Look to see how each number is related to the preceding number. The number of points for each level is ☐ more than the preceding level.

150   250   350   450   ☐   ☐

Answer: To pass Level 5 you need ☐ points and to pass Level 6 you need ☐ points.

Guided Practice

9. Cleaning A window cleaner plans to clean all the windows at an office building. One bucket of cleaning solution cleans 25 windows. How many buckets of cleaning solution does the window cleaner need to clean 130 windows?

Describe the pattern. Then find the next two numbers.

10. 2, 7, 12, 17, _?_, _?_	**11.** 56, 52, 48, 44, _?_, _?_
12. 2, 6, 18, 54, _?_, _?_	**13.** 243, 81, 27, 9, _?_, _?_

LESSON 1.2

Whole Number Estimation

Goal: Round to estimate with whole numbers.

Vocabulary

Leading digit: ______

Compatible numbers: ______

EXAMPLE 1 Estimating Sums and Differences

Comedy Club Tickets A comedy club sold 78 tickets for the 7 P.M. performance and 102 tickets for the 9 P.M. performance.

a. Estimate how many tickets the club sold altogether.

b. The next night, the club sold a total of 109 tickets for the 7 P.M. performance. Estimate the difference in the number of tickets for the 7 P.M. performance each night.

Solution

a. To estimate the total number of tickets sold, round the number of tickets sold for each performance to the same place value. Then add.

$$\begin{array}{r} 78 \\ +\ 102 \\ \hline \end{array} \quad \xrightarrow{\text{Round each number to the nearest ____.}} \quad \begin{array}{r} ____ \\ +\ ____ \\ \hline ____ \end{array}$$

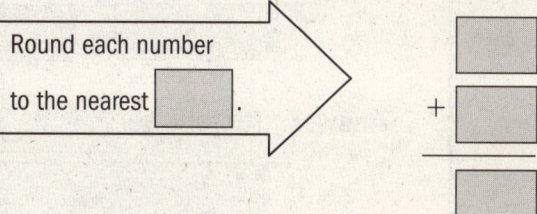

By rounding to the nearest ten, you get a closer estimate of the actual sum than you would get if you rounded to the nearest hundred.

Answer: The club sold about ______ tickets altogether.

b. To estimate the difference in the number of tickets sold for the 7 P.M. performance each night, round the number of tickets sold for each performance to the same place value. Then subtract.

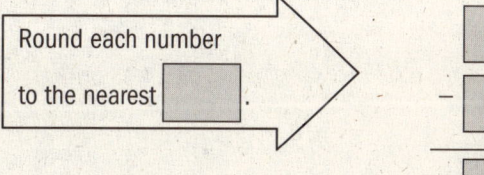

$$\begin{array}{r} 109 \\ -\ \ 78 \\ \hline \end{array} \quad \xrightarrow{\text{Round each number to the nearest ____.}} \quad \begin{array}{r} ____ \\ -\ ____ \\ \hline ____ \end{array}$$

Answer: The club sold about ______ more tickets the next night.

Guided Practice Estimate the sum or difference.

1. 37 + 92	2. 43 + 279	3. 521 + 584
4. 41 − 16	5. 713 − 34	6. 907 − 244

EXAMPLE 2 Estimating Products

Estimate to tell whether the given answer is reasonable.

a. 134 × 16; 2144

☐ × ☐ = ☐   Round both numbers to ☐.

Answer: The answer ☐ reasonable because ☐.

b. 2361 × 6; 8266

☐ × ☐ = ☐   Round ☐ to its leading digit.

Answer: The answer ☐ reasonable because ☐.

Use an estimate when you do not need an exact answer or when you need to check whether an answer is reasonable.

6 | Chapter 1 Notetaking Guide

EXAMPLE 3 Standardized Test Practice

The attendance at a high school basketball game is 635 people. A total of 79 people can sit in a section of the gym. About how many sections of the gym are needed to seat the people?

A 5   **B** 6   **C** 8   **D** 11

Solution

The symbol ≈ can be read "is about equal to."

635 ÷ 79 ≈ ☐ ÷ ☐   Round the ☐ to its leading digit.

≈ ☐ ÷ ☐   Replace the ☐ with a close number that is compatible with ☐.

= ☐   Divide. The quotient 635 ÷ 79 is about ☐.

Answer: About ☐ sections of the gym are needed to seat the people.

The correct answer is ☐.   **A** **B** **C** **D**

Guided Practice Estimate the product or quotient.

7. 23 × 77	8. 784 × 42	9. 292 × 6
10. 133 ÷ 17	11. 311 ÷ 48	12. 896 ÷ 9

Lesson 1.2 Whole Number Estimation

Powers and Exponents

Goal: Find values of powers.

Vocabulary

Factor:

Power:

Base:

Exponent:

Powers, Bases, and Exponents

The base of a power is the [ ] and the exponent is the [ ].

$9^4 = 9 \times 9 \times 9 \times 9$

[ ]   There are [ ] factors.

EXAMPLE 1 Writing a Power

Metric System In the metric system of measurement, there are $1{,}000{,}000 = 10 \times 10 \times 10 \times 10 \times 10 \times 10$ millimeters in one kilometer. Write the number of millimeters in one kilometer as a power.

$1{,}000{,}000 = 10 \times 10 \times 10 \times 10 \times 10 \times 10$ There are [ ] factors.

$= $ [ ]

Answer: There are [ ] millimeters in one kilometer.

8 | Chapter 1 Notetaking Guide

Guided Practice Write the product as a power.

1. 3 × 3 × 3 × 3 × 3 × 3 × 3	**2.** 5 × 5 × 5 × 5	**3.** 40 × 40 × 40

EXAMPLE 2 Finding the Value of a Power

a. Find the value of nine squared.

☐ = ☐   Write ☐ as a factor ☐ times.

  = ☐   Multiply.

b. Find the value of three to the fourth power.

☐ = ☐   Write ☐ as a factor ☐ times.

  = ☐   Multiply.

EXAMPLE 3 Powers in Real-World Problems

Movie Theaters A movie theater has 12 rows of seats. In each row there are 12 seats. How many seats are in the movie theater altogether?

Solution

☐ × ☐ = ☐ = ☐

  Number of seats in one row   Number of rows

In some cases, it may be helpful to draw a diagram so you can visualize the problem.

Answer: There are ☐ seats in the movie theater.

Guided Practice Write the power as a product. Then find the value.

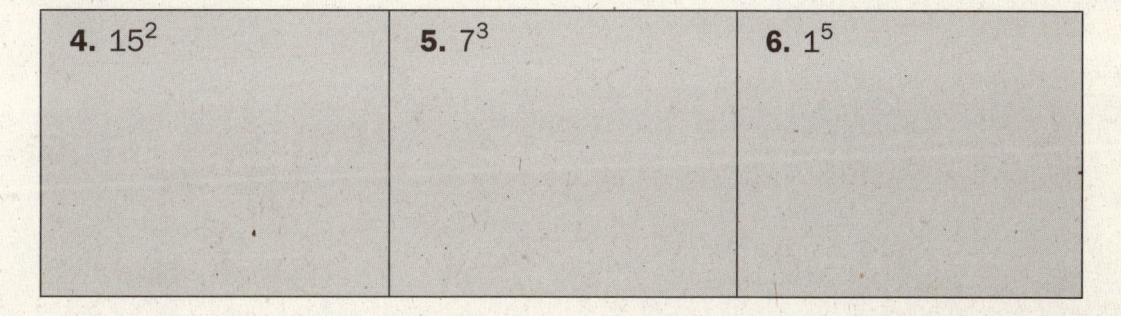

4. 15^2	**5.** 7^3	**6.** 1^5

Lesson 1.3 Powers and Exponents

7. 10^4

8. 8 cubed

9. 2 to the sixth power

Order of Operations

Goal: Evaluate expressions using the order of operations.

Vocabulary

Numerical expression: _____

Grouping symbols: _____

Evaluate: _____

Order of operations: _____

Order of Operations

1. Evaluate _____ .
2. Evaluate _____ .
3. _____ and _____ from left to right.
4. _____ and _____ from left to right.

EXAMPLE 1 Using the Order of Operations

WATCH OUT!
In part (a) of Example 1, divide *before* multiplying because the division is on the left. In part (b), subtract *before* adding because the subtraction is on the left.

a. $16 \div 8 \times 7 =$ _____   First _____ .
   $=$ _____   Then _____ .

b. $21 - 13 + 4 =$ _____   First _____ .
   $=$ _____   Then _____ .

c. $15 + 8 \div 4 - 9 =$ _____   First _____ .
   $=$ _____   Next _____ .
   $=$ _____   Then _____ .

Lesson 1.4 Order of Operations 11

EXAMPLE 2 **Powers and Grouping Symbols**

a. $20 - 4^2 = $ ☐   First ☐.
   $= $ ☐   Then ☐.

b. $(5 + 2) \times 6 = $ ☐   First ☐.
   $= $ ☐   Then ☐.

c. $\dfrac{3 + 9}{7 - 4} = $ ☐   First evaluate ☐.
   $= $ ☐   Then ☐.

Guided Practice Evaluate the expression.

1. $6 + 4 - 7$	2. $14 - 2 \times 3$	3. $32 - 3 \times 5 + 8$
4. $42 - 5^2$	5. $10 \times (4 + 5)$	6. $(15 - 9) \times 4 + 3$
7. $8 + 2 \times 7^2$	8. $\dfrac{21 - 9}{4}$	9. $\dfrac{13 + 2}{10 - 7}$

EXAMPLE 3 Standardized Test Practice

Ski Trip You and four of your family members are planning a ski vacation during an upcoming 3-day weekend. The ski rental is $14 each day for adult skis and $12 each day for junior skis. Your family needs to rent 3 pairs of junior skis and 2 pairs of adult skis. How much will the ski rental cost for the entire weekend?

- **A** $64
- **B** $192
- **C** $6048
- **D** $9072

Solution

1. ▢ to find the cost of adult skis for three days.

   ▢ adults · $ ▢ per adult per day ▢ · ▢ days = $ ▢

2. ▢ to find the cost of junior skis for three days.

   ▢ juniors · $ ▢ per junior per day ▢ · ▢ days = $ ▢

3. ▢ the adult cost and the junior cost to find the total cost.

   $ ▢ ▢ $ ▢ = $ ▢

Answer: The total cost for ski rental is $ ▢ .

The correct answer is ▢ .   Ⓐ Ⓑ Ⓒ Ⓓ

Guided Practice Use the situation in Example 3.

10. If 3 more adults decide to go on the trip, what will be the new total cost for ski rental?

11. If the cost of a junior rental goes down by $1, what will be the new total cost for the original group?

Lesson 1.4 Order of Operations **13**

Lesson 1.5 Variables and Expressions

Goal: Evaluate expressions that involve variables.

Vocabulary

Variable: _____

Variable expression: _____

EXAMPLE 1 Evaluating Expressions

a. Evaluate $12 - n$, when $n = 5$.

$12 - n = $ ☐   Substitute ☐ for ☐.

$= $ ☐   Subtract.

b. Evaluate $x \div 6$, when $x = 72$.

$x \div 6 = $ ☐   Substitute ☐ for ☐.

$= $ ☐   Divide.

Guided Practice Evaluate the expression.

1. $t + 13$, when $t = 8$	2. $17 - a$, when $a = 12$
3. $y - 4$, when $y = 11$	4. $s \div 5$, when $s = 40$

14 | Chapter 1 Notetaking Guide

EXAMPLE 2 Solve a Multi-Step Problem

Bowling A bowling alley charges $1 for shoe rental and $4 for each game. The expression $4g + 1$ can be used to find the total cost of playing g games at the bowling alley. Find the total cost of playing 3, 4, and 5 games.

1. Choose values for g (number of games).
2. Substitute for g in the expression $4g + 1$.
3. Evaluate the expressions to find the total costs of the games.

Answer: It costs $ ☐ to play three games. It costs $ ☐ to play four games. It costs $ ☐ to play five games.

EXAMPLE 3 Expressions with Two Variables

Evaluate the expression when $x = 3$ and $y = 7$.

a. $x + y =$ ☐   Substitute ☐ for ☐ and ☐ for ☐.
       $=$ ☐   Add.

b. $x^2 - y =$ ☐   Substitute ☐ for ☐ and ☐ for ☐.
         $=$ ☐   Evaluate the power.
         $=$ ☐   Subtract.

You may want to include part (b) in your notebook as a reminder to use the order of operations when evaluating a variable expression.

Guided Practice Evaluate the expression when $p = 12$ and $q = 5$.

5. $4p$	6. $15q$	7. $3q + 2$	8. $38 - 2p$
9. $p - q$	10. $p + 6q$	11. $50 - q^2$	12. $p + 8 - q$

Lesson 1.5 Variables and Expressions | 15

Equations and Mental Math

Goal: Solve equations using mental math.

Vocabulary

Equation:

Solution:

Solve:

EXAMPLE 1 Guess, Check, and Revise

Email You have a 4-digit password for your email account. The first three digits are 2, 3, and 7. The product of all the digits is 336. What is the last digit?

Solution

To answer this question, you can use the problem solving strategy *guess, check,* and *revise*.

When using guess, check, and revise, use the information given in the problem to make an educated first guess.

1. Try the digit 5, which is halfway between 1 and 9.

   This product is [ ] 336.

2. Try the digit 9, which is greater than 5.

   This product is [ ] 336.

3. Try the digit 8, which is less than 9.

   This product is [ ] 336.

Answer: The last digit is [ ].

EXAMPLE 2 Checking a Possible Solution

Tell whether the given number is a solution of the equation.

a. $8m = 82$; 9

☐ $\stackrel{?}{=}$ ☐

☐ ☐ ☐

Answer: 9 ☐ a solution.

b. $x - 7 = 18$; 25

☐ $\stackrel{?}{=}$ ☐

☐ ☐ ☐

Answer: 25 ☐ a solution.

Properties of 0 and 1

Identity Property of Addition   The sum of any number and 0 is ☐.

Multiplication Property of 0   The product of any number and 0 is ☐.

Identity Property of Multiplication   The product of any number and 1 is ☐.

EXAMPLE 3 Using Mental Math to Solve Equations

In your notes for this lesson, you may want to include examples showing equations rewritten as questions.

Equation → Question → Solution → Check

a. $y - 6 = 14$ ☐ minus ☐ equals ☐ ?   ☐   ☐

b. $15r = 45$ ☐ times ☐ equals ☐ ?   ☐   ☐

c. $b \div 7 = 8$ ☐ divided by ☐ equals ☐ ?   ☐   ☐

d. $z + 9 = 9$ ☐   ☐   ☐

e. $12 \cdot c = 12$ ☐   ☐   ☐

Lesson 1.6   Equations and Mental Math   17

Guided Practice Solve the equation using mental math.

1. $n + 13 = 22$	2. $17x = 17$	3. $t - 9 = 27$
4. $6p = 42$	5. $34 \div d = 2$	6. $3s = 0$

EXAMPLE 4 Solving Problems Using Mental Math

Baseball Cards Together, you and a friend have 250 baseball cards. You have 178 baseball cards. Use mental math to solve the equation $c + 178 = 250$ to find the number of cards c your friend has.

Solution

Think of the equation as a question.

Equation

↓

Question ?

↓

Solution .

Answer: Your friend has ☐ baseball cards.

18 | Chapter 1 Notetaking Guide

1.7 A Problem Solving Plan

Goal: Use a problem solving plan.

Vocabulary

Verbal model:

EXAMPLE 1 Understanding and Planning

Book Sales A discount bookstore sells paperback books for $5 each and hardcover books for $9 each. At the end of the day, the store has sold 325 paperback books and 175 hardcover books. How much money did the bookstore make by the end of the day?

Solution

To solve the problem, first make sure you understand the problem. Then make a plan for solving the problem.

Read and Understand

What do you know?

What do you want to find out?

Make a Plan

How can you relate what you know to what you want to find out?
Write a *verbal model* to describe how the values in this problem are related.

☐ = ☐ + ☐

Lesson 1.7 A Problem Solving Plan | 19

Guided Practice Use the information from Example 1.

1. How can you figure out how much money was made from paperback books?

2. How can you figure out how much money was made from hardcover books?

EXAMPLE 2 Solving and Looking Back

Book Sales To solve the problem from Example 1 about bookstore sales, you need to carry out your plan from Example 1 and then check the answer.

Solve the Problem
Write a verbal model to relate the amount of money made by the end of the day to the amount of money made from selling each kind of book. Then substitute values into the verbal model.

☐ = ☐ + ☐

☐ = ☐ + ☐

☐ = ☐ + ☐

☐ = ☐

Answer: The bookstore made $ ☐ by the end of the day.

Look Back
Make sure your answer is reasonable. Estimate the amount of money made by the end of the day. This number should be close to your answer.

☐ + ☐ ≈ ☐ + ☐

= ☐ + ☐

= ☐ ✓

Guided Practice Use Example 2 above.

3. If hardcover books sold for $10 each instead of $9 each, how much would the store have made by the end of the day?

A Problem Solving Plan

1. Read and Understand

2. Make a Plan

3. Solve the Problem

4. Look Back

EXAMPLE 3 **Draw a Diagram**

Tennis You and a friend are going to play tennis at the courts near your homes. You leave your house and walk 4 blocks north and then 2 blocks east to your friend's house. From your friend's house, you get to the courts by walking 1 block south and 3 blocks east. How many blocks do you have to walk to get back to your house from the tennis courts?

Here is a list of some common problem solving strategies.
Guess, Check, and Revise
Draw a Diagram
Perform an Experiment
Make a List
Work Backward
Look for a Pattern
Solve a Simpler Problem
Make a Model
Break into Parts
Use an Equation
Act It Out

Solution

Read and Understand

What do you know and what do you want to find out?

Make a Plan

Draw a diagram to show ⬚ ⬚. Use the diagram to solve the problem.

Solve the Problem

Draw the path on a piece of graph paper.

Answer: From the diagram, you can see that you will have to walk ⬚ blocks to get home.

Look Back

You walked ⬚ blocks to get to the tennis courts from your house via your friend's house. Because ⬚, the answer is reasonable.

Lesson 1.7 A Problem Solving Plan 21

Guided Practice The grid shows the locations of different places in your neighborhood.

4. You leave home to drop off some books at the library, stop at the store for some items, and then return home. How many blocks do you walk during the trip?

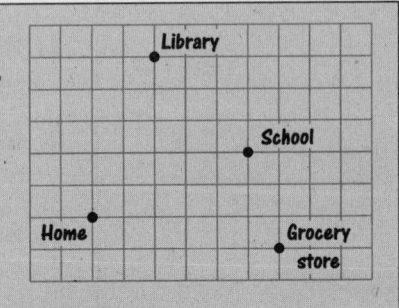

5. Write directions for your friend to get from school to your house.

6. If you walk to and from school every day, how many blocks do you walk between Monday and Friday?

Chapter 1 Words to Review

Give an example of the vocabulary word.

Leading digit

Compatible numbers

Factor

Power

Base

Exponent

Numerical expression

Grouping symbols

Evaluate

Order of operations

Variable

Variable expression

Equation

Solution

Solve

Verbal model

Review your notes and Chapter 1 by using the Chapter Review on pages 47–50 of your textbook.

LESSON 2.1

Measuring Lengths

Goal: Measure length using customary and metric units.

Vocabulary

Inch:

Foot:

Yard:

Mile:

Millimeter:

Centimeter:

Meter:

Kilometer:

EXAMPLE 1 **Using Customary Units of Length**

Find the length of the leaf to the nearest inch.

Line up one end of the leaf at the mark for ☐.

The other end is between the ☐ and ☐ marks and is closer to ☐ inches.

Answer: The leaf is about ☐ long.

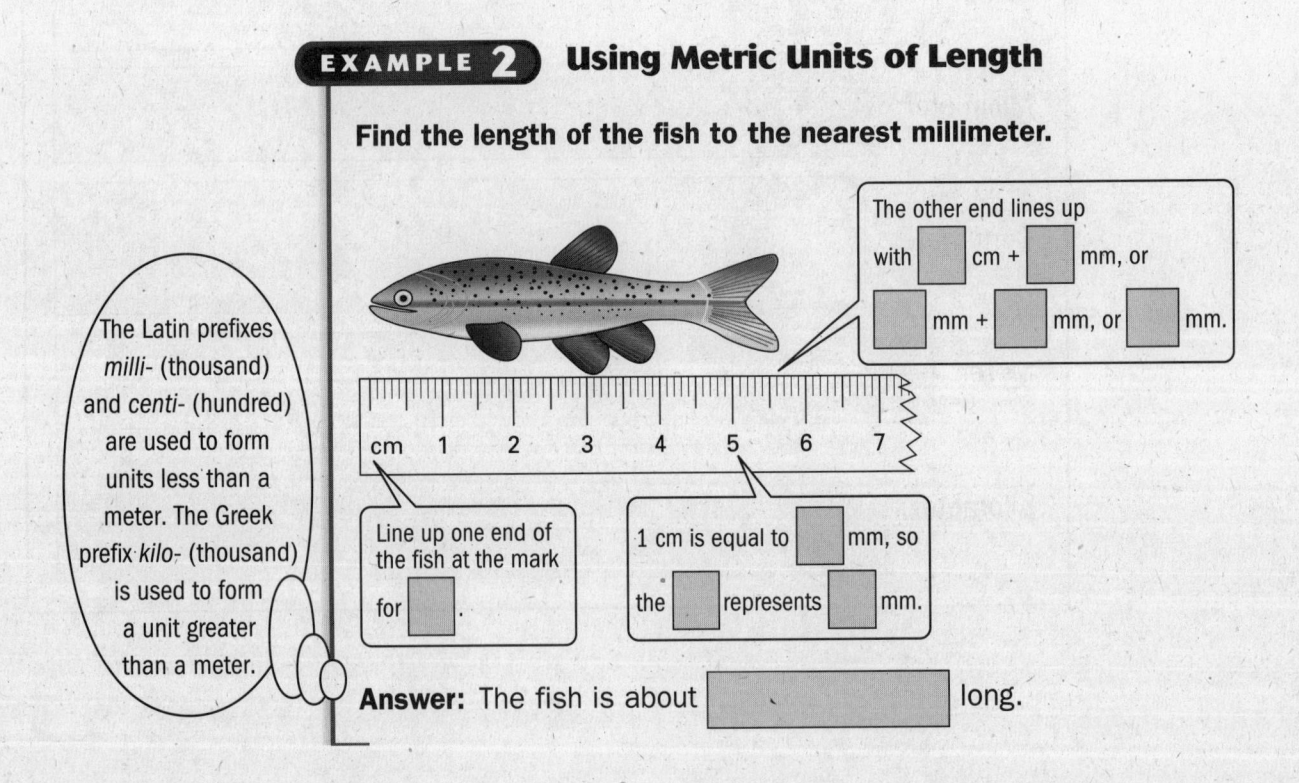

EXAMPLE 2 **Using Metric Units of Length**

Find the length of the fish to the nearest millimeter.

The other end lines up with ☐ cm + ☐ mm, or ☐ mm + ☐ mm, or ☐ mm.

Line up one end of the fish at the mark for ☐.

1 cm is equal to ☐ mm, so the ☐ represents ☐ mm.

The Latin prefixes *milli-* (thousand) and *centi-* (hundred) are used to form units less than a meter. The Greek prefix *kilo-* (thousand) is used to form a unit greater than a meter.

Answer: The fish is about ☐ long.

26 | Chapter 2 Notetaking Guide

EXAMPLE 3 Choosing Appropriate Units

Choose an appropriate customary unit and metric unit for the length.

   a. height of a cell phone tower   b. length of the Mississippi River

Solution

   a. The height of a cell phone tower is much greater than _____ _____, and much less than _____. So, you should use _____.

   b. The length of the Mississippi River is much greater than _____ _____. So, you should use _____.

Guided Practice Measure the object to the nearest whole unit.

1. width of a CD case (millimeters)

2. width of a piece of letter-size paper (inches)

3. length of your shoe (centimeters)

Guided Practice Choose an appropriate customary unit and metric unit for the length. Explain your reasoning.

4. length of a ski

5. width of a milk carton

Lesson 2.1 Measuring Lengths 27

Benchmarks for Units of Length

A benchmark [_____].

Customary Units

An **inch** is about the same as [_____].

A **foot** is about the same as [_____].

A **yard** is about the same as [_____].

Metric Units

A **millimeter** is about the same as [_____].

A **centimeter** is about the same as [_____].

A **meter** is about the same as [_____].

EXAMPLE 4 Estimating Length Using Benchmarks

Estimate the height of the volleyball net below in meters. Measure to check.

Solution

1. To estimate, imagine how high the volleyball net is in "chairs."

2. To check your estimate, measure the volleyball net with a meterstick.

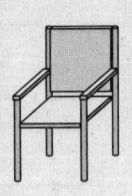

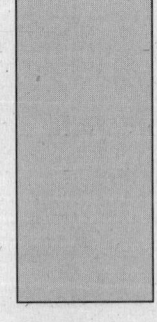

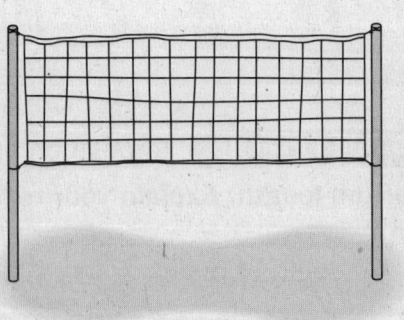

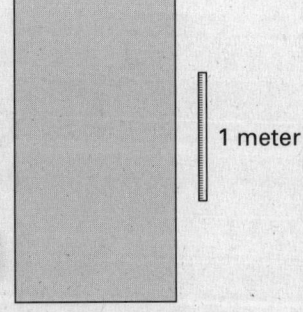

You can use your own height as a benchmark when estimating.

1 meter

Answer: The volleyball net is about [___] "chairs" high, which is about [___] meters. The height of the volleyball net is just over [___] meters.

28 | Chapter 2 Notetaking Guide

LESSON 2.2

Perimeter and Area

Goal: Use formulas to find perimeter and area.

Vocabulary

Perimeter: ⬜

Area: ⬜

Perimeter of a Rectangle

Words Perimeter = ⬜

Algebra P = ⬜

EXAMPLE 1 Finding the Perimeter of a Rectangle

Flower Box You are making a flower box using recycled railroad ties. The flower box will be 9 feet long and 4 feet wide. How many feet of railroad ties will you need to make the flower box?

Solution

To answer the question, find the perimeter.

P = ⬜ Write the formula for perimeter of a rectangle.

= ⬜ Substitute ⬜ for ⬜ and ⬜ for ⬜.

= ⬜ Multiply.

= ⬜ Add.

Answer: You need ⬜ of railroad ties to make the flower box.

Guided Practice Find the perimeter of the rectangle with the given dimensions.

1. length = 4 yd, width = 7 yd

2. length = 17 cm, width = 12 cm

Area of a Rectangle

Words   Area = _____

Algebra   A = _____

EXAMPLE 2 Finding the Area of a Rectangle

Find the area of the flower box from Example 1.

A = _____   Write the formula for area of a rectangle.

= _____   Substitute ___ for ___ and ___ for ___.

= _____   Multiply.

Answer: The area of the flower box is _____.

WATCH OUT!
The units of the answer are square feet, not linear feet. To help you remember this, think of multiplying the units: $\ell w = ft \times ft = ft^2$.

EXAMPLE 3 Perimeter and Area of a Square

Find the perimeter and area of a 70-foot by 70-foot playground.

Perimeter = _____   Area = _____

= _____   = _____

= _____   = _____

Answer: The perimeter is _____. The area is _____.

30 | Chapter 2 Notetaking Guide

Guided Practice Tell whether to find the *perimeter* or the *area* to help you decide how much of the item to buy. Then find the measurement.

3. fabric for a 30-inch by 30-inch tablecloth

4. string to mark the outside border of an 18-meter by 9-meter volleyball court

EXAMPLE 4   Solving for an Unknown Dimension

Algebra Write and solve an equation to find the length of a rectangle. Its area is 234 square millimeters and its width is 13 millimeters.

☐ = ☐   Write the formula for the ☐ of a rectangle.

☐ = ☐   Substitute ☐ for ☐ and ☐ for ☐.

☐ = ☐   Write the related ☐ equation.

☐ = ☐   .

Answer: The length of the rectangle is ☐.

Need help with thinking of a related equation? See page 740 of your textbook.

Guided Practice Write and solve an equation to find the length.

5. Area of rectangle = 575 in.², width = __?__, length = 25 in.

6. Perimeter of square = 480 m, side length = __?__

Lesson 2.3 Scale Drawings

Goal: Use scale drawings to find actual lengths.

Vocabulary

Scale drawing:

Scale:

EXAMPLE 1 Interpreting Scale Drawings

Floor Plan Find the actual lengths that correspond to 6 inches, 8 inches, and 13 inches on the scale drawing for the first floor of a house. What is the length and width of the first floor of the house?

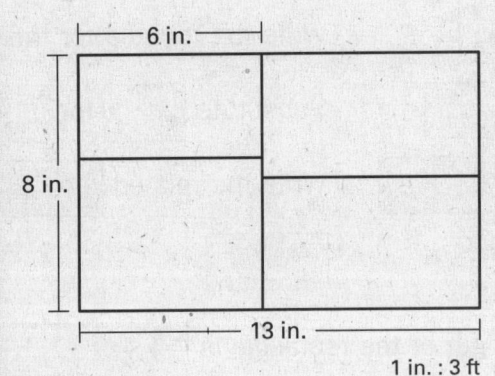

1 in. : 3 ft

Solution

Make a table. The scale of the drawing is ☐. Each inch on the drawing represents ☐ of the house.

Scale drawing length (inches)	Dimension × ☐	Actual length (feet)
6	☐ × ☐	18
8	☐ × ☐	24
13	☐ × ☐	39

Answer: The actual length and width of the first floor of the house are ☐ and ☐.

EXAMPLE 2 Standardized Test Practice

Model Car A model car is 8 inches long. The scale used to create the car is 2 in. : 48 in. How long is the actual car?

Ⓐ 96 in.   Ⓑ 192 in.   Ⓒ 288 in.   Ⓓ 384 in.

The standard way to write a scale is scale model : actual object.

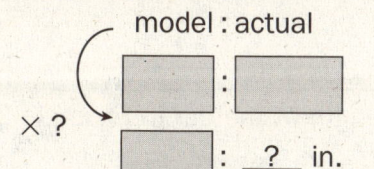

Solution

Find the relationship between the known length and the scale.

model : actual

☐ : ☐   Write the scale.

× ?

☐ : ? in.   Ask, "_____"

Because ☐ × ☐ = ☐, you multiply by ☐ to find the actual length.

model : actual

☐ : ☐   Write the scale.

× ☐

☐ : ☐

Answer: The actual car is _____ long. The correct answer is ☐.

Ⓐ Ⓑ Ⓒ Ⓓ

EXAMPLE 3 Using a Scale to Build a Model

Model Bridge You are building a model of the George Washington Bridge using a scale of 1 in. : 500 ft. The actual bridge is 3500 feet long. How long do you make your model?

Solution

Find the relationship between the known length and the scale.

model : actual

☐ : ☐   Write the scale.

× ?

? in. : ☐   Ask, "_____"

Because ☐ × ☐ = ☐, you multiply by ☐ to find the length of the model: ☐ × ☐ = ☐

Answer: You make your model _____ long.

Lesson 2.3 Scale Drawings 33

Guided Practice Refer to Examples 1–3.

1. Find the length and width of the house in Example 1 using the scale 1 in. : 5 ft.

2. Find the actual length of the car in Example 2 if the model of the car is 6 inches long.

3. Find the length of your model in Example 3 if the scale is 1 in. : 700 ft.

Lesson 2.4 Frequency Tables and Line Plots

Goal: Create and interpret frequency tables and line plots.

Vocabulary

Data:

Frequency table:

Line plot:

EXAMPLE 1 Making a Frequency Table

Family Vacation Students were asked to identify the month their family took a summer vacation. Make a frequency table of the data. In which month did most of the families take their vacation?

June, June, June, July, August, June, August, July, July, June, August, June, August, July, August

Solution

Month	Tally	Frequency
June		
July		
August		

Answer: Most of the families took their vacation in ☐.

Guided Practice

1. For a long list of data, explain why it is helpful to record the data as tally marks and then count the tally marks for the frequency.

2. Make a frequency table of the letters that occur in the word "Albuquerque." Which letter occurs most often?

EXAMPLE 2 Making a Line Plot

House Plants The frequency table shows the numbers of house plants people have in their house.

a. Make a line plot of the data.

b. Use the line plot to find the total number of people.

c. Use the line plot to find how many people have less than three plants.

Plants	Tally	Frequency
0	III	3
1	IIII I	6
2	IIII	4
3	IIII	5
4	II	2
5	I	1

Solution

a.

The X marks above the number line show the _____.

Number of Plants

Need help with number lines? See page 741 of your textbook.

The number line includes the different _____.

b. There are ☐ X marks in all, so the total number of people is ☐.

c. The total number of X marks ☐ the numbers ☐ is ☐, so ☐ people have less than three plants.

Lesson 2.4 Frequency Tables and Line Plots 37

Guided Practice The following data show the numbers of brothers and sisters in students' families. Use the data in Exercises 3–5.

4, 0, 1, 1, 2, 0, 3, 3, 4, 5, 2, 2, 1, 0, 0, 0, 5, 2, 2, 4

3. Make a frequency table of the data.

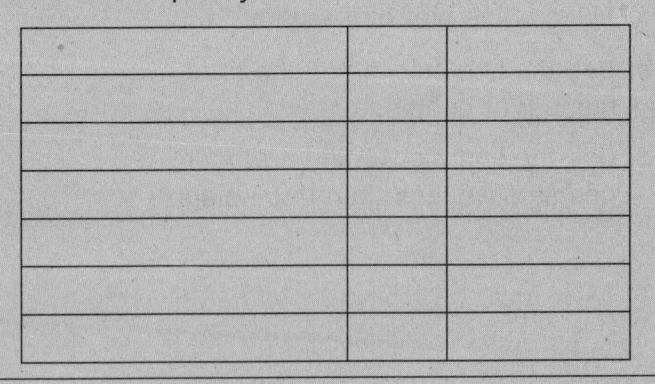

4. Make a line plot of the data.

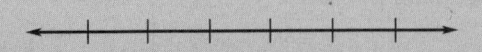

5. Choose one of the displays and use it to find out whether more students had 2 brothers and sisters or more than 3 brothers and sisters. Which display did you choose and how did you use it to answer the question?

Lesson 2.5 Bar Graphs

Goal: Display data using bar graphs.

Vocabulary

Bar graph:

Double bar graph:

EXAMPLE 1 Making a Bar Graph

Speed Limits The numbers of states with a given speed limit on an urban interstate are shown in the table. Make a bar graph of the data.

Urban Interstates	
Speed Limit (miles per hour)	States
50	1
55	20
60	3
65	19
70	7

Solution

1. Decide how far to extend the scale. Start the scale at ☐. The greatest data value is ☐, so end the scale at a value greater than ☐, such as ☐.

2. Choose the increments for the scale. Use 3 to 10 equal increments for the scale. Choose an increment that is easy to work with and compatible with ☐, such as increments of ☐.

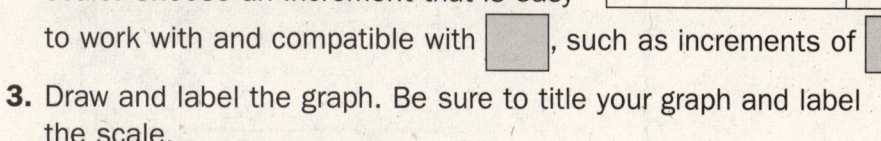

3. Draw and label the graph. Be sure to title your graph and label the scale.

Need help with reading a bar graph? See page 757 of your textbook.

EXAMPLE 2 **Making a Double Bar Graph**

Radio Stations Make a double bar graph of the radio station data in the table.

Radio station format	Stations in 1999	Stations in 2001
Country	2305	2190
Rock	730	760
Top 40	401	468
R & B	278	301
Jazz	72	81

Solution

1. Draw the first set of bars using the [ ] data, leaving room for the [ ] bars.

   The greatest data value in the table is [ ], so end the scale at [ ].

2. Draw the [ ] bars [ ] the [ ] bars and shade them a different color. Add a [ ] and a [ ].

40 | Chapter 2 Notetaking Guide

Guided Practice Make a double bar graph of the data.

1.

United States Crop Production (millions of metric tons)						
Crop	Corn	Soybeans	Wheat	Cotton	Milled Rice
1999	240	72	63	14	7
2000	253	75	61	17	6

Lesson 2.6 — Coordinates and Line Graphs

Goal: Plot points on coordinate grids and make line graphs.

Vocabulary

Ordered pair:

Coordinates:

Line graph:

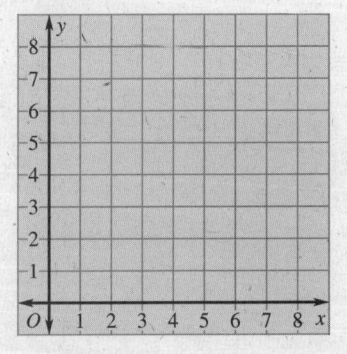

EXAMPLE 1   Graphing Points

a. Graph the point (2, 5) on a coordinate grid.

Start at ____. Move ____ units to the right and ____ units up.

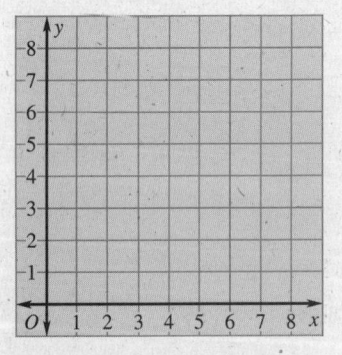

b. Graph the point (4, 0) on a coordinate grid.

Start at ____. Move ____ units to the right and ____ units up.

Guided Practice Graph the points on the same coordinate grid. Label the coordinates.

1. (0, 3) **2.** (4, 1) **3.** (5, 0) **4.** (2, 2)

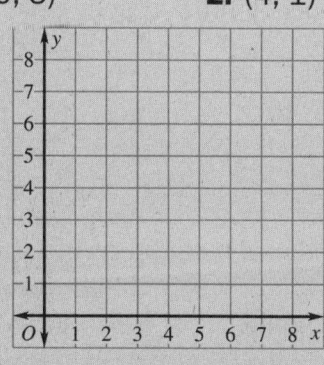

5. In Exercises 1–4, the first coordinate is the number of years a copier has been owned by a company. The second coordinate is the worth of the copier in hundreds of dollars. What is the copier worth after 4 years?

EXAMPLE 2 Making a Line Graph

Newspapers Make a line graph of the newspaper data below.

U.S. Weekly Newspapers						
Year	1975	1980	1985	1990	1995	2000
Newspapers	7612	7954	7704	7606	8453	7689

Solution

1. Make a list of ordered pairs. Think of each column of the table as an ordered pair: (_____ , _____).

2. Choose a scale that includes all the _____ values in your table.

3. Graph _____ .

4. Connect the points by _____ .

When choosing a scale for a graph with a break, make sure that the range of the scale can be divided into an even number of units.

Lesson 2.6 Coordinates and Line Graphs 43

Guided Practice In Exercise 6, use the graph in Example 2.

6. During which years was the decrease in the number of newspapers the least? How can you tell from the graph?

7. Make a line graph of the population of the U.S. Virgin Islands.

Population of U.S. Virgin Islands					
Year	1960	1970	1980	1990	2000
Population (thousands)	33	63	100	104	121

LESSON 2.7

Circle Graphs

Goal: Interpret circle graphs and make predictions.

Vocabulary

Circle graph: _____

EXAMPLE 1 **Interpreting a Circle Graph**

Paper A group of students are asked what kind of paper they use when taking notes in class. Their answers are shown in the circle graph.

a. How many students prefer using wide-ruled paper?

b. How many students do not use wide-ruled paper?

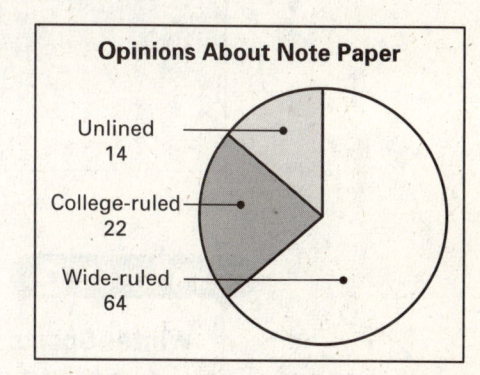

Opinions About Note Paper

Unlined 14
College-ruled 22
Wide-ruled 64

Solution

a. To find out how many students prefer using wide-ruled paper, find the data value in the section labeled _____.

   Answer: The number who prefer using wide-ruled paper is ____.

b. To find out how many students do not prefer using wide-ruled paper, add the values in the _____ and _____ sections:

   ____ + ____ = ____.

   Answer: The number who do not prefer using wide-ruled paper is ____.

Lesson 2.7 Circle Graphs 45

Guided Practice In Exercises 1–3, use the circle graph that shows how many teenagers out of 100 prefer using a bike, a scooter, a skateboard, or in-line skates.

1. Which item is most popular?

2. How many teenagers do not prefer skateboards?

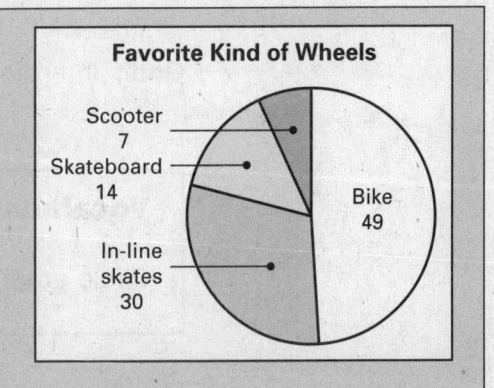

Favorite Kind of Wheels
- Scooter 7
- Skateboard 14
- Bike 49
- In-line skates 30

3. Is it reasonable to say that the scooter is the least popular choice? Explain.

EXAMPLE 2 Using a Graph

Writing down key facts as you read a problem can help you solve it. In Example 2, you know: 100 students were surveyed, 48 of them like skiing, and 200 people are in the group you're predicting for.

Winter Sports The circle graph shows the favorite winter sport of 100 students. Predict how many students out of 200 you would expect to respond "Skiing."

Favorite Winter Sport
- Snowboarding 33
- Skiing 48
- Ice skating 19

Solution

Find the relationship between the number of students surveyed and the number of students in the group you're making a prediction for:

☐ × ☐ = ☐.

Multiply the number of students who prefer skiing by ☐ to predict the number of students out of the group of 200 that will respond "Skiing":

☐ × ☐ = ☐.

Answer: About ☐ students in a group of 200 should respond "Skiing."

46 | Chapter 2 Notetaking Guide

Guided Practice Use the circle graph in Example 2.

4. Predict the number of students out of 500 you would expect to respond "Snowboarding."

Lesson 2.8 Mean, Median, and Mode

Goal: Describe data using mean, median, mode, and range.

Vocabulary

Mean:

Median:

Mode:

Range:

EXAMPLE 1 Finding a Mean

CD Collections The numbers of CDs in students' collections are listed below. Find the mean of the data.

35   30   34   30   33   34   28

Solution

To find the mean of the numbers of CDs, ☐ the numbers of CDs in the students' collections. Then divide by ☐, the number of collections.

$$\text{Mean} = \frac{\rule{2cm}{0.4pt}}{\rule{2cm}{0.4pt}} = \frac{\square}{\square} = \square$$

Answer: The mean of the numbers of CDs is ☐ CDs.

48 | Chapter 2 Notetaking Guide

EXAMPLE 2 Finding Median, Mode, and Range

CD Collections Find the median, mode(s), and range of the CD collections in Example 1.

Solution

Put the numbers of CDs in order from ☐ to ☐.

☐ ☐ ☐ ☐ ☐ ☐ ☐

Median: The middle number is ☐, so the median is ☐.

Mode: ☐ and ☐ occur ☐. There are ☐ mode(s): ☐.

Range: Range = Largest number of CDs − Smallest number of CDs

= ☐ − ☐

= ☐

EXAMPLE 3 Solving a Multi-Step Problem

Baseball The total numbers of runs in a series of baseball games are listed below. Choose the best average(s) for the data.

10   3   0   8   15   3   11   6

Solution

Mean: ☐ ÷ ☐ = ☐. The mean is _____ the data values.

Median: ☐ ÷ ☐ = ☐. The median is _____ the data values.

Mode: The mode is ☐. The mode is _____ the data values.

Answer: The _____ is not representative of the data.

The _____ best represent the data.

Be sure your notes include an example with an even number of data values, such as Example 3. Make note of the fact that the median is the mean of the two middle numbers.

Guided Practice Find the mean, median, mode(s), and range.

1. 15, 24, 17, 14, 21, 26, 30	**2.** 42, 35, 40, 28, 35
3. 4, 13, 9, 5, 5, 14, 6, 8	**4.** 89, 104, 98, 90, 89, 96, 110, 100
5. Choose the best average(s) to represent the data in Exercise 4.	

Chapter 2 Words to Review

Give an example of the vocabulary word.

Inch

Foot

Yard

Mile

Millimeter

Centimeter

Meter

Kilometer

Perimeter

Area

Scale drawing

Scale

Data

Frequency table

Line plot

Bar graph

Double bar graph

Ordered pair

Coordinates

Line graph

Circle graph

Mean

Median

Mode

Range

Review your notes and Chapter 2 by using the Chapter Review on pages 106–110 of your textbook.

Chapter 2 Words to Review

Lesson 3.1 Decimals and Place Value

Goal: Read and write decimals.

Vocabulary

Decimal: _____

EXAMPLE 1 Expressing a Number in Different Ways

a. Write 50 hundredths using only tenths.

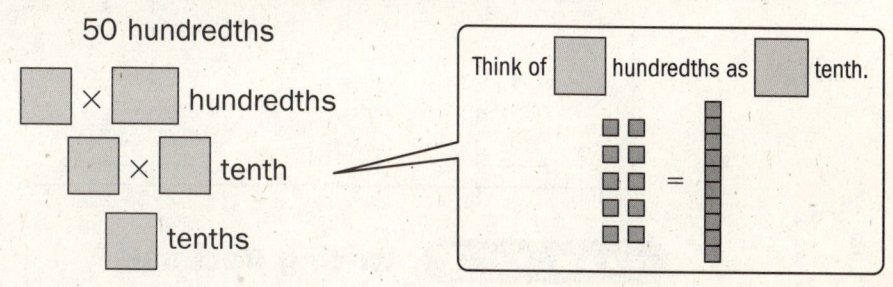

50 hundredths

☐ × ☐ hundredths

☐ × ☐ tenth

☐ tenths

Think of ☐ hundredths as ☐ tenth.

You might want to record relationships between base-ten pieces in your notebook, such as 1 one = 10 tenths.

b. Write 1 one and 7 tenths using only tenths.

1 one and 7 tenths

☐ tenths and ☐ tenths

☐ tenths

Use the fact that 1 one equals ☐ tenths.

Guided Practice Copy and complete the statement.

1. 800 hundredths = __?__ tenths

2. 3 ones and 5 tenths = __?__ tenths

Decimals and Place Value

Word form

[   ]

Decimal form

4.16

```
|   |   |   |   | 4 . 1 | 6 |   |   |
```

[   ] (read as *and*)

Expanded form

[ ] ones + [ ] tenth + [ ] hundredths

[ ] + [ ] + [ ]

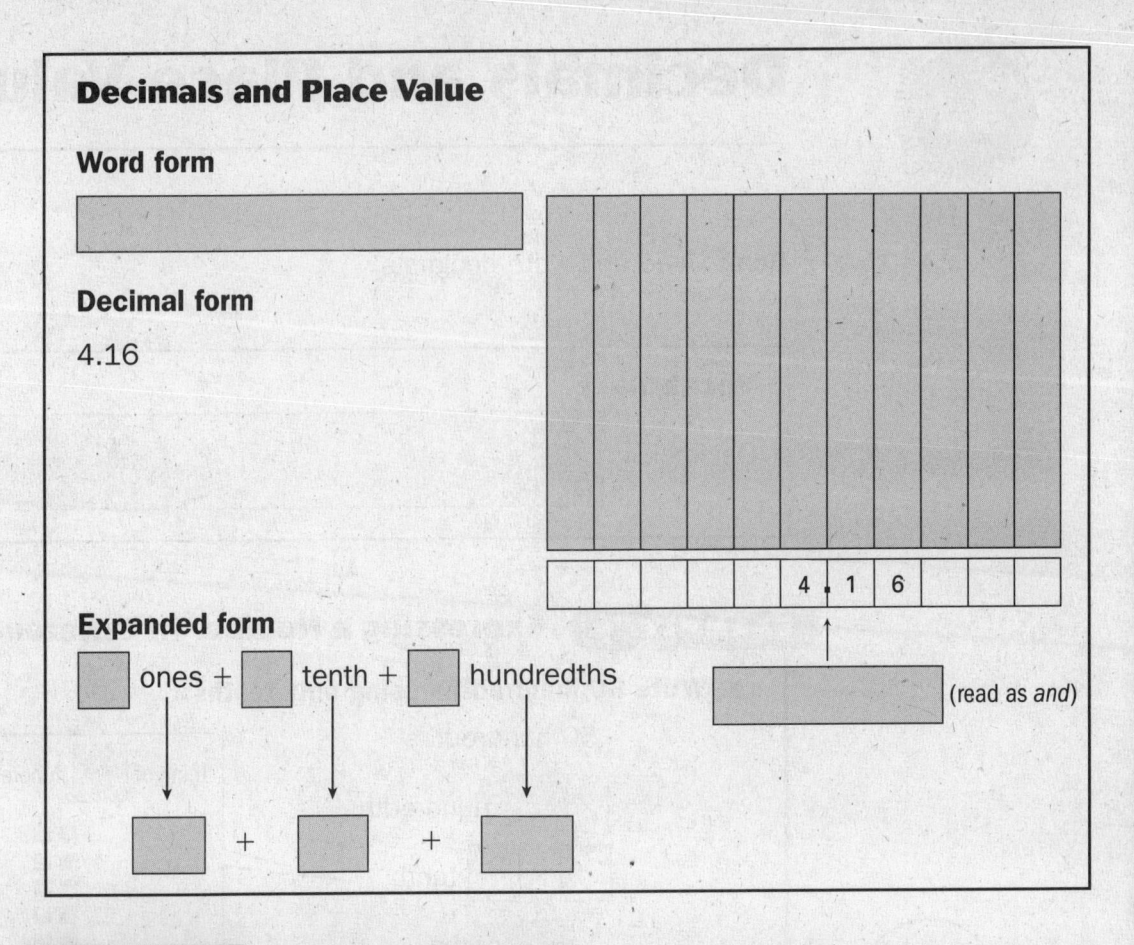

EXAMPLE 2 Writing Decimals

Distance A friend tells you that the distance between her house and your house is thirty-two and seven tenths miles. Write this distance as a decimal.

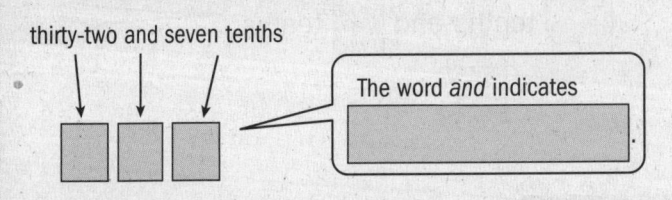

thirty-two and seven tenths

[ ] [ ] [ ]

The word *and* indicates [   ].

EXAMPLE 3 Reading Decimals

Orbit Earth makes one complete trip around the Sun in 356.256 days. Write the number of days in one complete trip in words.

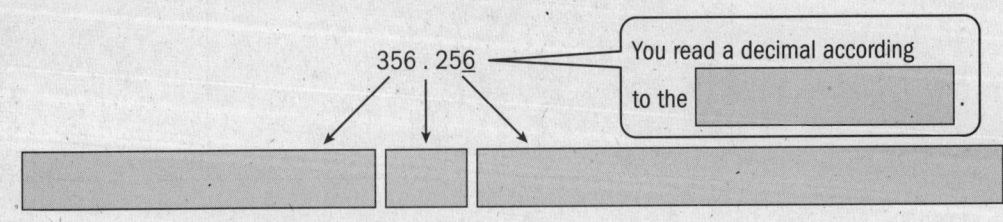

356 . 256

You read a decimal according to the [   ].

[   ] [   ] [   ]

56 | Chapter 3 Notetaking Guide

Guided Practice

3. Write *forty-one and nine hundred-thousandths* as a decimal.

4. Write 8.032 in words.

5. Write 505.83 in words.

Lesson 3.2

Measuring Metric Lengths

Goal: Use decimals to express metric measurements.

EXAMPLE 1 Writing Measurements as Decimals

Lizards A zoo keeper is recording information about the zoo's lizards. One of the lizards has a tail that is about 10 centimeters long. What is a more precise measurement for the lizard's tail?

Solution

To answer the question about the lizard's tail, use a metric ruler and write your answer as a decimal number of centimeters.

Remember that when measuring an object, line up one end of the object with the zero mark on the ruler.

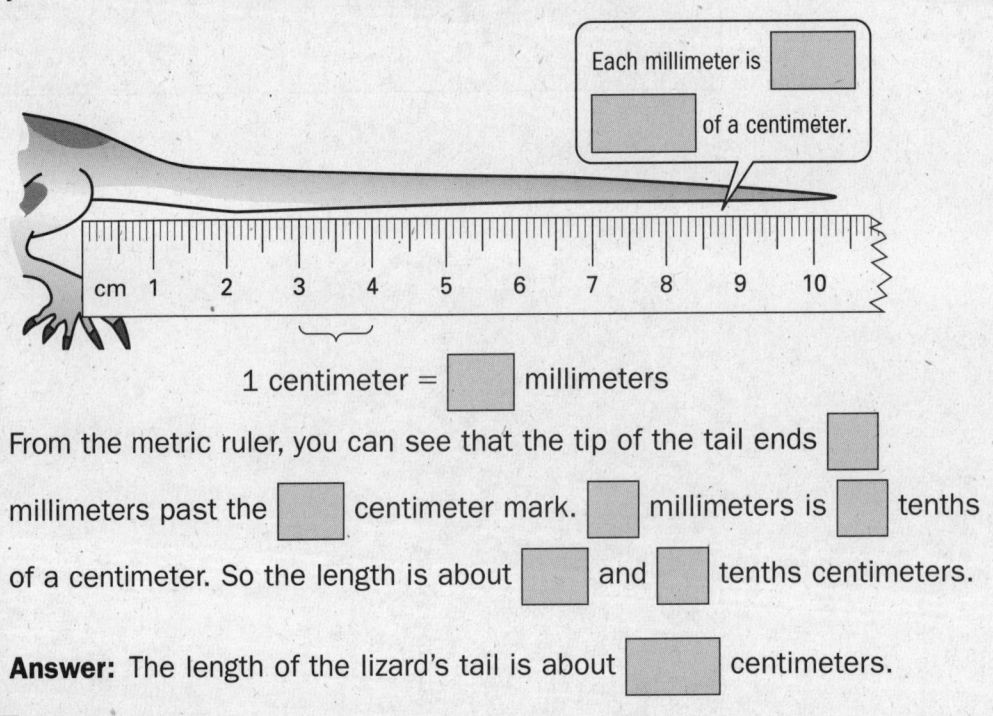

Each millimeter is ☐ of a centimeter.

1 centimeter = ☐ millimeters

From the metric ruler, you can see that the tip of the tail ends ☐ millimeters past the ☐ centimeter mark. ☐ millimeters is ☐ tenths of a centimeter. So the length is about ☐ and ☐ tenths centimeters.

Answer: The length of the lizard's tail is about ☐ centimeters.

Guided Practice Write the length of the line segment as a decimal number of centimeters.

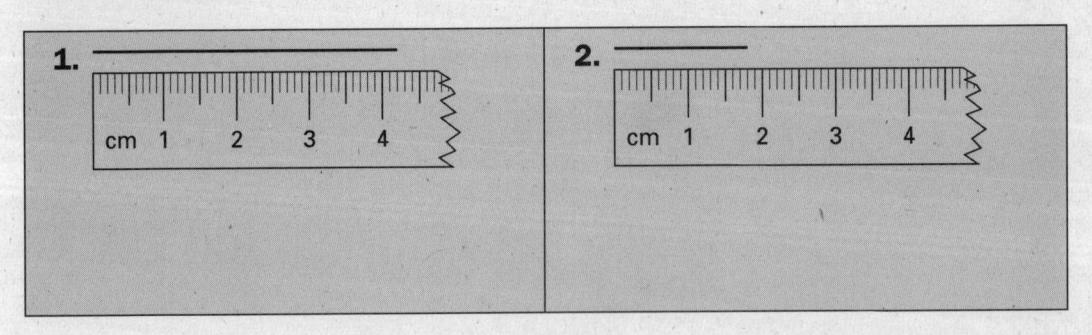

1.

2.

58 | Chapter 3 Notetaking Guide

Metric Units of Length

millimeter (mm)	centimeter (cm)	meter (m)
1 mm = ☐ cm	1 cm = ☐ mm	1 m = ☐ mm
1 mm = ☐ m	1 cm = ☐ m	1 m = ☐ cm
		1 m = ☐ km

EXAMPLE 2 Measuring in Centimeters

Find the length of the line segment to the nearest tenth of a centimeter.

☐ and ☐ tenths centimeters

Need help with metric units of length? See page 60 of your textbook.

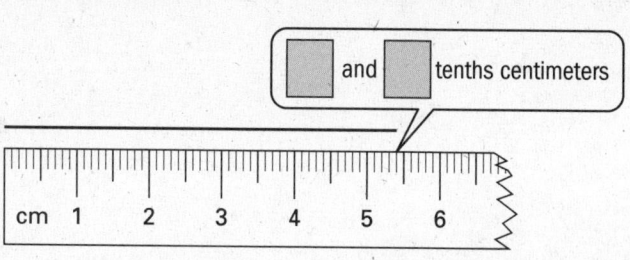

Answer: The length of the line segment is about ☐.

EXAMPLE 3 Measuring in Meters

Lizards Find the length of the lizard to the nearest hundredth of a meter.

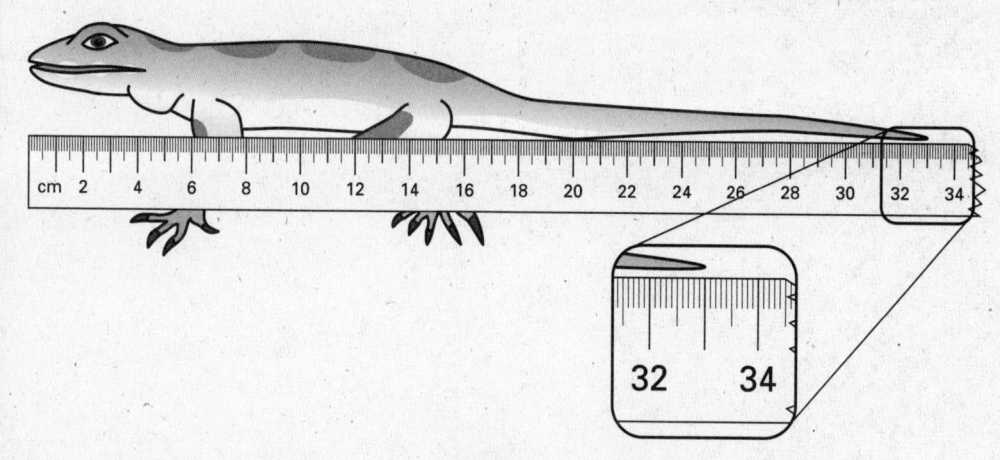

It takes more of a smaller unit of length to equal a measurement written in a larger unit of length. For example, it takes 300 cm to equal 3 m.

The length of the lizard is about ☐ centimeters. Because 1 centimeter is ☐ hundredth of a meter, ☐ centimeters is ☐ hundredths of a meter.

Answer: The length of the lizard is about ☐ meter.

Lesson 3.2 Measuring Metric Lengths 59

Guided Practice Find the length of the line segment to the given unit.

3. to the nearest tenth of a centimeter	4. to the nearest hundredth of a meter
————————	————————

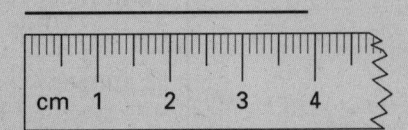

60 | Chapter 3   Notetaking Guide

Lesson 3.3 — Ordering Decimals

Goal: Compare and order decimals.

EXAMPLE 1 Comparing Metric Lengths

Writing Utensils Carolyn has a pen and a mechanical pencil in her book bag. The pen measures 15.7 centimeters and the mechanical pencil measures 15.3 centimeters. Which writing utensil is longer, the pen or the mechanical pencil?

Solution

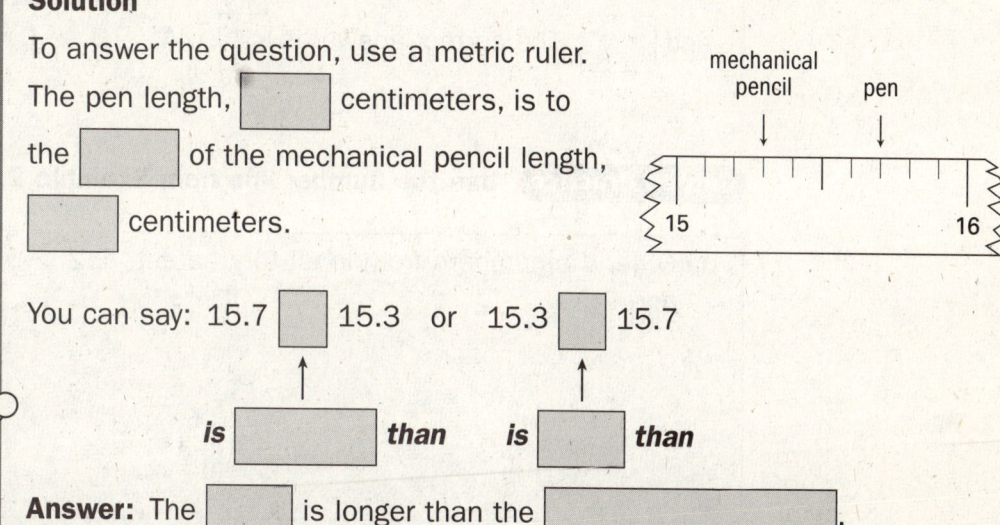

To answer the question, use a metric ruler. The pen length, ____ centimeters, is to the ____ of the mechanical pencil length, ____ centimeters.

You can say: 15.7 ____ 15.3   or   15.3 ____ 15.7

     is ____ than   is ____ than

> *Less than* and *greater than* symbols always point to the lesser number.

Answer: The ____ is longer than the ____.

EXAMPLE 2 Standardized Test Practice

Order the numbers from least to greatest: 2.3, 2.18, 2.06, 2, and 2.25.

Ⓐ 2.3, 2.25, 2.18, 2.06, 2
Ⓑ 2, 2.3, 2.06, 2.18, 2.25
Ⓒ 2, 2.06, 2.18, 2.25, 2.3
Ⓓ 2.06, 2, 2.18, 2.25, 2.3

Solution

Graph each number on a number line. Begin by marking tenths from ☐ to ☐. Then mark hundredths by dividing each tenth into ☐ sections.

The numbers on a number line ☐ from left to right.

☐ ☐ ☐ ☐ ☐
☐ ☐ ☐ ☐

> By writing the numbers above their plotted points on the number line, you can easily order the numbers.

Answer: An ordered list of the numbers is ☐, ☐, ☐, ☐, and ☐. The correct answer is ☐. Ⓐ Ⓑ Ⓒ Ⓓ

Guided Practice Use the number line from Example 2.

1. Order the numbers from least to greatest: 2.2, 2.09, 2.1, 2.01, and 2.29.

2. Write three numbers that are greater than 5.7 and less than 5.8.

Steps for Comparing Decimals

1. Write the decimals in a ☐, lining up the ☐.

2. If necessary, write ☐ to the right of the decimals so that all decimals ☐.

3. Compare place values from ☐ to ☐.

EXAMPLE 3 Comparing Decimals

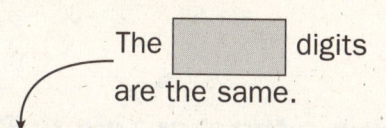

Copy and complete the statement with <, >, or =.

a. 6.398 _?_ 6.406

The [ ] digits are the same.

6.398
6.406

The [ ] digits are different: 3 [ ] 4.

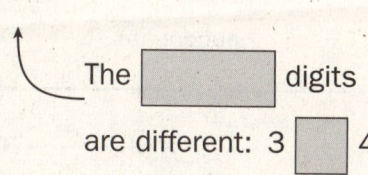

Answer: 6.398 [ ] 6.406

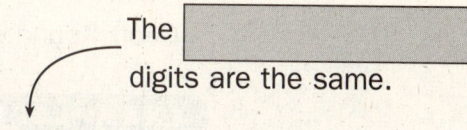

b. 3.72 _?_ 3.7

The [ ] digits are the same.

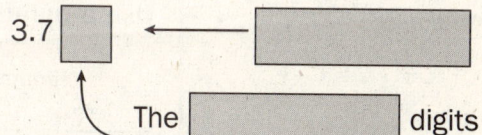

3.72
3.7 ← [ ]

The [ ] digits are different: 2 [ ] 0.

Answer: 3.72 [ ] 3.7

EXAMPLE 4 Ordering Decimals

Order the countries by the price for one gallon of gasoline from greatest to least.

The digits are the same through the [ ] place. Compare [ ]: 1.**8**0, 1.**7**2, 1.**5**1, and 1.**1**7.

Country	Price (in dollars)
Australia	1.72
Canada	1.51
Mexico	1.80
United States	1.17

Answer: The countries, from the greatest price to the least price, are [ ], [ ], [ ], and [ ].

Guided Practice Copy and complete the statement with <, >, or =.

3. 8.21 _?_ 8.12

4. 9.3 _?_ 9.30

5. 0.207 _?_ 0.213

Lesson 3.3 Ordering Decimals 63

Lesson 3.4 Rounding Decimals

Goal: Round decimals.

EXAMPLE 1 — Using a Number Line to Round

Use a number line to round 5.26 to the nearest tenth.

The decimal 5.26 is closer to [ ] than to [ ].

Answer: The decimal 5.26 rounds [ ] to [ ].

Guided Practice — Use a number line to round the decimal as specified.

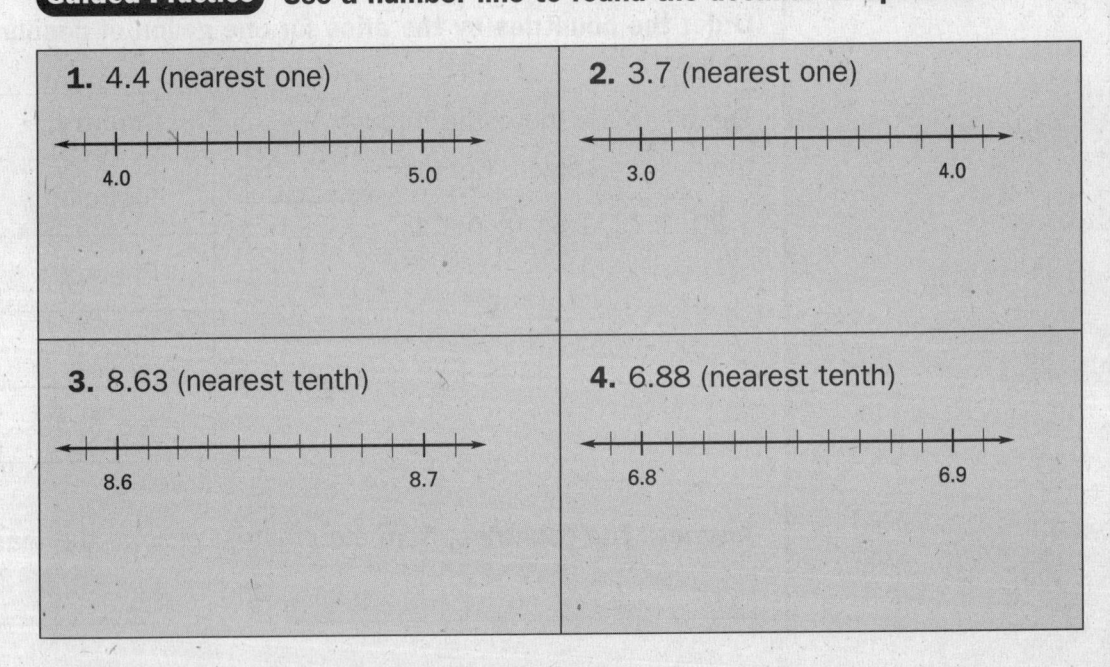

1. 4.4 (nearest one)

2. 3.7 (nearest one)

3. 8.63 (nearest tenth)

4. 6.88 (nearest tenth)

Rule for Rounding Decimals

To round a decimal to a given place value, look at the digit in the place to the [ ].

- If the digit is 4 or less, round [ ].
- If the digit is 5 or greater, round [ ].

64 | Chapter 3 Notetaking Guide

EXAMPLE 2 Rounding Decimals

Round the decimal to the place value of the underlined digit.

a. 1.<u>4</u>1 → ⬚ The digit to the ⬚ of 4 is ⬚, so round ⬚.

b. 9.3<u>7</u>6 → ⬚ The digit to the ⬚ of 7 is ⬚, so round ⬚.

c. 3.92<u>8</u>17 → ⬚ The digit to the ⬚ of 8 is ⬚, so round ⬚.

d. 7.<u>9</u>53 → ⬚ The digit to the ⬚ of 9 is ⬚, so round ⬚.

WATCH OUT!
In rounding problems like part (d) of Example 2, do not drop the final zero. Keep it to mark the place value you rounded to.

Guided Practice Round the decimal as specified.

5. 7.39 (nearest tenth)	6. 3.097 (nearest hundredth)
7. 5.47 (nearest one)	8. 2.9885 (nearest thousandth)

EXAMPLE 3 Rounding to the Leading Digit

Sand A grain of sand has a diameter of 0.0008512 inch. Round the diameter of the grain of sand to the leading digit.

Solution

The first ⬚ digit at the left of 0.0008512 is ⬚, and it is in the ⬚ place. You should round the diameter to the nearest ⬚.

0.0008512 ⬚ is in the ⬚ place.

Because ⬚ is to the right of the ⬚ place, round ⬚ to ⬚.

Answer: The diameter of the grain of sand rounded to the leading digit is ⬚ inch.

Lesson 3.4 Rounding Decimals 65

Guided Practice Round the decimal to the leading digit.

9. 0.069	**10.** 0.0082	**11.** 0.0971	**12.** 0.008419

EXAMPLE 4 Using Decimals for Large Numbers

Big Cities The populations of the four largest cities in the United States in a recent year are shown below. Round each population to the nearest hundred thousand. Then write each rounded population as a decimal number of millions. Display your results in a bar graph.

Solution

City	Population	Round	Write in millions
New York	8,008,278		____ million
Los Angeles	3,694,820		____ million
Chicago	2,896,016		____ million
Houston	1,953,631		____ million

As you work on the exercises, remember to write down any questions you want to ask your teacher.

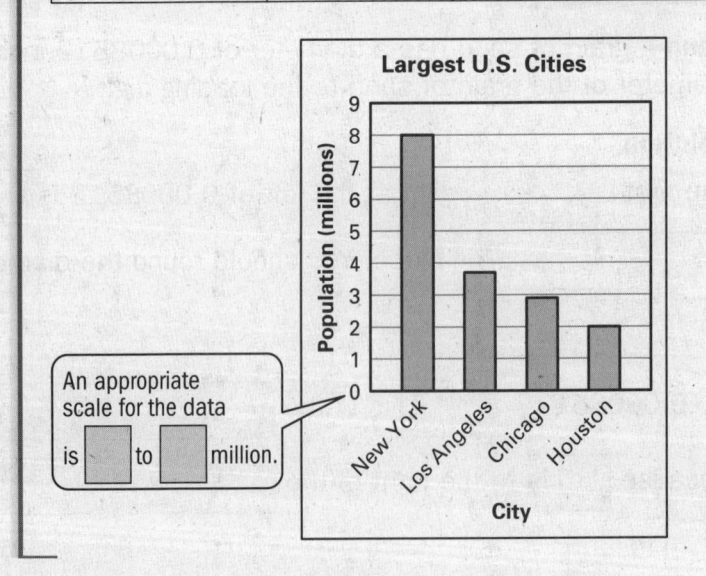

Largest U.S. Cities

An appropriate scale for the data is ____ to ____ million.

66 | Chapter 3　Notetaking Guide

LESSON 3.5

Decimal Estimation

Goal: Estimate sums and difference of decimals.

Vocabulary

Front-end estimation: _____

EXAMPLE 1 Estimating Sums and Differences

Vehicle Production The table shows the number of passenger cars and commercial vehicles made by different countries in a recent year. About how many vehicles were made in the United States altogether? About how many more passenger cars did Japan produce than Germany?

Country	Passenger cars (millions)	Commercial vehicles (millions)
Germany	4.8	0.4
Japan	8.4	1.8
United States	5.5	7.2

Solution

a. To estimate the answer to the first question, round each decimal to the nearest whole number. Then add.

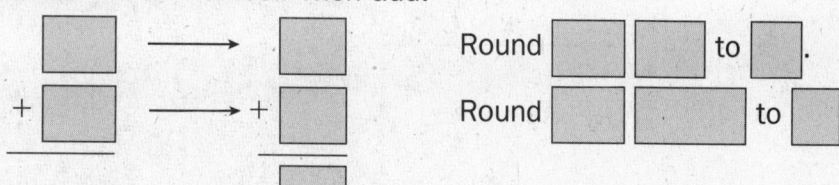

☐ ⟶ ☐
+ ☐ ⟶ + ☐
          ☐

Round ☐ ☐ to ☐.
Round ☐ ☐ to ☐.

Answer: About ☐ million total vehicles were made in the United States.

b. To estimate the answer to the second question, round each decimal to the nearest whole number. Then subtract.

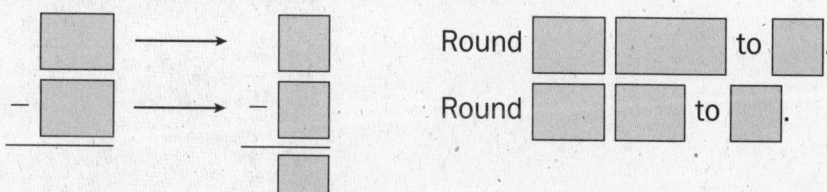

☐ ⟶ ☐
− ☐ ⟶ − ☐
          ☐

Round ☐ ☐ to ☐.
Round ☐ ☐ to ☐.

Answer: Japan made about ☐ million more passenger cars than Germany.

When answering a question, make sure that you include the correct number of units. In Example 1, the numbers of vehicles are given in millions *of vehicles.*

Lesson 3.5   Decimal Estimation   67

Guided Practice Use the information provided in Example 1.

1. Estimate the total number of vehicles made in Japan.

2. Estimate how many more commercial vehicles than passenger cars were made in the United States.

EXAMPLE 2 **Predicting Results**

Writing You spent 12 hours researching for a report for one of your classes. You spent a total of 8.3 hours writing the report. Estimate how much more time you spent on researching than on writing. Is this estimate *high* or *low*?

Round ☐ ☐ to ☐.

Before rounding, it can be helpful to use zeros to write each decimal with the same number of decimal places.

Answer: You spent about ☐ more hours on researching than on writing.

This estimate is ☐ because ☐ ☐.

68 | Chapter 3 Notetaking Guide

EXAMPLE 3 Using Front-End Estimation

Mail You are mailing a package of books to your brother in college. You have enough money to mail a 6-pound package. The books weigh 1.25 pounds, 1.72 pounds, 1.54 pounds, and 0.45 pound. Can you mail the package?

Solution

Find the sum of all the weights.

1. Add the front-end digits.
2. Estimate the sum of the remaining digits.
3. Add your results.

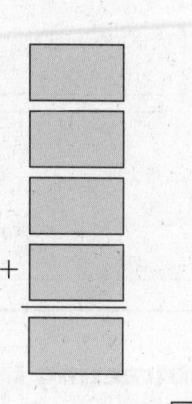

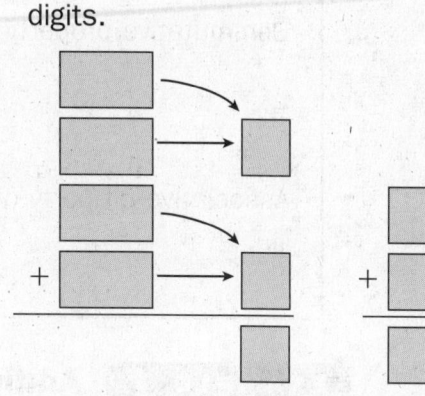

Answer: You ☐ mail the package.

Guided Practice Use front-end estimation to estimate the sum.

3. 5.74 + 8.32 + 2.54 + 1.51

4. 4.48 + 2.46 + 5 + 3.13

5. How can you estimate the difference in Example 2 so that your answer is a low estimate?

Lesson 3.5 Decimal Estimation 69

LESSON 3.6 Adding and Subtracting Decimals

Goal: Add and subtract decimals.

Vocabulary

Commutative property of addition:

Associative property of addition:

You can add zeros following the last digit to the right of the decimal point to help you line up the decimal points.

EXAMPLE 1 Adding and Subtracting Decimals

a. $7.6 + 3.28$

b. $9 - 2.15$

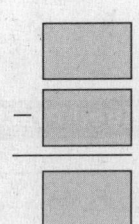

EXAMPLE 2 Evaluating Algebraic Expressions

Evaluate $30 - x$ when $x = 6.14$.

$30 - x = $ ☐   Substitute ☐ for ☐.

$= $ ☐

Guided Practice Evaluate the expression when $x = 8.25$ and $y = 4.2$.

1. $2.9 + x$	2. $14.38 - y$	3. $x - y$

70 | Chapter 3 Notetaking Guide

EXAMPLE 3 Using Mental Math to Add Decimals

Building Materials Find the total cost for a bag of nails that is $1.75, two pieces of wood that are $10.15 each, and a can of paint that is $8.25.

List the prices: **Rearrange the prices and group pairs of prices.**

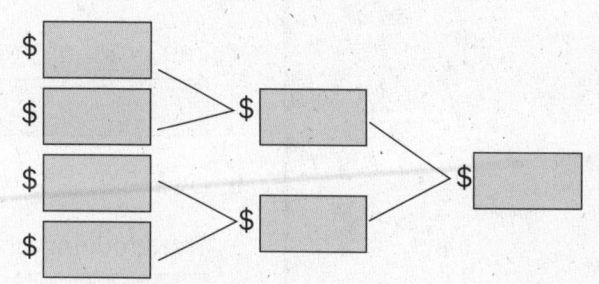

$ [ ]
$ [ ]
$ [ ]
$ [ ]

$ [ ]
$ [ ] $ [ ]
$ [ ] $ [ ]
$ [ ] $ [ ]

Answer: The building materials will cost $ [ ].

Properties of Addition

Commutative Property You can add numbers [ ].

Numbers [ ] = 8 + 3   **Algebra** x + y = [ ]

Associative Property The value of a sum does not depend on [ ].

Numbers [ ] = 5 + (1 + 7)   **Algebra** (x + y) + z = [ ]

Guided Practice Tell which property is illustrated. Then find the sum.

4. 6.2 + 3.7 = 3.7 + 6.2

5. (1.9 + 4.4) + 8.6 = 1.9 + (4.4 + 8.6)

Lesson 3.6 Adding and Subtracting Decimals | 71

EXAMPLE 4 Using Properties of Addition

Tell whether the *commutative* or *associative* property of addition allows you to rewrite the problem as shown. *Explain* your choice.

a. $7 + 3.8 + 16 = 3.8 + 7 + 16$

The order of the numbers has changed. This is allowed by the ⬜ property of addition.

b. $(2.6 + 9) + 2 = 2.6 + (9 + 2)$

The grouping of the numbers has changed. This is allowed by the ⬜ property of addition.

EXAMPLE 5 Standardized Test Practice

Rivers The Mississippi River is about 3765.86 kilometers long. The Potomac River is about 616.38 kilometers long. The St. Lawrence River is about 1287.48 kilometers long. How much longer is the Mississippi River than the Potomac River and St. Lawrence River combined?

- Ⓐ 1862 km
- Ⓑ 1903.86 km
- Ⓒ 2478.38 km
- Ⓓ 3149.48 km

Solution

Write a verbal model to help you find the difference in the lengths.

$$\begin{array}{l} \text{Difference in length} = \text{Length of Mississippi} - (\text{Length of Potomac} + \text{Length of St. Lawrence}) \\ = \boxed{} - (\boxed{} + \boxed{}) \quad \text{Substitute.} \\ = \boxed{} - \boxed{} \quad \text{Add.} \\ = \boxed{} \quad \text{Subtract.} \end{array}$$

Answer: The Mississippi River is ⬜ kilometers longer than the Potomac River and the St. Lawrence River combined. The correct answer is ⬜. Ⓐ Ⓑ Ⓒ Ⓓ

Need help with the order of operations? See page 21 of your textbook.

✓ **Check** Use estimation to check that your answer is reasonable. Round 3765.86 to ⬜, 616.38 to ⬜, and 1287.48 to ⬜. Because ⬜ − (⬜ + ⬜) = ⬜, the answer ⬜ reasonable.

Chapter 3 Words to Review

Give an example of the vocabulary word.

Decimal

Front-end estimation

Commutative property of addition

Associative property of addition

Review your notes and Chapter 3 by using the Chapter Review on pages 157–160 of your textbook.

Lesson 4.1 Multiplying Decimals and Whole Numbers

Goal: Multiply decimals and whole numbers.

Vocabulary

Commutative property of multiplication: ⬜

Associative property of multiplication: ⬜

EXAMPLE 1 Multiplying Decimals by Whole Numbers

Find the product 8×0.009.

Because 0.009 has ⬜ decimal places, the answer will have ⬜ decimal places.

⬜
$\times$ ⬜
―――
⬜

Write a ⬜ as a placeholder so that the answer has ⬜ decimal places.

You may want to think of Example 1 in words. 8 times 9 thousandths is ? thousandths. Then you can see why a zero is needed as a placeholder in the product.

Guided Practice Find the product. Then write the product in words.

1. 2×0.007	2. 6×0.018	3. 3.4×9	4. 7.14×5

EXAMPLE 2 Solving a Problem

Spaghetti Sauce A food company packages its spaghetti sauce in jars that weigh 1.625 pounds. The jars are then shipped in cases that contain 12 jars of sauce each. How much does one case of spaghetti sauce weigh?

Solution

Multiply the weight of one jar by the number of jars in one case.

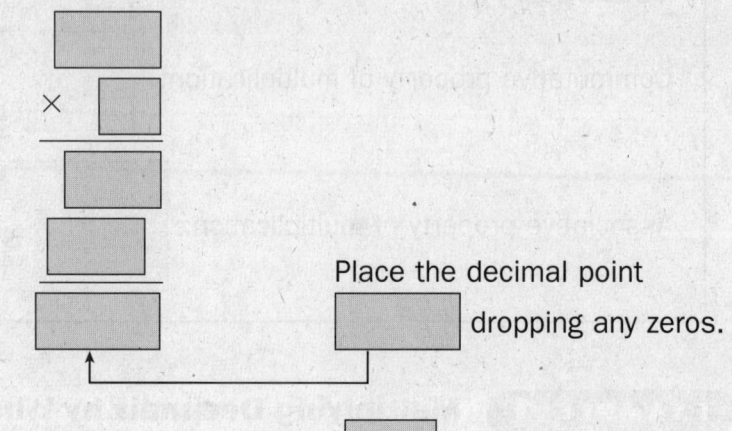

$$\begin{array}{r} \boxed{} \\ \times \boxed{} \\ \hline \boxed{} \\ \boxed{} \\ \hline \boxed{} \end{array}$$

Place the decimal point _____ dropping any zeros.

Answer: One case weighs _____ pounds.

EXAMPLE 3 Checking for Reasonableness

When estimating the product of a decimal and a whole number, you only need to round the decimal and not the whole number.

Use estimation to check that the answer to Example 2 is reasonable.

Weight of one case = _____ × _____

≈ _____ × _____   Round _____ to _____.

= _____

Answer: Because _____ is close to _____, the weight is reasonable.

Guided Practice Find the product.

5. 0.6 × 70	**6.** 3.602 × 9	**7.** 4.23 × 85	**8.** 7.75 × 33

76 | Chapter 4 Notetaking Guide

Guided Practice Use estimation to check whether the answer is reasonable.

9. 4.135 × 17; 70.295	10. 19.309 × 6; 1158.54

11. Explain why the answer 312 is *not* reasonable for the product 8 × 3.9.

12. Explain why the answer 2.34 *is* reasonable for the product 3 × 0.78.

Properties of Multiplication

Commutative Property You can multiply numbers _____.

Numbers 7 × 5.4 = _____   **Algebra** _____ = b • a

Associative Property Changing the grouping of factors
_____.

Numbers (7 × 5.4) × 3 = _____

Algebra _____ = a • (b • c)

EXAMPLE 4 Using Properties of Multiplication

Tell whether the *commutative* or *associative* property of multiplication allows you to rewrite the problem as shown. Explain your choice.

a. 8 × 6.34 × 5 = 6.34 × 8 × 5

_____ has changed, so this is an example of the _____ property of multiplication.

b. (6.34 × 8) × 5 = 6.34 × (8 × 5)

_____ have changed, so this is an example of the _____ property of multiplication.

Lesson 4.1 Multiplying Decimals and Whole Numbers | 77

Lesson 4.2 The Distributive Property

Goal: Use the distributive property to evaluate expressions.

Vocabulary

Distributive property:

Numbers $7(3 + 4) = \boxed{}(\boxed{}) + \boxed{}(\boxed{}); \boxed{}(\boxed{}) = 4(9) - 4(5)$

Algebra $\boxed{}(\boxed{} + \boxed{}) = ab + ac \qquad a(b - c) = \boxed{} - \boxed{}$

EXAMPLE 1 Standardized Test Practice

Amusement Park Tickets A family of six is going to an amusement park. The admission is $42 per person, but the family has a coupon for $5 off each ticket. Which equation can be used to find t, the total cost of admission to the amusement park?

Ⓐ $t = 6(42 - 5)$ Ⓑ $t = 6(42) - 5$

Ⓒ $t = 6(42) + 6(5)$ Ⓓ $t = 42 - 5$

Solution

Method 1 Write an expression for the cost of one ticket using a coupon. Then multiply by the number of family members.

t = Number of family members × Cost of one ticket using coupon

$= \boxed{} \times (\boxed{}) = \boxed{}(\boxed{}) = \boxed{}$

Remember that a(b) is another way to write a × b.

Method 2 First write expressions for the cost without the coupon and the value of the coupon. Then find the difference.

t = Cost without using coupon − Total worth of coupon

$= (\boxed{} \times \boxed{}) - (\boxed{} \times \boxed{}) = \boxed{} - \boxed{} = \boxed{}$

Answer: The family will pay $\boxed{}$ altogether for admission to the park.

An equation for the total cost of admission is $\boxed{}$. The correct answer is $\boxed{}$. Ⓐ Ⓑ Ⓒ Ⓓ

EXAMPLE 2 Using the Distributive Property

a. $3(40 + 9) = \square(\square) + \square(\square)$
$= \square + \square$
$= \square$

b. $20(7.2 - 3.9) = \square(\square) - \square(\square)$
$= \square - \square$
$= \square$

Guided Practice Use the distributive property to evaluate.

1. $3(15 + 8)$	2. $9(30 - 4)$	3. $100(7.6 - 5)$	4. $0.4(25 + 17)$

EXAMPLE 3 Evaluating Using Mental Math

a. To find 8(59), rewrite $\square$.

$8(59) = \square(\square - \square)$
$= \square(\square) - \square(\square)$
$= \square - \square$
$= \square$

Another way to solve Example 3(a) would be to rewrite 59 as the sum 50 + 9.

b. To find 6(7.2), rewrite $\square$.

$\square(\square) = \square(\square + \square)$
$= \square(\square) + \square(\square)$
$= \square + \square$
$= \square$

Lesson 4.2 The Distributive Property 79

EXAMPLE 4 **Using a Formula**

Serving Platter A rectangular serving platter is 14 inches long and 10.5 inches wide. What is the area of the serving platter?

Solution

Use the formula *Area = length × width*.

Area = ☐(☐)   Use ☐ for the length and ☐ for the width.

= ☐(☐ + ☐)   Rewrite 10.5 as ☐ + ☐.

= ☐(☐) + ☐(☐)   Use the distributive property.

= ☐ + ☐   Multiply.

= ☐   Add.

Answer: The area of the serving platter is ☐ square inches.

Guided Practice Use mental math to find the product.

5. 7(43)	6. 3(98)	7. 4(14.5)	8. 9(2.3)

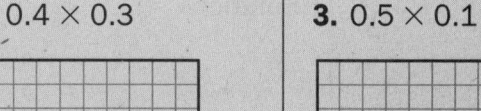

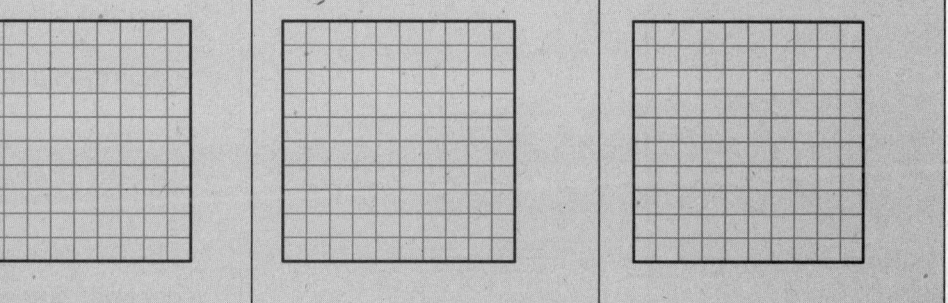

Lesson 4.3 Multiplying Decimals

Goal: Multiply decimals by decimals.

EXAMPLE 1 Using a Model to Multiply Decimals

Rainfall Shawna has been recording the amount of rainfall in her town for a science project. The first week she recorded 0.7 inch of rain. The amount of rainfall for the second week was 0.5 times the amount of rain that fell during the first week. How much rain fell during the second week?

Solution

To find the amount of rain that fell during the second week, use a model to find the product 0.7 × 0.5.

1. Draw a 10 × 10 square. The whole square represents ☐. The width of each row or column is ☐ tenth, or ☐.

2. Shade a rectangle that is ☐ by ☐. Each small square represents ☐ hundredth, or ☐. The area is ☐ hundredths, because ☐ small squares are shaded. So, 0.7 × 0.5 = ☐.

Answer: During the second week, ☐ inch of rain fell.

Guided Practice Draw a model to find the product.

1. 0.2 × 0.9
2. 0.4 × 0.3
3. 0.5 × 0.1

Multiplying Decimals

Words Multiply decimals as you do whole numbers. Then place the decimal point. The number of decimal places in the product is _____.

Numbers   6.92   ×   12.3   =   ☐

☐ places   ☐ place   ☐ places

EXAMPLE 2 Placing a Decimal Point in a Product

Place the decimal point in the correct location.

342.89   ×   0.908   =   ☐

☐ places   ☐ places   ☐ places

The first factor has ☐ decimal places. The second factor has ☐ decimal places. Because ☐ + ☐ = ☐, the answer has ☐ decimal places.

Answer: 342.89 × 0.908 = ☐

✓ **Check** Estimate using compatible numbers.

342.89 × 0.908 ≈ ☐ × ☐ = ☐.

So, the product ☐ is reasonable.

> When you estimate to check a decimal product, you can use compatible numbers or round each decimal to its leading digit. Another estimate in Example 2 would be 300 × 1 = 300.

EXAMPLE 3 Multiplying Decimals

Find the product.

a. 6.05 × 3.7   b. 1.732 × 0.04   c. 6.345 × 4.4

Solution

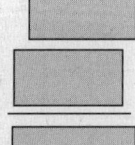

a.   6.05   ☐ decimal places
    ×   3.7   + ☐ decimal place
    ─────────
        ☐
        ☐   ☐ decimal places

82 | Chapter 4 Notetaking Guide

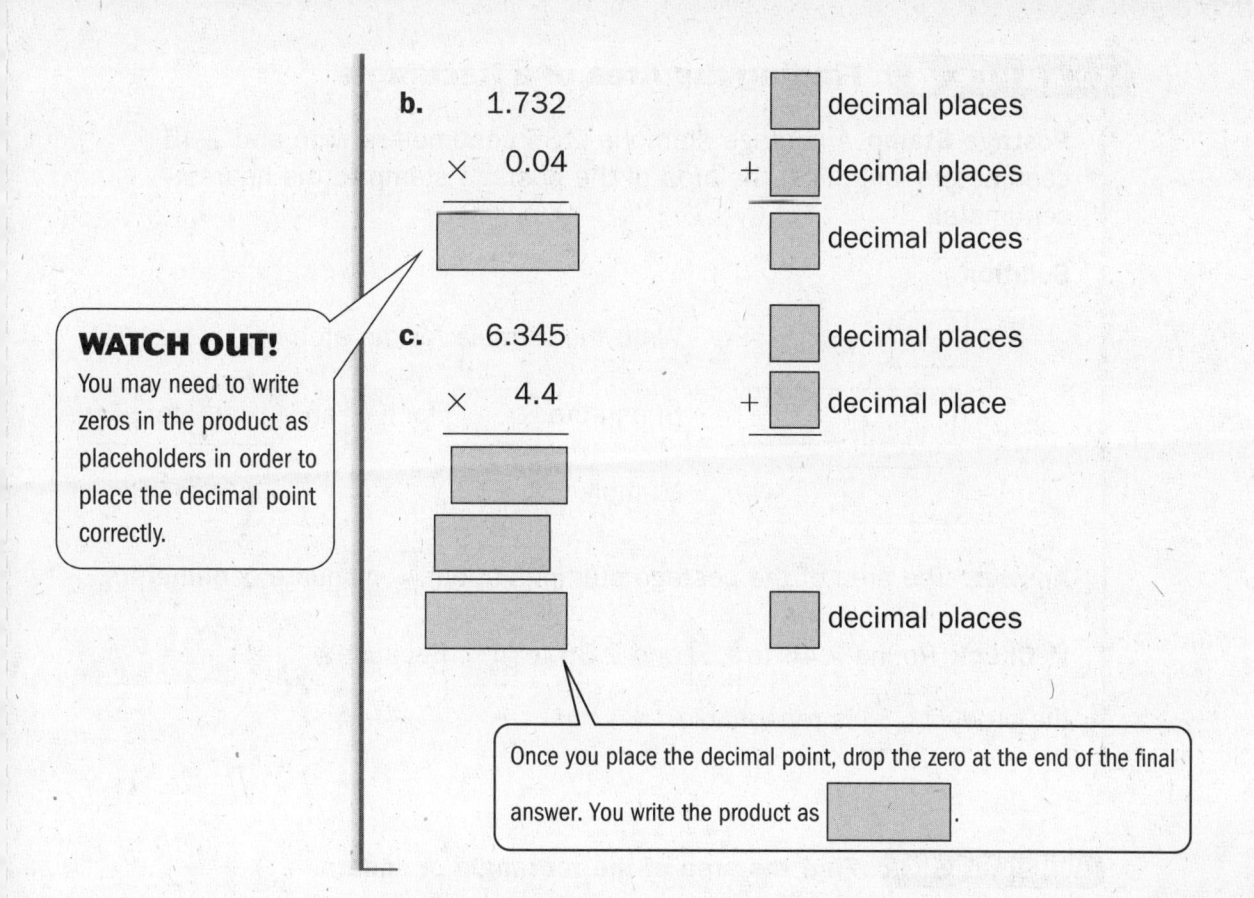

b. 1.732   ☐ decimal places
   × 0.04   + ☐ decimal places
   ☐   ☐ decimal places

WATCH OUT! You may need to write zeros in the product as placeholders in order to place the decimal point correctly.

c. 6.345   ☐ decimal places
   × 4.4   + ☐ decimal place
   ☐
   ☐
   ☐   ☐ decimal places

Once you place the decimal point, drop the zero at the end of the final answer. You write the product as ☐ .

Guided Practice — Multiply. Use estimation to check your answer.

4. 4.75 × 5.6	**5.** 16.8 × 3.7	**6.** 7.178 × 0.3	**7.** 0.84 × 0.06

Lesson 4.3 Multiplying Decimals 83

EXAMPLE 4 **Finding the Area of a Rectangle**

Postage Stamp A postage stamp is 2.35 centimeters wide and 2.45 centimeters long. Find the area of the postage stamp to the nearest centimeter.

Solution

$A = \boxed{}$ Write the formula for the area of a rectangle.

$= (\boxed{})(\boxed{})$ Substitute $\boxed{}$ for $\boxed{}$ and $\boxed{}$ for $\boxed{}$.

$= \boxed{}$ Multiply.

Answer: The area of the postage stamp is about $\boxed{}$ square centimeters.

✓ **Check** Round 2.45 to $\boxed{}$ and 2.35 to $\boxed{}$. Because $\boxed{} \times \boxed{} = \boxed{}$, the product $\boxed{}$ is reasonable.

Guided Practice Find the area of the rectangle or square.

8. A square with side length 4.5 feet

9. A rectangle with length 7.6 centimeters and width 2.32 centimeters

Lesson 4.4

Dividing by Whole Numbers

Goal: Divide decimals by whole numbers.

Dividing a Decimal by a Whole Number

Words When dividing a decimal by a whole number, place the decimal point in the quotient _____.

Numbers

$$4\overline{)27.2}^{\,6.8}$$

Place the decimal point in the quotient _____.

EXAMPLE 1 Dividing a Decimal by a Whole Number

CDs A computer store charges $9.95 for a 5-pack of rewritable CDs. How much does one CD cost at this price?

Solution

To answer the question, find $9.95 \div 5$.

1. Place the decimal point.

    $5\overline{)9.95}$

2. Then divide.

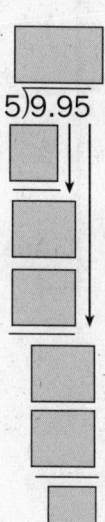

    $5\overline{)9.95}$

Answer: One CD costs $ _____ .

Guided Practice Find the quotient.

| 1. 4)30.4 | 2. 3)27.9 | 3. 9)4.77 |

EXAMPLE 2 Writing Additional Zeros

Find the quotient 13 ÷ 4.

1. Place the decimal point and begin dividing.

    4)13.

2. Write additional zeros in the dividend as needed.

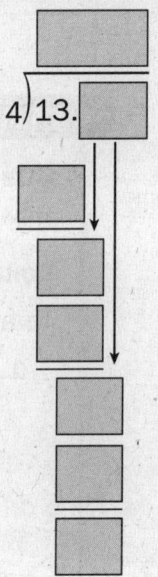

    4)13.

Answer: 13 ÷ 4 = ☐

86 | Chapter 4 Notetaking Guide

EXAMPLE 3   Using Zeros as Placeholders

Road Trip Three people are going on a 425-mile trip. They want to divide the driving up evenly among the three people. How far does each person have to drive? Round your answer to the nearest tenth of a mile.

Solution

3)425.☐

Write zeros in the dividend as needed.

> To round to a given decimal place, divide until the quotient has one more decimal place than needed. Then round back.

Stop when the quotient reaches the ☐ place.

Answer: Each person has to drive about ☐ miles.

Guided Practice   Divide. Round to the nearest thousandth if necessary.

4. 6)45	**5.** 8)26	**6.** 7)30.52	**7.** 13)38.56

Lesson 4.4   Dividing by Whole Numbers

Lesson 4.5 Multiplying and Dividing by Powers of Ten

Goal: Use mental math to help multiply and divide.

Multiplying by Powers of Ten

Multiplying by Whole Number Powers of 10 Move the decimal point one place *to the* [____] for each [____] in the whole number power of 10.

Numbers 4.278 × 100 = [____]

Multiplying by Decimal Powers of 10 Move the decimal point one place *to the* [____] for each [_____] in the decimal power of 10.

Numbers 427.8 × 0.001 = [____]

EXAMPLE 1 Multiply Decimals Using Mental Math

When you move a decimal point to the right or left, you may need to write zeros as placeholders.

a. 0.008 × 1000 = [____] Move [__] places to the [____].

b. 85.96 × 0.0001 = [____] Move [__] places to the [____].

Guided Practice Find the product using mental math.

1. 17.34 × 10	2. 4.03 × 1000	3. 218.8 × 0.01	4. 18 × 0.001

EXAMPLE 2 — Multiply Decimals by Powers of Ten

Airports The graph shows the number of people that traveled through airports during 2000. How many people traveled through Chicago's O'Hare airport?

Airport Traffic in 2000

Hartsfield International (Atlanta)	👤👤👤👤👤👤👤👤	8.02
O'Hare (Chicago)	👤👤👤👤👤👤👤	7.21
Los Angeles	👤👤👤👤👤👤	6.85

👤 = 10,000,000 people

> When multiplying by powers of 10, first determine the direction in which you should move the decimal point, and then determine how many places to move the decimal point.

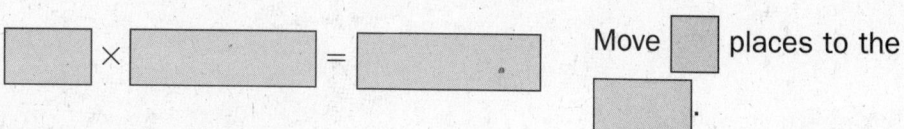

[ ] × [ ] = [ ]   Move [ ] places to the [ ].

Answer: In 2000, [ ] people traveled through O'Hare airport.

Dividing by Powers of Ten

Dividing by Whole Number Powers of 10 Move the decimal point one place *to the* [ ] for each [ ] in the whole number power of 10.

Numbers $78 \div 100 =$ [ ]

Dividing by Decimal Powers of 10 Move the decimal point one place *to the* [ ] for each [ ] in the decimal power of 10.

Numbers $78 \div 0.001 =$ [ ]

EXAMPLE 3 — Divide Decimals Using Mental Math

a. $907.4 \div 10 =$ [ ]   Move [ ] place to the [ ].

b. $907.4 \div 0.01 =$ [ ]   Move [ ] places to the [ ].

Lesson 4.5 Multiplying and Dividing by Powers of Ten

Guided Practice Find the quotient using mental math.

5. 38.7 ÷ 100	6. 704 ÷ 1000	7. 2 ÷ 0.1	8. 1.9 ÷ 0.001

Lesson 4.6 — Dividing by Decimals

Goal: Divide by decimals.

Dividing by a Decimal

Words When you divide by a decimal, multiply both the divisor and the dividend by [____] that will make the [____] a whole number.

Numbers 4.5)6.75   Multiply 4.5 and 6.75 by [____].

$$ \xrightarrow{} 45)\overline{}\ 1.5$$

EXAMPLE 1 Writing Divisors as Whole Numbers

Rewrite the division problem so that the divisor is a whole number.

a. 4.27 ÷ 3.6

3.6)4.27 ← Multiply the divisor and dividend by [____].

Answer: [____] ÷ [____]

b. 8 ÷ 0.42

0.42)8.[____] ← Write [____] as placeholders.

↑ Multiply the divisor and dividend by [____].

Answer: [____] ÷ [____]

> When you divide by a decimal with one decimal place, multiply the divisor and the dividend by 10. For a divisor with two decimal places, multiply by 100, and so on.

Guided Practice

Rewrite the division problem so that the divisor is a whole number.

1. 0.5)7.8	2. 4.1)8.97	3. 0.33)0.59	4. 0.024)679

WATCH OUT! Sometimes you need to place zeros as placeholders in the quotient.

EXAMPLE 2 Using Zeros While Dividing

Find the quotient.

a. $0.96 \div 1.5$

$1.5 \overline{)0.96}$ Multiply the divisor and the dividend by ☐.

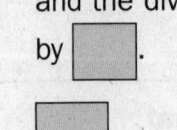

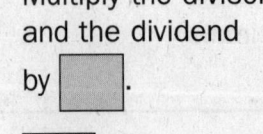

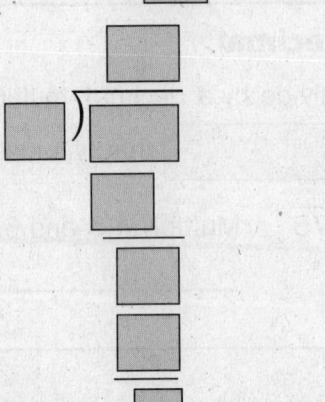

Answer: $0.96 \div 1.5 =$ ☐

b. $42 \div 0.03$

$0.03 \overline{)42}$ Multiply the divisor and the dividend by ☐.

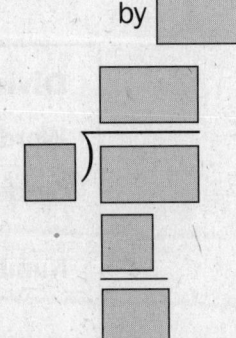

Answer: $42 \div 0.03 =$ ☐

EXAMPLE 3 Solving Problems Involving Decimals

Potatoes While at the grocery store, you buy $6.25 worth of potatoes. If one pound of potatoes costs $1.25, how many pounds of potatoes did you buy?

Solution

Divide the total cost of the potatoes by the cost of one pound of potatoes.

Divide $☐ by $☐.

$1.25 \overline{)6.25}$ Multiply the divisor and dividend by ☐.

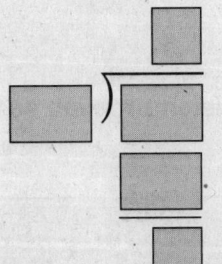

Answer: You bought ☐ pounds of potatoes.

✓ **Check** Estimate: $6.25 \div 1.25 \approx$ ☐ $\div$ ☐ $=$ ☐. So, the answer of ☐ pounds is reasonable.

92 | Chapter 4 Notetaking Guide

Guided Practice Divide. Round to the nearest tenth.

5. 0.4)0.94	6. 1.7)4.35	7. 0.36)31.8	8. 3.2)28

9. You buy $5.20 worth of apples. If apples cost $1.60 a pound, how many pounds of apples did you buy?

Lesson 4.7 Mass and Capacity

Goal: Use metric units of mass and capacity.

Vocabulary

mass:

gram:

milligram:

kilogram:

capacity:

liter:

milliliter:

kiloliter:

EXAMPLE 1 Choosing Units of Mass

An item has a mass of 6.4 kilograms. Is it a *videotape* or a *guitar*? Explain.

The mass of a _____ is about 1 kilogram, so 6.4 kilograms is the mass of about 6 _____. The mass of a _____ is closest to the mass of 6 _____, so the item is a _____.

As you preview this lesson, you may want to review what you learned about benchmarks for metric units of length in Lesson 2.1.

EXAMPLE 2 **Choosing Units of Capacity**

Tell whether the most appropriate unit to measure the capacity of the item is *milliliters*, *liters*, or *kiloliters*.

　　a. mixing bowl　　　　　　　　b. swimming pool

Solution

a. The capacity of a mixing bowl is closest to the capacity of ☐ ☐. You should use ☐.

b. The capacity of a swimming pool is closest to the capacity of ☐. You should use ☐.

EXAMPLE 3 **Choosing Metric Units**

Choose an appropriate metric unit to measure the item.

　　a. mass of a refrigerator magnet　　b. capacity of a measuring spoon

Solution

a. The mass of a refrigerator magnet is much greater than ☐ and less than ☐. So, you should use a ☐.

b. The capacity of a measuring spoon is much less than ☐ ☐. So, you should use a ☐.

When choosing an appropriate metric unit, use your benchmarks as a guide.

Guided Practice Choose an appropriate metric unit to measure the item.

1. mass of a stone statue	2. capacity of a food storage bag

Lesson 4.7　Mass and Capacity　95

Lesson 4.8 Changing Metric Units

Goal: Change from one metric unit of measure to another.

EXAMPLE 1 Changing Units Using Multiplication

Change 0.52 L to milliliters.

Solution

1. Decide whether to multiply or divide.
2. Select the power of 10.

Answer: 0.52 L = [ ] mL

Change to a smaller unit by [ ].

mL ← 0.52 [ ] [ ] = [ ] → L

EXAMPLE 2 Standardized Test Practice

Change 42.7 g to kilograms.

Ⓐ 42,700 kg   Ⓑ 4.27 kg   Ⓒ 0.427 kg   Ⓓ 0.0427 kg

Solution

1. Decide whether to multiply or divide.
2. Select the power of 10.

Answer: 42.7 g = [ ] kg

Change to a larger unit by [ ].

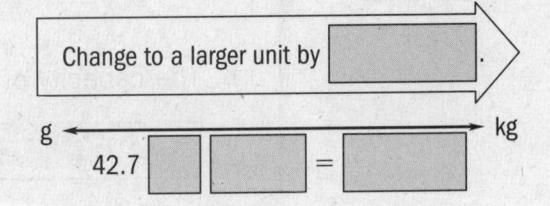

g ← 42.7 [ ] [ ] = [ ] → kg

The correct answer is [ ]. Ⓐ Ⓑ Ⓒ Ⓓ

Guided Practice Copy and complete the statement.

1. 540 g = __?__ kg	2. 1.8 mL = __?__ L	3. 0.37 m = __?__ cm

EXAMPLE 3 Comparing Measures

Which is longer, 340 m or 0.35 km?

Change 340 m to kilometers so the units are the same for both measures.

340 m = (340 · ☐) km   ☐ m = ☐ km

= ☐ km

Then compare measures.

Because ☐ km ☐ 0.35 km, you know that 340 m ☐ 0.35 km.

Answer: ☐ is longer than ☐.

> You can change either unit to the other. In Example 3, you could have changed 0.35 kilometers to meters instead.

Guided Practice Copy and complete the statement with <, >, or =.

4. 80 mm __?__ 6.7 cm	5. 620 mL __?__ 7 L	6. 0.03 kg = __?__ 30 g

Lesson 4.8 Changing Metric Units

EXAMPLE 4 Solve a Multi-Step Problem

Shelving A storage shelf can hold up to 39.8 kg of materials. A paint can has a mass of about 995 g. How many paint cans can four storage shelves hold?

Solution

1. Write a verbal model to find the number of cans that one shelf can hold.

   Number of cans on one shelf = [ ] ÷ [ ]

2. Change 39.8 kg to grams.

   39.8 kg = (39.8 [ ] [ ]) g = [ ] g

3. Substitute the given values into the verbal model.

   Number of cans on one shelf = [ ] ÷ [ ]

   = [ ]

4. Find the number of paint cans that four shelves can hold by multiplying the number of shelves by the number of paint cans that one shelf can hold.

   [ ] × [ ] = [ ]

Answer: Four storage shelves can hold [ ] paint cans.

Whenever you are solving problems involving units of measure, check to see if you need to convert any of the units.

Chapter 4 Words to Review

Give an example of the vocabulary word.

Commutative property of multiplication

Associative property of multiplication

Distributive property

Mass

Gram

Milligram

Kilogram

Capacity

Liter

Milliliter

Kiloliter

Review your notes and Chapter 4 by using the Chapter Review on pages 214–218 of your textbook.

Lesson 5.1 — Prime Factorization

Goal: Write whole numbers as the product of prime factors.

Vocabulary

Divisible:

Prime number:

Composite number:

Prime factorization:

Factor tree:

EXAMPLE 1 Finding Factors

Gardening You are planting tulip bulbs in rows in your garden. The bulbs will be arranged so that each row contains the same number of bulbs. Can 15 tulip bulbs or 18 tulip bulbs be arranged in more ways?

Solution

To answer the question, list all the factors of 15 and 18 by writing each number as a product of two numbers in as many ways as possible.

15: ☐ × ☐
    ☐ × ☐
    ☐ × ☐

18: ☐ × ☐
    ☐ × ☐
    ☐ × ☐
    ☐ × ☐

Stop when a pair of factors repeats.

The factors of 15 are _____.

The factors of 18 are _____.

Answer: ☐ bulbs can be arranged in more ways than ☐ bulbs, because ☐ has more ☐ than ☐.

Divisibility Rules for 2, 3, 5, 6, 9, and 10

A whole number is divisible by:
- 2 if the number is ____.
- 3 if the sum of ____ is divisible by ____.
- 5 if it ends with ____.
- 6 if it is ____.
- 9 if the sum of ____ is divisible by ____.
- 10 if it ends with ____.

EXAMPLE 2 Using Divisibility Rules

Test 120 for divisibility by 2, 3, 5, 6, 9, and 10.

120 ____ divisible by 2 because it ____.

120 ____ divisible by 3 because ____ + ____ + ____ = ____, which ____ divisible by ____.

120 ____ divisible by 5 because it ends with ____.

120 ____ divisible by 6 because it is ____ and divisible by ____.

120 ____ divisible by 9 because ____ + ____ + ____ = ____, which ____ divisible by ____.

120 ____ divisible by 10 because it ends with ____.

Answer: 120 is divisible by ____.

Guided Practice List all the factors of the number.

1. 10	2. 16	3. 20	4. 22

Test the number for divisibility by 2, 3, 5, 6, 9, and 10.

5. 80	6. 126	7. 585	8. 1296

EXAMPLE 3 **Classifying as Prime or Composite**

Tell whether the number is *prime* or *composite*.

a. 63   b. 71

Solution

a. List the factors of 63: _____.

   Answer: The number 63 is _____. It has factors _____ 1 and itself.

b. List the factors of 71: _____.

   Answer: The number 71 is _____. Its factors _____ 1 and itself.

> Another way to tell if a number is composite is to use divisibility rules. For example, 21 is divisible by 3. So, 3 is a factor of 21 and 21 is composite.

Guided Practice Tell whether the number is *prime* or *composite*.

9. 17	10. 16	11. 23	12. 28

EXAMPLE 4 **Standardized Test Practice**

Write the prime factorization of 80.

Ⓐ 2×5 Ⓑ 16×5
Ⓒ $2^4 \times 5$ Ⓓ $2^3 \times 10$

Solution

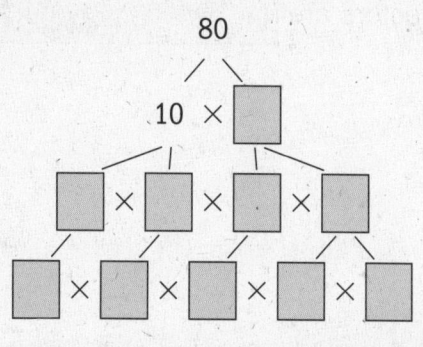

80
10 × ☐
☐ × ☐ × ☐ × ☐
☐ × ☐ × ☐ × ☐ × ☐

Write the original number.

Factor 80 as 10 times ☐.

Factor 10 and ☐.

Factor ☐.

Answer: The prime factorization of 80 is _____. The correct answer is ☐. Ⓐ Ⓑ Ⓒ Ⓓ

> Only prime and composite numbers are used in a factor tree. So, the number 1 is not used in a factor tree.

Lesson 5.1 Prime Factorization

LESSON 5.2 Greatest Common Factor

Goal: Find the greatest common factor of two or more numbers.

Vocabulary

Common factor: ⬚

Greatest Common Factor (GCF): ⬚

EXAMPLE 1 Multiple Representations

Drawing Class You are preparing kits for a drawing class. The kits will contain sheets of blank paper and sheets of grid paper. You have 180 sheets of blank paper and 96 sheets of grid paper. You want each kit to have the same number of each kind of paper, and you want to use all of the paper. What is the greatest number of kits you can make?

Solution

The greatest number of kits that you can make is the GCF of 96 and 180. Two methods for finding the GCF are shown.

Method 1 List all the factors of 96 and 180.

Factors of 96: ⬚

Factors of 180: ⬚

The common factors are ⬚. The GCF is ⬚.

Keep in mind that you can use the divisibility tests from Lesson 5.1 to help you find the factors of 96 and 180.

Method 2 Write the prime factorizations of 96 and 180. Then find the ☐ of the common prime factors.

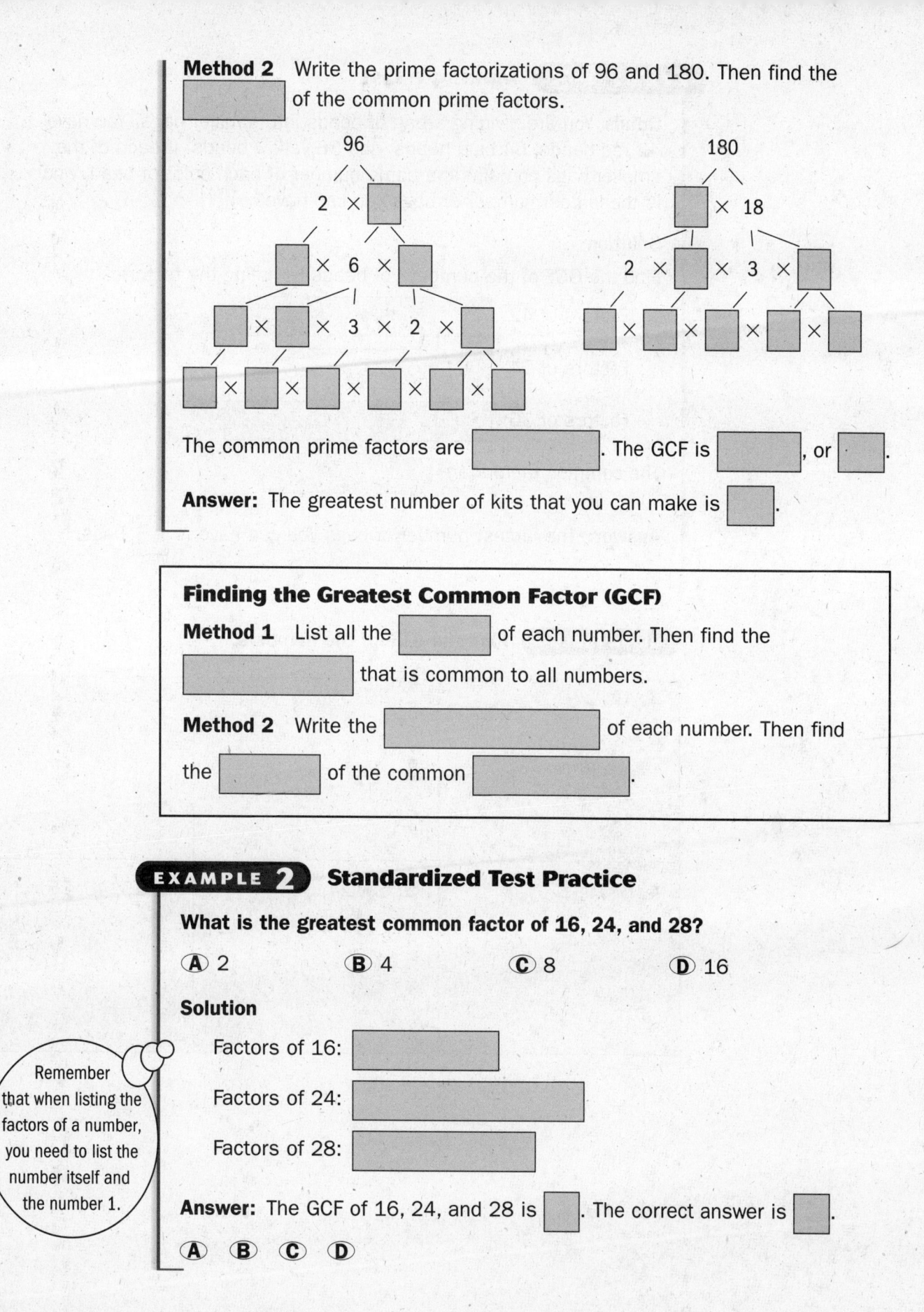

[Factor trees for 96 and 180]

The common prime factors are ☐. The GCF is ☐, or ☐.

Answer: The greatest number of kits that you can make is ☐.

Finding the Greatest Common Factor (GCF)

Method 1 List all the ☐ of each number. Then find the ☐ that is common to all numbers.

Method 2 Write the ☐ of each number. Then find the ☐ of the common ☐.

EXAMPLE 2 **Standardized Test Practice**

What is the greatest common factor of 16, 24, and 28?

Ⓐ 2   Ⓑ 4   Ⓒ 8   Ⓓ 16

Solution

Factors of 16: ☐

Factors of 24: ☐

Factors of 28: ☐

Answer: The GCF of 16, 24, and 28 is ☐. The correct answer is ☐.

Ⓐ Ⓑ Ⓒ Ⓓ

Remember that when listing the factors of a number, you need to list the number itself and the number 1.

Lesson 5.2 Greatest Common Factor 105

EXAMPLE 3 **Making a List**

Beads You are dividing a bag of beads into smaller bags. You have 42 red beads, 54 blue beads, and 36 yellow beads. If each of the smaller bags contains the same number of each color of bead, what is the largest number of bags you can have?

Solution

Find the GCF of the numbers of beads by listing the factors.

Factors of 42: [ ]

Factors of 54: [ ]

Factors of 36: [ ]

The common factors are [ ].

Answer: The largest number of bags you can have is [ ] bags.

Guided Practice Find the GCF of the numbers.

1. 12, 27	**2.** 20, 36	**3.** 24, 90
4. 6, 10, 12	**5.** 16, 24, 36	**6.** 15, 45, 75

106 | Chapter 5 Notetaking Guide

Lesson 5.3 Equivalent Fractions

Goal: Write equivalent fractions.

Vocabulary

Fraction:

Equivalent fractions:

Simplest form:

EXAMPLE 1 Writing Equivalent Fractions

Write two fractions that are equivalent to $\frac{1}{6}$.

$\frac{1}{6} = \frac{\square \times \square}{\square \times \square} = \frac{\square}{\square}$ Multiply the numerator and denominator by 2.

$\frac{1}{6} = \frac{\square \times \square}{\square \times \square} = \frac{\square}{\square}$ Multiply the numerator and denominator by 3.

In your notebook, you might want to record models of the equivalent fractions shown in Example 1.

Answer: The fractions $\frac{\square}{\square}$ and $\frac{\square}{\square}$ are equivalent to $\frac{1}{6}$.

Guided Practice Write two fractions that are equivalent to the given fraction.

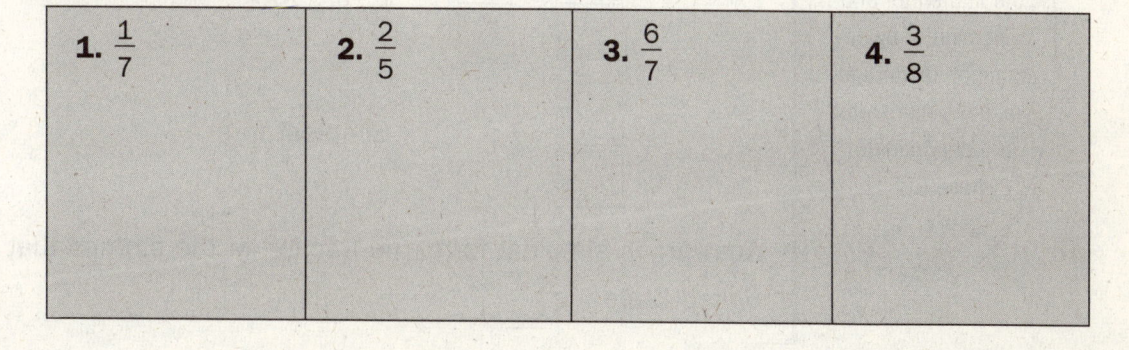

1. $\frac{1}{7}$
2. $\frac{2}{5}$
3. $\frac{6}{7}$
4. $\frac{3}{8}$

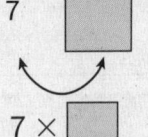

> **EXAMPLE 2** **Completing Equivalent Fractions**

Complete the equivalent fraction.

a. $\dfrac{4}{7} = \dfrac{20}{?}$

$4 \times \boxed{}$

$\dfrac{4}{7} = \dfrac{20}{\boxed{}}$

$7 \times \boxed{}$

You multiply $\boxed{}$ by $\boxed{}$ to get $\boxed{}$, so $\boxed{}$ the denominator by $\boxed{}$.

b. $\dfrac{21}{24} = \dfrac{?}{8}$

$21 \div \boxed{}$

$\dfrac{21}{24} = \dfrac{\boxed{}}{8}$

$24 \div \boxed{}$

You divide $\boxed{}$ by $\boxed{}$ to get $\boxed{}$, so $\boxed{}$ the numerator by $\boxed{}$.

> **Guided Practice** Copy and complete the statement.

5. $\dfrac{2}{9} = \dfrac{8}{?}$	6. $\dfrac{7}{10} = \dfrac{?}{40}$	7. $\dfrac{18}{24} = \dfrac{?}{4}$	8. $\dfrac{10}{45} = \dfrac{2}{?}$

> **EXAMPLE 3** **Simplifying Fractions**

Stamps In a grab bag of 100 stamps, 26 of the stamps are from the United States. Write this as a fraction in simplest form.

Solution

Write "26 out of 100" as a fraction. Then simplify.

$\dfrac{26}{100} = \dfrac{\boxed{} \times \boxed{}}{\boxed{} \times \boxed{}}$ Use the GCF to write the numerator and denominator as products.

$= \dfrac{\boxed{} \times \boxed{}}{\boxed{} \times \boxed{}}$ Divide the numerator and denominator by the GCF.

$= \dfrac{\boxed{}}{\boxed{}}$ Simplest form

Answer: In simplest form, the fraction of the stamps that are from the United States is $\boxed{}$.

If the numerator and denominator are large numbers, you could start by dividing the numerator and denominator by any common factor until you get a numerator and denominator whose GCF is easier to find.

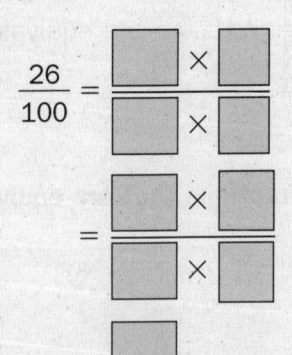

Guided Practice Write the fraction in simplest form.

9. $\frac{6}{24}$	10. $\frac{4}{32}$	11. $\frac{12}{18}$	12. $\frac{27}{54}$

EXAMPLE 4 Simplifying Fractions

Stickers You bought a pack of 100 stickers. Write a fraction in simplest form to describe the portion of each kind of sticker in the pack.

a. There are 12 frog stickers in the pack.

$$\frac{12}{\square} = \frac{\square \times \square}{\square \times \square} = \frac{\square}{\square}$$

☐ of the stickers are frogs.

b. There are 18 turtle stickers in the pack.

$$\frac{\square}{100} = \frac{\square \times \square}{\square \times \square} = \frac{\square}{\square}$$

☐ of the stickers are turtles.

c. There are 70 fish stickers in the pack.

$$\frac{70}{\square} = \frac{\square \times \square}{\square \times \square} = \frac{\square}{\square}$$

☐ of the stickers are fish.

Lesson 5.3 Equivalent Fractions

Lesson 5.4

Least Common Multiple

Goal: Find least common multiples.

Vocabulary

Multiple: _____

Common multiple: _____

Least Common Multiple (LCM): _____

EXAMPLE 1 Finding a Common Multiple

Haircuts You get your hair cut every 6 weeks and your brother gets his hair cut every 4 weeks. If you both get your hair cut today, when will you get your hair cut on the same day in the next 48 weeks?

Solution

You can use common multiples to answer the question about haircuts. Begin by writing the multiples of 6 and 4. Then identify the common multiples through 48.

Multiples of 6: _____

Multiples of 4: _____

The common multiples of 6 and 4 are _____.

Answer: You and your brother will get your hair cut on the same day in _____ weeks.

Guided Practice Find two common multiples of the numbers.

1. 2, 5	2. 3, 4	3. 8, 12	4. 4, 16

110 | Chapter 5 Notetaking Guide

5. A garbage company picks up nonrecyclable items every 7 days and recyclable items every 12 days. If the company picks up both kinds of items today, in how many days will the company pick up both kinds of items next?

Finding the Least Common Multiple (LCM)

The least common multiple of two or more numbers is the _____ of the common _____. Below are two methods to find the LCM.

Method 1 Start listing the _____ of each number. Then find the _____ of the common _____.

Method 2 Write the _____ of the numbers. Multiply together the _____. Use each _____ the _____ number of times it is a factor of any of the numbers.

EXAMPLE 2 Using Multiples

If the only common factor of two numbers is 1, then their least common multiple is the product of the two numbers.

Find the LCM of 6 and 16.

Multiples of 6: ___, ___, ___, ___, ___, ___, ___, ___, . . .

Multiples of 16: ___, ___, ___, ___, ___, ___, . . .

Answer: The LCM of 6 and 16 is ___.

Lesson 5.4 Least Common Multiple 111

EXAMPLE 3 Using Prime Factorization

Find the LCM of 30 and 36 using prime factorization.

1. Write the prime factorizations. Circle any common factors.

    30 = _____

    36 = _____

2. Multiply together the _____, using each circled factor the _____ number of times it occurs in either factorization.

    _____ = _____

Answer: The LCM of 30 and 36 is _____.

Guided Practice Find the LCM of the numbers.

6. 6, 15	7. 5, 8, 10	8. 40, 70

112 | Chapter 5 Notetaking Guide

LESSON 5.5 Ordering Fractions

Goal: Compare and order fractions.

Vocabulary

Least Common Denominator (LCD): _____

EXAMPLE 1 Comparing Fractions Using the LCD

Compare $\frac{3}{4}$ and $\frac{5}{6}$.

You can use any common denominator to compare two fractions, but it is usually easiest to use the LCD.

1. Find the LCD: Because the LCM of ☐ and ☐ is ☐, the LCD is ☐.

2. Use the LCD to write equivalent fractions.

$$\frac{3}{4} = \frac{\square \times \square}{\square \times \square} = \frac{\square}{\square} \qquad \frac{5}{6} = \frac{\square \times \square}{\square \times \square} = \frac{\square}{\square}$$

3. Compare: Because ☐☐☐, you know that ☐☐.

So, ☐☐☐.

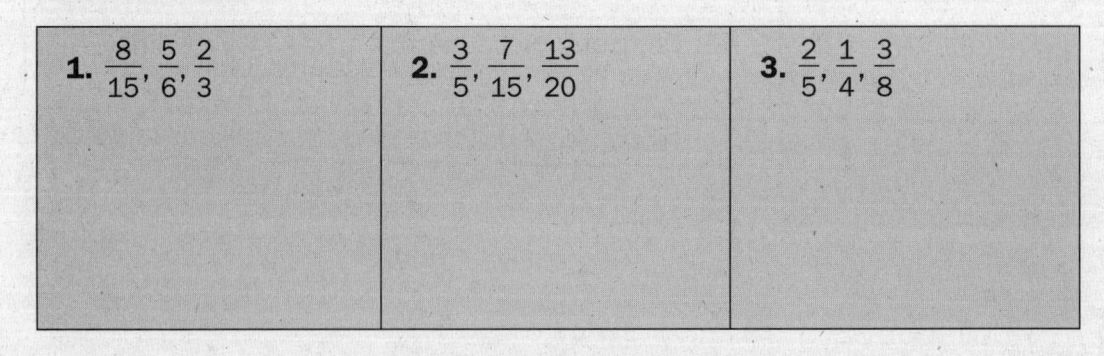

EXAMPLE 2 Ordering Fractions

Order the fractions $\frac{5}{6}$, $\frac{3}{8}$, and $\frac{7}{12}$ from least to greatest.

1. Find the LCD: Because the LCM of ☐, ☐, and ☐ is ☐, the LCD is ☐.

2. Use the LCD to write equivalent fractions.

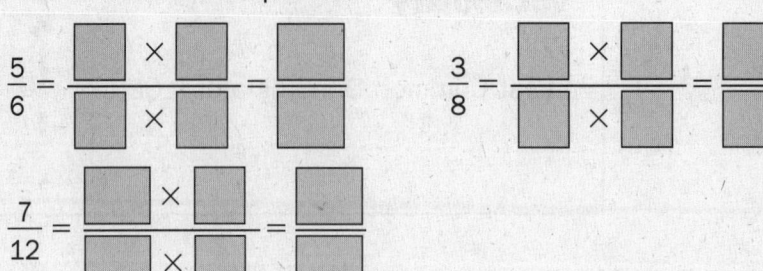

$$\frac{5}{6} = \frac{\Box \times \Box}{\Box \times \Box} = \frac{\Box}{\Box} \qquad \frac{3}{8} = \frac{\Box \times \Box}{\Box \times \Box} = \frac{\Box}{\Box}$$

$$\frac{7}{12} = \frac{\Box \times \Box}{\Box \times \Box} = \frac{\Box}{\Box}$$

3. Compare: Because ☐ < ☐, you know that ☐ < ☐.

    Because ☐ < ☐, you know that ☐ < ☐.

Answer: The fractions, from least to greatest, are ☐, ☐, and ☐.

WATCH OUT!
Don't forget to multiply the numerator by the same number you multiply the denominator by when writing an equivalent fraction.

Guided Practice   Order the fractions from least to greatest.

1. $\frac{8}{15}, \frac{5}{6}, \frac{2}{3}$

2. $\frac{3}{5}, \frac{7}{15}, \frac{13}{20}$

3. $\frac{2}{5}, \frac{1}{4}, \frac{3}{8}$

EXAMPLE 3 Ordering Fractions to Solve a Problem

Chair Repair You are replacing the screws in a chair. You tried a screw that was $\frac{3}{4}$ inch long, but it was too long. Should you try a screw that is $\frac{9}{16}$ inch long or a screw that is $\frac{7}{8}$ inch long?

Solution

Order the fractions from least to greatest:

1. Find the LCD: Because the LCM of ☐, ☐, and ☐ is ☐, the LCD is ☐.

2. Use the LCD to write equivalent fractions.

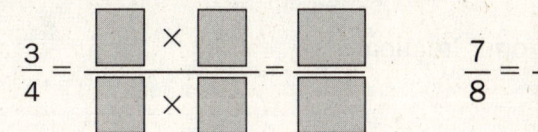

$\frac{3}{4} = \dfrac{☐ \times ☐}{☐ \times ☐} = \dfrac{☐}{☐}$ $\frac{7}{8} = \dfrac{☐ \times ☐}{☐ \times ☐} = \dfrac{☐}{☐}$

3. Order the fractions: The fractions, from least to greatest, are ☐, ☐, and ☐.

Answer: You should try the screw that is ☐ inch long.

LESSON 5.6
Mixed Numbers and Improper Fractions

Goal: Rewrite mixed numbers and improper fractions.

Vocabulary

Mixed number:

Improper fraction:

EXAMPLE 1 Measuring to a Fraction of an Inch

Picture Frame You need to measure the length of a photo so that you can buy the correct size of frame for the photo. Write the length as a mixed number and as an improper fraction.

Solution

Measure the photo and write the length as a mixed number: inches.

Then count eighths to write the length as an improper fraction: inches.

There are eighths in .

116 Chapter 5 Notetaking Guide

Guided Practice Draw a line segment that has the given length.

1. $\frac{5}{2}$ in.

2. $3\frac{3}{8}$ in.

EXAMPLE 2 Rewriting Mixed Numbers

Write $6\frac{3}{7}$ as an improper fraction.

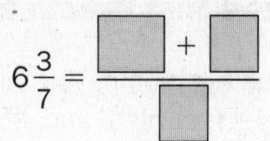

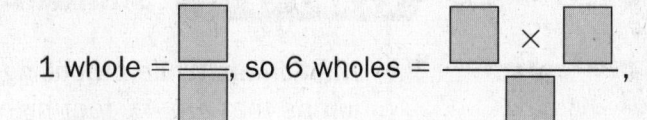

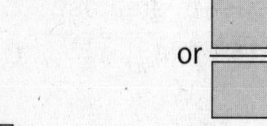

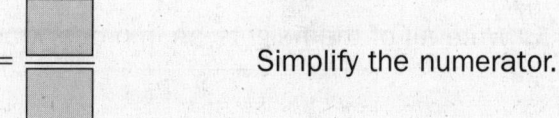

$6\frac{3}{7} = \frac{\square + \square}{\square}$ 1 whole = $\frac{\square}{\square}$, so 6 wholes = $\frac{\square \times \square}{\square}$, or $\frac{\square}{\square}$.

$= \frac{\square}{\square}$ Simplify the numerator.

WATCH OUT!
In Example 2, don't forget to add the fraction part after you write the whole part as a fraction.

EXAMPLE 3 Rewriting Improper Fractions

Write $\frac{18}{5}$ as a mixed number.

1. Divide 18 by 5.

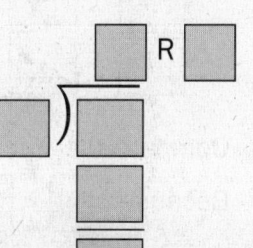

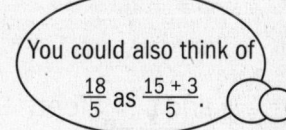

$\square \overline{)\square} \; R \; \square$

You could also think of $\frac{18}{5}$ as $\frac{15 + 3}{5}$.

2. Write the mixed number. $\square + \square = \square$

Lesson 5.6 Mixed Numbers and Improper Fractions 117

Guided Practice Write the mixed number as an improper fraction.

3. $2\frac{3}{5}$	4. $3\frac{1}{8}$	5. $5\frac{4}{9}$

Write the improper fraction as a mixed number.

6. $\frac{24}{7}$	7. $\frac{48}{15}$	8. $\frac{52}{11}$

EXAMPLE 4 Standardized Test Practice

High Jump While practicing the high jump, you take three practice jumps that are $4\frac{3}{8}$ feet high, $4\frac{1}{4}$ feet high, and $\frac{18}{4}$ feet high. Order the heights from least to greatest.

Ⓐ $4\frac{3}{8}, 4\frac{1}{4}, \frac{18}{4}$ Ⓑ $\frac{18}{4}, 4\frac{1}{4}, 4\frac{3}{8}$ Ⓒ $\frac{18}{4}, 4\frac{3}{8}, 4\frac{1}{4}$ Ⓓ $4\frac{1}{4}, 4\frac{3}{8}, \frac{18}{4}$

Solution

1. Write all of the heights as improper fractions.

$$4\frac{3}{8} = \frac{\Box + \Box}{\Box} = \frac{\Box}{\Box} \qquad 4\frac{1}{4} = \frac{\Box + \Box}{\Box} = \frac{\Box}{\Box} \qquad \frac{18}{4}$$

2. Rewrite all of the heights using the LCD, $\Box$.

$$\frac{\Box}{\Box} = \frac{\Box \times \Box}{\Box \times \Box} = \frac{\Box}{\Box} \qquad \frac{18}{4} = \frac{\Box \times \Box}{\Box \times \Box} = \frac{\Box}{\Box}$$

3. Compare the fractions.

Because $\Box < \Box$ and $\Box < \Box$, you know that $\Box < \Box$ and $\Box < \Box$.

Answer: The heights, from least to greatest, are $\Box$, $\Box$, and $\Box$ feet. The correct answer is $\Box$. Ⓐ Ⓑ Ⓒ Ⓓ

LESSON 5.7

Changing Decimals to Fractions

Goal: Write a decimal as a fraction.

EXAMPLE 1 **Writing Decimals as Fractions**

Write the decimal as a fraction in simplest form.

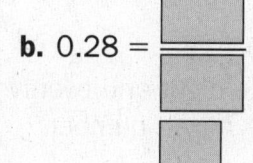

a. $0.6 = \dfrac{\boxed{}}{\boxed{}}$ Write six $\boxed{}$ as a fraction.

   $= \dfrac{\boxed{}}{\boxed{}}$ Simplify.

b. $0.28 = \dfrac{\boxed{}}{\boxed{}}$ Write twenty-eight $\boxed{}$ as a fraction.

   $= \dfrac{\boxed{}}{\boxed{}}$ Simplify.

Lesson 5.7 Changing Decimals to Fractions | 119

EXAMPLE 2 **Writing Decimals as Mixed Numbers**

Precipitation The total amounts of precipitation in Portland, Oregon, and Albuquerque, New Mexico, in 2000 are given below. Write each amount as a mixed number in simplest form.

a. Amount of precipitation in Portland, Oregon: 30.2 inches
b. Amount of precipitation in Albuquerque, New Mexico: 8.24 inches

> With practice, you will learn to recognize the fraction forms of several common decimals. Here are some examples.
> $0.5 = \frac{1}{2}$
> $0.2 = \frac{1}{5}$
> $0.25 = \frac{1}{4}$
> $0.125 = \frac{1}{8}$
> $0.75 = \frac{3}{4}$
> $0.4 = \frac{2}{5}$

Solution

a. $30.2 = \boxed{}\dfrac{\boxed{}}{\boxed{}}$ Write thirty and two $\boxed{}$ as a mixed number.

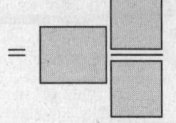

   $= \boxed{}\dfrac{\boxed{}}{\boxed{}}$ Simplify.

Answer: The amount of precipitation in Portland was $\boxed{}$ inches.

b. $8.24 = \boxed{}\dfrac{\boxed{}}{\boxed{}}$ Write eight and twenty-four $\boxed{}$ as a mixed number.

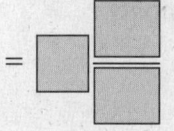

   $= \boxed{}\dfrac{\boxed{}}{\boxed{}}$ Simplify.

Answer: The amount of precipitation in Albuquerque was $\boxed{}$ inches.

EXAMPLE 3 Decimals with Zeros

Write the decimal as a fraction or mixed number in simplest form.

> Recall that you read a decimal according to its last place value. For example, 2.007 is read "two and seven thousandths."

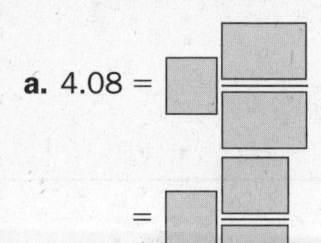

a. $4.08 = \dfrac{\square}{\square}$ Write four and eight _____ as a mixed number.

$= \dfrac{\square}{\square}$ Simplify.

b. $0.312 = \dfrac{\square}{\square}$ Write three hundred twelve _____ as a fraction.

$= \dfrac{\square}{\square}$ Simplify.

Guided Practice Write the decimal as a fraction or mixed number in simplest form.

1. 0.2	2. 1.48	3. 3.004	4. 0.806

Lesson 5.7 Changing Decimals to Fractions | 121

Lesson 5.8 Changing Fractions to Decimals

Goal: Write fractions as decimals.

Vocabulary

Terminating decimal: _____

Repeating decimal: _____

EXAMPLE 1 Writing a Fraction as a Decimal

U.S. Government In the 107th Congress, fourteen out of the fifty states had 10 or more representatives in the House of Representatives. This can be written as the fraction $\frac{14}{50}$. Write this fraction as a decimal.

Solution

To answer the question, write the fraction $\frac{14}{50}$ as a decimal by dividing 14 by 50.

$50 \overline{)14.00}$

← The remainder is ____.

Answer: The quotient is ____, so ____ of the states had 10 or more representatives.

Need help with division? See page 187 of your textbook.

Writing a Fraction as a Decimal

Words To write a fraction as a decimal, divide the _____ by the _____.

Numbers $\frac{2}{5}$ means ____ ÷ ____   **Algebra** $\frac{}{}$ means $a \div b$ $(b \neq 0)$

Guided Practice Write the fraction as a decimal.

| 1. $\frac{1}{5}$ | 2. $\frac{7}{10}$ | 3. $\frac{3}{4}$ | 4. $\frac{5}{8}$ |

EXAMPLE 2 — Writing a Mixed Number as a Decimal

Write $4\frac{7}{8}$ as a decimal.

1. Divide 7 by 8.

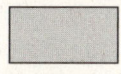

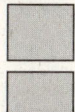

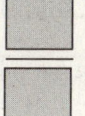

   ☐
   8)7.000
   ☐
   ──
   ☐
   ☐
   ☐
   ☐
   ☐ ← The remainder is ☐.

2. Add the whole number and the decimal.

   ☐ + ☐ = ☐

Answer: The mixed number $4\frac{7}{8}$, written as a decimal, is ☐.

Lesson 5.8 Changing Fractions to Decimals | 123

EXAMPLE 3 **Repeating Decimals**

a. Write $\dfrac{11}{6}$ as a decimal.   **b.** Write $1\dfrac{4}{11}$ as a decimal.

6)11.000   11)4.0000

The digit □ repeats.   The digits □ repeat.

> With practice, you will learn to recognize the decimal form of several common fractions. Here are some examples.
>
> $\dfrac{1}{2} = 0.5$
>
> $\dfrac{1}{5} = 0.2$
>
> $\dfrac{1}{4} = 0.25$
>
> $\dfrac{1}{3} = 0.\overline{3}$
>
> $\dfrac{1}{10} = 0.1$
>
> $\dfrac{1}{8} = 0.125$

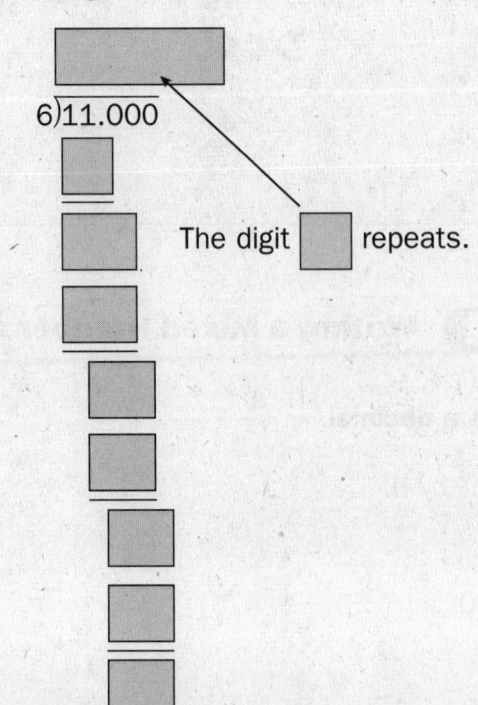

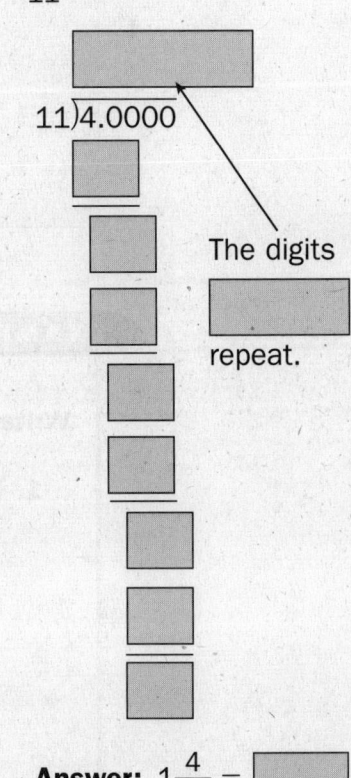

Answer: $\dfrac{11}{6} =$ □   **Answer:** $1\dfrac{4}{11} =$ □

Guided Practice Write the fraction or mixed number as a decimal.

5. $2\dfrac{4}{5}$	**6.** $3\dfrac{7}{8}$	**7.** $\dfrac{5}{9}$	**8.** $4\dfrac{5}{11}$

Chapter 5 Notetaking Guide

Chapter 5 Words to Review

Give an example of the vocabulary word.

Divisible

Prime number

Composite number

Prime factorization

Factor tree

Common factor

Greatest Common Factor (GCF)

Fraction

Equivalent fractions

Simplest form

Multiple

Common multiple

Least Common Multiple (LCM)

Least Common Denominator (LCD)

Mixed number

Improper fraction

Proper fraction

Terminating or repeating decimal

Review your notes and Chapter 5 by using the Chapter Review on pages 278–282 of your textbook.

Lesson 6.1

Fraction Estimation

Goal: Estimate with fractions and mixed numbers.

EXAMPLE 1   Rounding Fractions

Round the fraction.

a. $\dfrac{1}{9} \approx$ ☐   Because 1 is ☐ 9, round $\dfrac{1}{9}$ to ☐.

b. $\dfrac{6}{11} \approx$ ☐   Because 6 is ☐ 11, round $\dfrac{6}{11}$ to ☐.

c. $\dfrac{7}{8} \approx$ ☐   Because 7 is ☐ 8, round $\dfrac{7}{8}$ to ☐.

EXAMPLE 2   Rounding Mixed Numbers

Round the mixed number.

a. $5\dfrac{1}{4} \approx$ ☐   Because $\dfrac{1}{4}$ is ☐ $\dfrac{1}{2}$, round $5\dfrac{1}{4}$ ☐ to ☐.

b. $6\dfrac{2}{3} \approx$ ☐   Because $\dfrac{2}{3}$ is ☐ $\dfrac{1}{2}$, round $6\dfrac{2}{3}$ ☐ to ☐.

If the fraction or mixed number that you are rounding is halfway between two numbers, you usually round to the greater number.

Guided Practice   Round the fraction or mixed number.

| 1. $\dfrac{1}{5}$ | 2. $\dfrac{9}{10}$ | 3. $1\dfrac{7}{12}$ | 4. $3\dfrac{2}{5}$ |

EXAMPLE 3 **Estimating a Difference**

Estimate the difference $7\frac{1}{3} - 2\frac{5}{6}$.

$7\frac{1}{3} - 2\frac{5}{6} \approx \boxed{} - \boxed{}$ Round each mixed number.

$\phantom{7\frac{1}{3} - 2\frac{5}{6}} = \boxed{}$ Find the difference.

EXAMPLE 4 **Estimating a Sum**

Home Repair You are replacing the wood frame around a door. You need $13\frac{1}{4}$ feet of wood for the sides and $3\frac{7}{8}$ feet of wood for the top of the frame. You want to know how much wood you need.

a. Should your estimate of the amount of wood be *high* or *low*?

b. Estimate the amount of wood needed.

Solution

a. Your estimate of the amount of wood you need should be $\boxed{}$ so that you will $\boxed{}$.

b. Estimate the sum $13\frac{1}{4} + 3\frac{7}{8}$.

$13\frac{1}{4} + 3\frac{7}{8} \approx \boxed{} + \boxed{}$ Round each fraction $\boxed{}$ to get a $\boxed{}$ estimate.

$\phantom{13\frac{1}{4} + 3\frac{7}{8}} = \boxed{}$ Find the sum.

Answer: You will need about $\boxed{}$ feet of wood.

> Usually when you are estimating a sum involving fractions or mixed numbers, you want to round to the nearest half or nearest whole number. In real-life situations, however, you may want to round all fractions or mixed numbers up (or down) to get a high (or low) estimate.

Guided Practice Estimate the sum or difference.

5. $\frac{2}{3} + \frac{6}{7}$	6. $\frac{7}{13} - \frac{1}{6}$	7. $5\frac{1}{8} - 3\frac{9}{14}$	8. $2\frac{8}{9} + 4\frac{1}{2}$

Chapter 6 Notetaking Guide

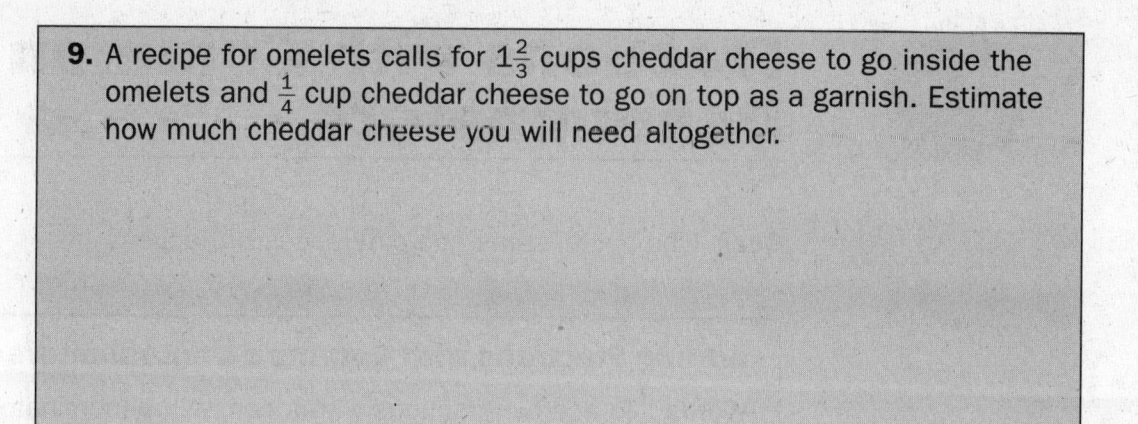

9. A recipe for omelets calls for $1\frac{2}{3}$ cups cheddar cheese to go inside the omelets and $\frac{1}{4}$ cup cheddar cheese to go on top as a garnish. Estimate how much cheddar cheese you will need altogether.

Lesson 6.2 Fractions with Common Denominators

Goal: Find actual sums and differences of fractions.

Adding Fractions with Common Denominators

Words To add two fractions with a common denominator, write the ☐ of the ☐ over the ☐.

Numbers $\frac{2}{9} + \frac{5}{9} = \frac{\square}{\square}$ **Algebra** $\frac{\square}{\square} + \frac{\square}{\square} = \frac{a+b}{c}$ $(c \neq 0)$

EXAMPLE 1 Adding Fractions

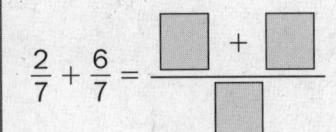

$\frac{2}{7} + \frac{6}{7} = \frac{\square + \square}{\square}$ Add the numerators.

$= \frac{\square}{\square}$ Simplify the numerator.

$= \square \frac{\square}{\square}$ Rewrite the improper fraction as a mixed number.

Need help with rewriting improper fractions as mixed numbers? See page 261 of your textbook.

Guided Practice Find the sum. Simplify if possible.

1. $\frac{1}{5} + \frac{2}{5}$	2. $\frac{4}{9} + \frac{2}{9}$	3. $\frac{3}{8} + \frac{7}{8}$	4. $\frac{11}{12} + \frac{5}{12}$

Subtracting Fractions with Common Denominators

Words To subtract two fractions with a common denominator, write the ☐ of the ☐ over the ☐.

Numbers $\dfrac{6}{7} - \dfrac{3}{7} = \dfrac{\Box}{\Box}$ **Algebra** $\dfrac{\Box}{\Box} - \dfrac{\Box}{\Box} = \dfrac{a-b}{c}\ (c \neq 0)$

EXAMPLE 2 Subtracting Fractions

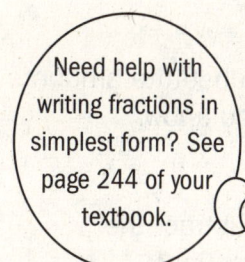

$\dfrac{9}{16} - \dfrac{3}{16} = \dfrac{\Box - \Box}{\Box}$ Subtract the numerators.

$= \dfrac{\Box}{\Box}$ Simplify the numerator.

$= \dfrac{\Box}{\Box}$ Simplify the fraction.

Need help with writing fractions in simplest form? See page 244 of your textbook.

Lesson 6.2 Fractions with Common Denominators | 131

EXAMPLE 3 Standardized Test Practice

Soil Particles The U.S. Bureau of Soils classifies soil particles according to their diameters. For example, a particle with a diameter of $\frac{6}{25}$ millimeter is called fine sand and a particle with a diameter of $\frac{1}{25}$ millimeter is called silt. How would you find the difference in the diameters of the particles?

Ⓐ Subtract $\frac{1}{25}$ from $\frac{6}{25}$. Ⓑ Add $\frac{6}{25}$ and $\frac{1}{25}$.

Ⓒ Multiply $\frac{6}{25}$ and $\frac{1}{25}$. Ⓓ Divide $\frac{6}{25}$ by $\frac{1}{25}$.

Solution

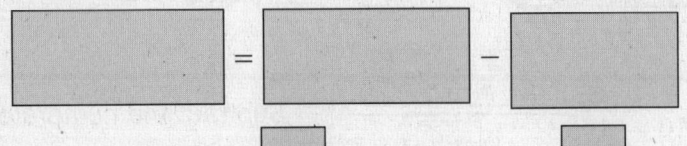

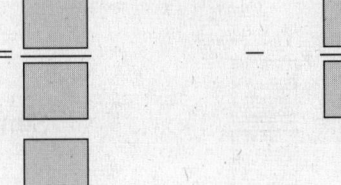

☐ = ☐ − ☐

= ☐/☐ − ☐/☐   Substitute amounts you know.

= ☐/☐   Subtract the fractions.

= ☐/☐   Simplify.

Answer: You need to ☐. The correct answer is ☐.

Ⓐ Ⓑ Ⓒ Ⓓ

Guided Practice Find the difference. Simplify if possible.

5. $\frac{6}{7} - \frac{5}{7}$	6. $\frac{3}{4} - \frac{1}{4}$	7. $\frac{9}{10} - \frac{7}{10}$	8. $\frac{11}{12} - \frac{5}{12}$

LESSON 6.3 Fractions with Different Denominators

Goal: Add and subtract fractions with different denominators.

Adding and Subtracting Fractions

1. Rewrite the fractions using the ☐.

2. ☐ the numerators.

3. Write the result over the ☐.

4. ☐ if possible.

EXAMPLE 1 Adding Fractions

Art Class You are buying art supplies for an art class. Of the total amount of money you will spend on supplies, $\frac{1}{4}$ of the total amount will be spent on paper and $\frac{3}{5}$ of the total amount will be spent on paints and charcoal pencils. How much of the total amount of money will you spend on paper, paints, and charcoal pencils?

Solution

To answer the question, find the sum $\frac{\Box}{\Box} + \frac{\Box}{\Box}$.

$$\frac{\Box \times \Box}{\Box \times \Box} = \frac{\Box}{\Box}$$ Rewrite both fractions using the LCD, ☐.

$$+ \frac{\Box \times \Box}{\Box \times \Box} = + \frac{\Box}{\Box}$$

$$\frac{\Box}{\Box}$$ Add the fractions.

Answer: You will spend ☐ of the total amount of money on paper, paints, and charcoal pencils.

Need help with rewriting fractions? See page 254 of your textbook.

EXAMPLE 2 Rewriting Sums of Fractions

Find the sum $\frac{5}{6} + \frac{2}{3}$.

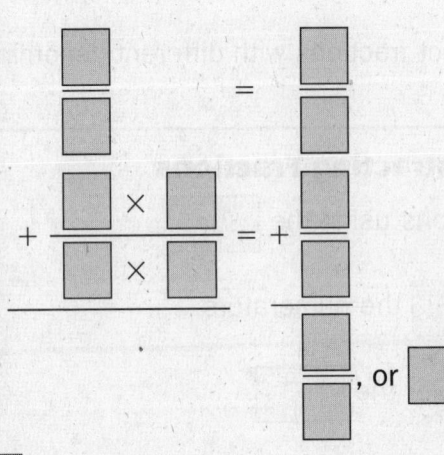

In your summary of this chapter, you may want to include examples of adding and subtracting fractions with common and different denominators.

$$\frac{\Box}{\Box} + \frac{\Box \times \Box}{\Box \times \Box} = \frac{\Box}{\Box} + \frac{\Box}{\Box}$$

Rewrite $\frac{\Box}{\Box}$ using the LCD, $\Box$.

$\frac{\Box}{\Box}$, or $\frac{\Box}{\Box}$ Add the fractions.

EXAMPLE 3 Subtracting Fractions

Science Project For a semester-long science project, you are recording the growth of your hair. During the month of September, your hair grew $\frac{5}{6}$ inch. In October, your hair grew $\frac{3}{4}$ inch. How much more did you hair grow in September than in October?

Solution

You need to find the difference $\frac{\Box}{\Box} - \frac{\Box}{\Box}$.

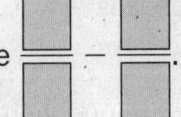

$$\frac{\Box \times \Box}{\Box \times \Box} = \frac{\Box}{\Box}$$
$$-\frac{\Box \times \Box}{\Box \times \Box} = -\frac{\Box}{\Box}$$

Rewrite both fractions using the LCD, $\Box$.

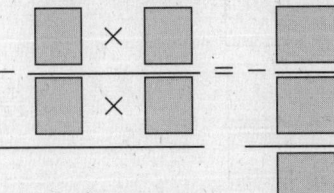

$$\frac{\Box}{\Box}$$

Subtract the fractions.

Answer: Your hair grew $\boxed{}$ inch longer in September.

Guided Practice Find the sum or difference. Simplify if possible.

1. $\frac{7}{8} - \frac{5}{6}$	2. $\frac{4}{9} + \frac{1}{3}$	3. $\frac{2}{3} + \frac{1}{5}$	4. $\frac{5}{9} - \frac{2}{15}$

5. You estimate that $\frac{3}{4}$ of a driving trip will be spent on the highway, $\frac{1}{5}$ on city streets, and the rest on country roads. How much greater of a portion of your trip will be spent on the highway than on city streets?

EXAMPLE 4 Standardized Test Practice

Homework You do your history homework for $\frac{2}{5}$ hour and do your math homework for $\frac{3}{10}$ hour. Which model represents the total time spent on homework?

Ⓐ   Ⓑ   Ⓒ   Ⓓ

Solution
You need to find the total amount of time, so add $\frac{2}{5}$ and $\frac{3}{10}$.

1. Draw models to represent the problem.
2. Redraw the models to divide them the same way.
3. Combine to find the sum.

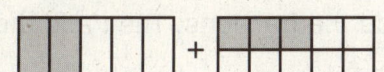

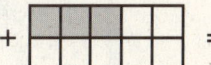

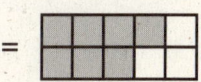

Answer: The total amount of time spent on your homework is ☐ hour.

The correct answer is ☐. Ⓐ Ⓑ Ⓒ Ⓓ

Lesson 6.3 Fractions with Different Denominators

LESSON 6.4 Adding and Subtracting Mixed Numbers

Goal: Add and subtract mixed numbers.

Adding and Subtracting Mixed Numbers

1. Rewrite the fractions using the [ ] if necessary.

2. Add or subtract the [ ].

3. Add or subtract the [ ].

4. [ ] if possible.

EXAMPLE 1 Adding Mixed Numbers

Guitar Practice Last week, you practiced playing the guitar for $6\frac{1}{5}$ hours. This week, you practiced for $8\frac{2}{5}$ hours. How much time did you spend practicing the guitar during the last two weeks?

Solution

Find the sum $[\;]\frac{[\;]}{[\;]} + [\;]\frac{[\;]}{[\;]}$.

$[\;]\frac{[\;]}{[\;]}$

$+[\;]\frac{[\;]}{[\;]}$

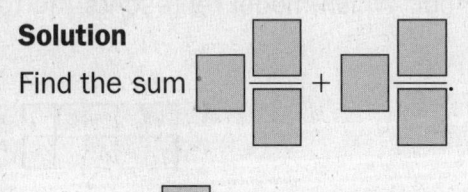

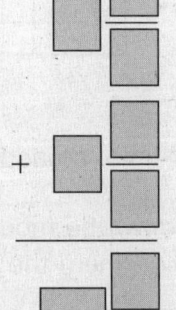

$[\;]\frac{[\;]}{[\;]}$

Add the fractions. Then add the whole numbers.

> Remember that when adding fractions, you write the sum of the numerators over the common denominator.

Answer: You spent [ ] hours practicing the guitar during the last two weeks.

---

136 | Chapter 6 | Notetaking Guide

Guided Practice Find the sum.

1. $3\frac{3}{5} + 2\frac{1}{5}$	2. $4\frac{2}{9} + 1\frac{5}{9}$	3. $6\frac{4}{7} + 5\frac{1}{7}$	4. $2\frac{4}{11} + 1\frac{6}{11}$

EXAMPLE 2 Simplifying Mixed Number Sums

Find the sum $2\frac{1}{6} + 1\frac{1}{3}$.

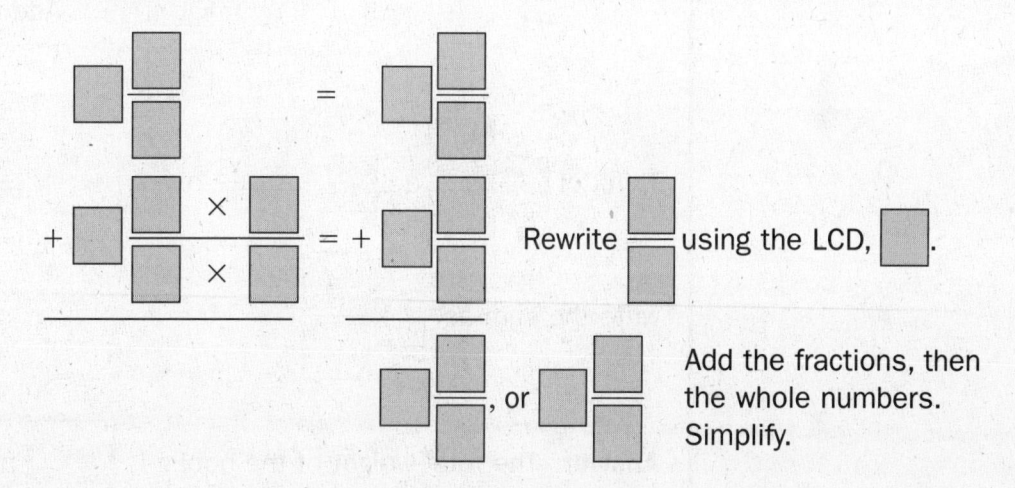

$$2\frac{1}{6} = 2\frac{\square}{\square}$$
$$+\, 1\frac{1 \times \square}{3 \times \square} = +\, 1\frac{\square}{\square} \quad \text{Rewrite } \frac{\square}{\square} \text{ using the LCD, } \square.$$

$$ \frac{\square}{\square}, \text{ or } \square\frac{\square}{\square} \quad \text{Add the fractions, then the whole numbers. Simplify.}$$

Lesson 6.4 Adding and Subtracting Mixed Numbers | 137

EXAMPLE 3 Solving Addition Problems

Books Your science book weighs $2\frac{3}{5}$ pounds and your history book weighs $3\frac{1}{2}$ pounds. What is the total weight of the books?

Solution

You need to find the sum $\boxed{}\frac{\boxed{}}{\boxed{}} + \boxed{}\frac{\boxed{}}{\boxed{}}$.

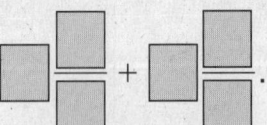

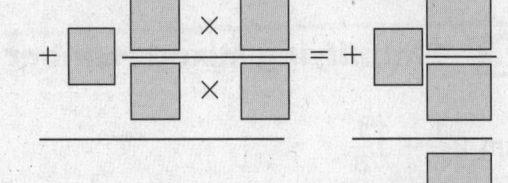

$\boxed{}\dfrac{\boxed{} \times \boxed{}}{\boxed{} \times \boxed{}} = \boxed{}\dfrac{\boxed{}}{\boxed{}}$ Rewrite both fractions using the LCD, $\boxed{}$.

$+ \boxed{}\dfrac{\boxed{} \times \boxed{}}{\boxed{} \times \boxed{}} = + \boxed{}\dfrac{\boxed{}}{\boxed{}}$

$\boxed{}\dfrac{\boxed{}}{\boxed{}}$ Add the fractions, then the whole numbers.

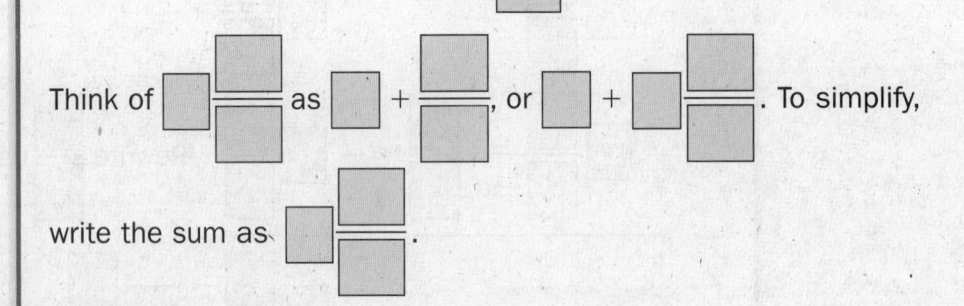

Think of $\boxed{}\dfrac{\boxed{}}{\boxed{}}$ as $\boxed{} + \dfrac{\boxed{}}{\boxed{}}$, or $\boxed{} + \boxed{}\dfrac{\boxed{}}{\boxed{}}$. To simplify, write the sum as $\boxed{}\dfrac{\boxed{}}{\boxed{}}$.

Answer: The total weight of the books is $\boxed{}$ pounds.

Guided Practice   Find the sum. Simplify if possible.

5. $1\frac{1}{2} + 2\frac{3}{8}$	6. $4\frac{2}{5} + 6\frac{1}{3}$	7. $5\frac{4}{9} + 8\frac{2}{3}$	8. $3\frac{5}{12} + 2\frac{5}{6}$

9. A plant stand is $16\frac{3}{5}$ inches tall. There is a plant on the top of the stand that is $5\frac{2}{3}$ inches tall. What is the total height of the plant and the stand?

10. It takes $3\frac{1}{2}$ hours to drive from your house to your cousin's house and the same time to return home. How long are you in the car for a round trip?

EXAMPLE 4 Subtracting Mixed Numbers

Racing The track at Pimlico Race Course in Baltimore, Maryland is $1\frac{3}{16}$ miles long. The track at Belmont Park in Elmont, New York is $1\frac{1}{2}$ miles long. How much longer is the track at Belmont Park?

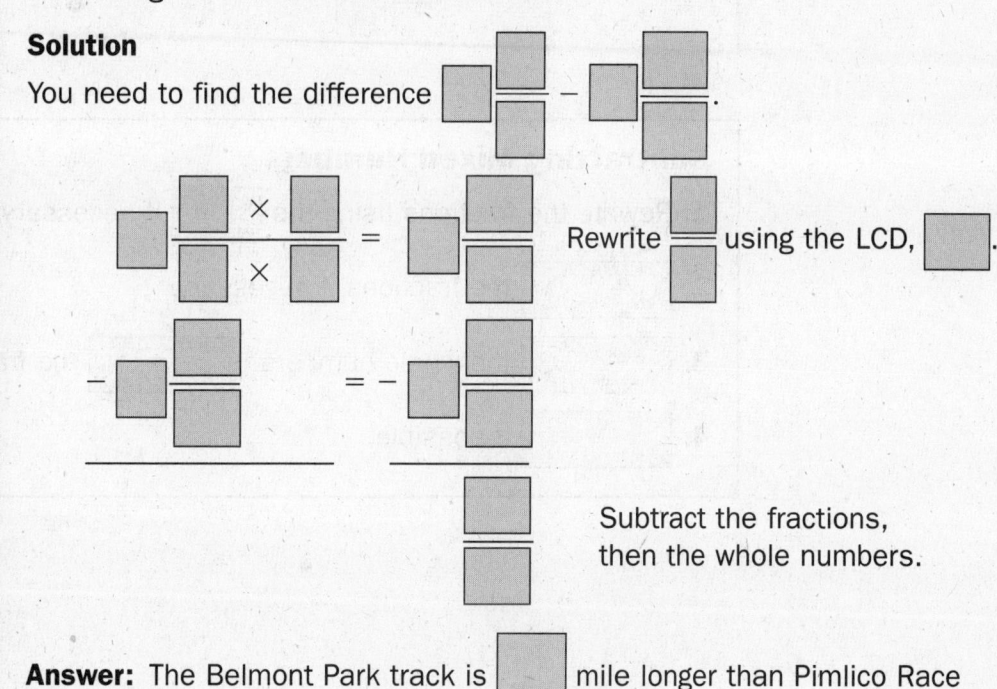

Solution

You need to find the difference $\boxed{}\frac{\boxed{}}{\boxed{}} - \boxed{}\frac{\boxed{}}{\boxed{}}$.

$\boxed{}\dfrac{\boxed{} \times \boxed{}}{\boxed{} \times \boxed{}} = \boxed{}\dfrac{\boxed{}}{\boxed{}}$ Rewrite $=$ using the LCD, $\boxed{}$.

$-\boxed{}\dfrac{\boxed{}}{\boxed{}} = -\boxed{}\dfrac{\boxed{}}{\boxed{}}$

$\dfrac{\boxed{}}{\boxed{}}$ Subtract the fractions, then the whole numbers.

Answer: The Belmont Park track is $\boxed{}$ mile longer than Pimlico Race Course track.

Lesson 6.5 Subtracting Mixed Numbers by Renaming

Goal: Subtract mixed numbers by renaming.

EXAMPLE 1 Subtracting Mixed Numbers

Find the difference $4\frac{1}{5} - 2\frac{3}{5}$.

Solution

You can't subtract $\frac{\square}{\square}$ from $\frac{\square}{\square}$. Think of $4\frac{1}{5}$ as $\square + \frac{\square}{\square} + \frac{\square}{\square}$.

$\frac{\square}{\square} = \frac{\square}{\square}$ Rename $\frac{\square}{\square}$ as $\frac{\square}{\square}$.

$-\frac{\square}{\square} = -\frac{\square}{\square}$

$\frac{\square}{\square}$ Subtract.

Subtracting Mixed Numbers

1. Rewrite the fractions using the [ ] if necessary.

2. [ ] the fractions if necessary.

3. [ ] the whole numbers. [ ] the fractions.

4. [ ] if possible.

Guided Practice Find the difference. Simplify if possible.

1. $6\frac{1}{6} - 4\frac{5}{6}$	2. $3\frac{1}{3} - 1\frac{2}{3}$	3. $5\frac{3}{8} - 2\frac{5}{8}$	4. $7\frac{2}{9} - 4\frac{7}{9}$

EXAMPLE 2 Subtracting from a Whole Number

Find the difference $7 - 2\frac{1}{8}$.

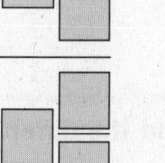

Think of 7 as ☐ + ☐, or ☐ + ☐/☐.

☐ = ☐/☐   Rename 7 as ☐/☐.

− ☐/☐ = − ☐/☐

─────────

= ☐/☐   Subtract.

When subtracting a mixed number from a whole number, rename one whole part as a fraction whose denominator is the same as the other denominator in the problem.

Lesson 6.5 Subtracting Mixed Numbers by Renaming 141

EXAMPLE 3 Solving Subtraction Problems

Solar Eclipse On April 8, 2005, a solar eclipse will occurred which lasted $\frac{7}{10}$ minute. A solar eclipse on December 4, 2002 lasted $2\frac{1}{15}$ minutes. How much longer was the December 4th eclipse?

Solution

> When subtracting mixed numbers, rewrite the mixed numbers with a common denominator before you determine if you need to rename.

You need to find the difference $\dfrac{\Box}{\Box} - \dfrac{\Box}{\Box}$. Use the LCD, $\Box$.

$\dfrac{\Box}{\Box} = \dfrac{\Box}{\Box} = \dfrac{\Box}{\Box}$ Rename $\dfrac{\Box}{\Box}$ as $\dfrac{\Box}{\Box}$.

$-\dfrac{\Box}{\Box} = -\dfrac{\Box}{\Box} = -\dfrac{\Box}{\Box}$

$\dfrac{\Box}{\Box}$ Subtract.

Answer: The December 4th eclipse lasted $\boxed{}$ minutes longer.

Guided Practice Find the difference. Simplify if possible.

5. $4 - 3\frac{1}{3}$	6. $10 - 8\frac{5}{6}$	7. $2\frac{1}{3} - 1\frac{1}{2}$	8. $5\frac{3}{8} - 3\frac{3}{4}$

Lesson 6.6 Measures of Time

Goal: Add and subtract measures of time.

Vocabulary

Elapsed time: _____

EXAMPLE 1 Adding Measures of Time

Marathon Your best running time in a marathon was 5 hours, 26 minutes, and 38 seconds. Your second best running time took 3 minutes and 25 seconds longer than your best time. What was your second best running time?

Solution

To answer the question, add 3 minutes and 25 seconds to 5 hours, 26 minutes, and 38 seconds.

☐ h ☐ min ☐ sec
+   ☐ min ☐ sec
―――――――――――――――
☐ h ☐ min ☐ sec   Add the hours, the minutes, and the seconds.

Think of ☐ sec as ☐ min ☐ sec. Then add ☐ min to ☐ min.

Answer: Your second best running time was ☐ hours, ☐ minutes, and ☐ seconds.

> When adding times vertically, make sure that you line up hours with hours, minutes with minutes, and seconds with seconds.

EXAMPLE 2 Subtracting Measures of Time

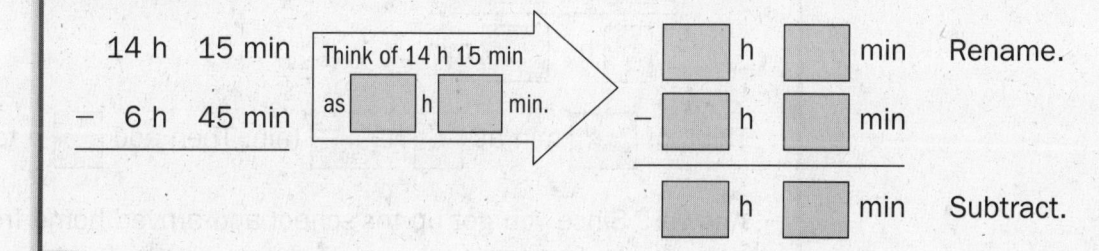

14 h 15 min   Think of 14 h 15 min   ☐ h ☐ min   Rename.
− 6 h 45 min   as ☐ h ☐ min.   − ☐ h ☐ min
                                            ――――――――――
                                             ☐ h ☐ min   Subtract.

Lesson 6.6 Measures of Time 143

Guided Practice Add or subtract the measures of time.

1. 3 h 42 min 12 sec + 1 h 33 min 19 sec	2. 6 min 24 sec − 3 min 50 sec

EXAMPLE 3   Solve a Multi-Step Problem

School You get up to go to school at 6:45 A.M. and arrive home from school at 3:55 P.M. How much time has passed since you got up for school and arrived home from school?

Solution

Break the problem into parts.

1. Find the elapsed time from 6:45 A.M. to 12:00 P.M.

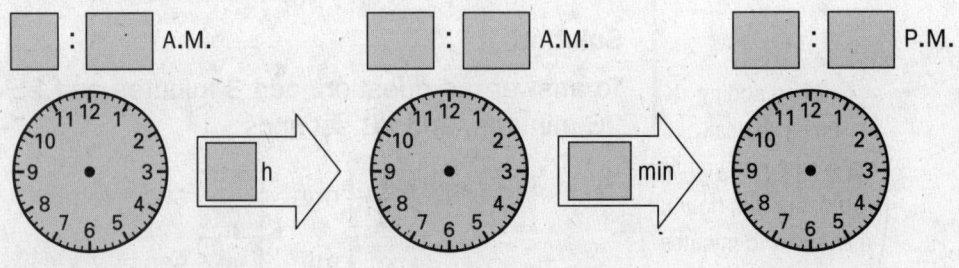

   ☐ : ☐ A.M.   ☐ : ☐ A.M.   ☐ : ☐ P.M.

   → ☐ h → ☐ min →

2. Find the elapsed time from 12:00 P.M. to 3:55 P.M.

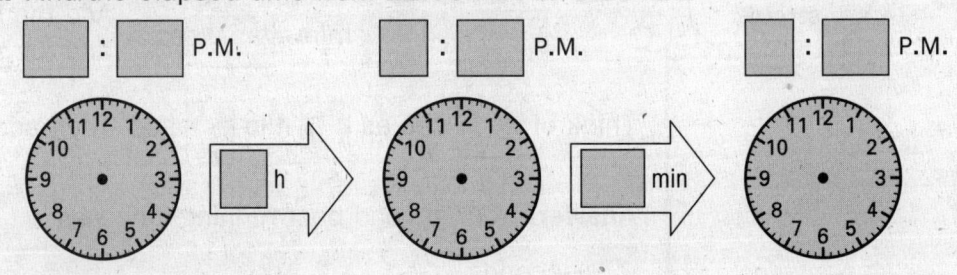

   ☐ : ☐ P.M.   ☐ : ☐ P.M.   ☐ : ☐ P.M.

   → ☐ h → ☐ min →

3. Add the two elapsed times.

       ☐ h   ☐ min
   + ☐ h   ☐ min
   ─────────────
       ☐ h   ☐ min

   Think of ☐ min as ☐ h ☐ min. Then add ☐ h to ☐ h.

Answer: Since you got up for school and arrived home from school, ☐ hours and ☐ minutes have passed.

WATCH OUT!
You can't always subtract two times to find elapsed time. For example, to find the elapsed time from 8:00 A.M. to 4:25 P.M., you can't compute 4 h 25 min − 8 h. You need to break the problem into parts.

144 | Chapter 6   Notetaking Guide

Guided Practice Find the elapsed time.

3. 4:00 A.M. to 10:00 A.M.	4. 6:30 A.M. to 10:45 A.M.
5. 11:35 A.M. to 4:10 P.M.	6. 9:40 P.M. to 2:10 P.M.

7. You make a long-distance phone call to your friend. The call begins at 7:43 P.M. and ends at 8:22 P.M. How long were you on the phone?

EXAMPLE 4 Standardized Test Practice

Health Club During a visit to a health club, Frank spent 43 minutes lifting weights, 62 minutes swimming, and 27 minutes running. About how much time in all did Frank spend at the health club?

Ⓐ 1 h 30 min   Ⓑ 1 h 50 min   Ⓒ 2 h 10 min   Ⓓ 2 h 30 min

Solution

You can estimate the total time by rounding.

43 min ≈ ☐ min

62 min ≈ ☐ min

27 min ≈ ☐ min

_____

☐ min = ☐ h ☐ min

Answer: The best estimate of the total time Frank spent at the health club is ☐ hours ☐ minutes. The correct answer is ☐.   Ⓐ Ⓑ Ⓒ Ⓓ

Lesson 6.6   Measures of Time   145

Words to Review

Give an example of the vocabulary word.

Fraction

Simplest form

Least common denominator

Mixed number

Improper fraction

Elapsed time

Round

Review your notes and Chapter 6 by using the Chapter Review on pages 329–332 of your textbook.

7.1 Multiplying Fractions and Whole Numbers

Goal: Multiply fractions and whole numbers.

Multiplying Fractions by Whole Numbers

Words To multiply a fraction by a whole number, multiply the _____ of the fraction by the _____ and write the _____ over the _____.

Numbers $4 \times \dfrac{2}{9} = \dfrac{\square}{\square}$

Algebra $a \cdot \dfrac{\square}{\square} = \dfrac{a \cdot b}{c}$ ($c \neq 0$)

EXAMPLE 1 Multiply Fractions by Whole Numbers

> When you write the rule for multiplying fractions by whole numbers in your notebook, you may want to include a model like the one in the activity on page 341 of your textbook.

$8 \times \dfrac{5}{6} = \dfrac{\square \times \square}{\square}$ Multiply the numerator by the whole number.

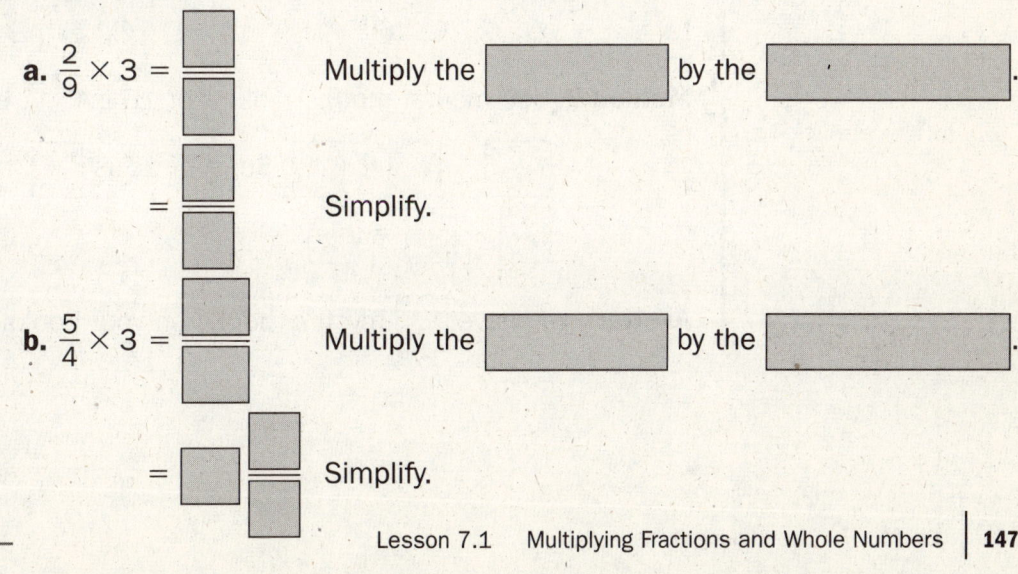

$= \dfrac{\square}{\square}$

$= \dfrac{\square}{\square}$, or $\dfrac{\square}{\square}$ Simplify.

EXAMPLE 2 Multiply Whole Numbers by Fractions

> You can find the product the same way whether the whole number is written on the left or right. In part (a) of Example 2, $\dfrac{2}{9} \times 3 = 3 \times \dfrac{2}{9}$.

a. $\dfrac{2}{9} \times 3 = \dfrac{\square}{\square}$ Multiply the _____ by the _____.

$= \dfrac{\square}{\square}$ Simplify.

b. $\dfrac{5}{4} \times 3 = \dfrac{\square}{\square}$ Multiply the _____ by the _____.

$= \dfrac{\square}{\square}$ Simplify.

Lesson 7.1 Multiplying Fractions and Whole Numbers

Guided Practice Find the product. Simplify if possible.

1. $3 \times \frac{2}{7}$	2. $8 \times \frac{2}{5}$	3. $\frac{4}{3} \times 4$	4. $\frac{7}{9} \times 3$

5. Look at the results in Example 2. Then predict whether the product will be *greater than 3* or *less than 3* when 3 is multiplied by $\frac{7}{8}$.

EXAMPLE 3 Using Mental Math or a Model

Books You have 15 books on your bookshelf, $\frac{2}{5}$ of which are mystery books. How many mystery books do you have on your bookshelf?

Solution

The number of mystery books you have is $\frac{2}{5}$ *of* 15, or $\frac{2}{5} \times 15$. The word *of* indicates multiplication. You can use a model or mental math to find this product.

Method 1 Use a model. Draw an array of ☐ circles. Divide them into ☐ equal parts. Circle ☐ of the ☐ parts.

Method 2 Use mental math. Think: $\frac{1}{5}$ of 15 is ☐, because ☐ ÷ ☐ = ☐. So, $\frac{2}{5}$ of 15 is ☐, because ☐ × ☐ = ☐.

Answer: You have ☐ mystery books on your bookshelf.

148 Chapter 7 Notetaking Guide

EXAMPLE 4 Estimating a Product

Saving Money Alicia has a summer job that pays $157 a week. Each week, she will put $\frac{3}{4}$ of her earnings in a savings account. Estimate how much money Alicia will put in the account each week.

Solution

Amount put into account = ☐ × ☐   Multiply fraction of earnings put into account by the weekly amount earned.

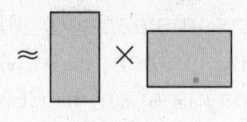

≈ ☐ × ☐   Replace ☐ with a number compatible with ☐.

= ☐   Think: $\frac{1}{4}$ of ☐ is ☐, so $\frac{3}{4}$ of ☐ is ☐.

Answer: Alicia will put about $☐ in the account each week.

Guided Practice Use mental math.

6. Find $\frac{4}{5}$ of 20.	7. Find $48 \times \frac{3}{8}$.	8. Estimate $\frac{2}{3} \times 19$.

Lesson 7.1 Multiplying Fractions and Whole Numbers   149

7.2 Multiplying Fractions

Goal: Multiply fractions.

EXAMPLE 1 Using a Model to Multiply Fractions

Sleep The average person sleeps for about $\frac{1}{3}$ of a 24-hour day. About $\frac{1}{5}$ of the time spent sleeping is spent in REM (rapid eye movement) sleep. What fraction of a 24-hour day is spent in REM sleep?

Solution
Use a model to find $\frac{1}{5}$ of $\frac{1}{3}$, or $\frac{1}{5} \times \frac{1}{3}$.

1. Draw a ☐ by ☐ rectangle to model ☐ and ☐. Each small square is ☐ of the whole.

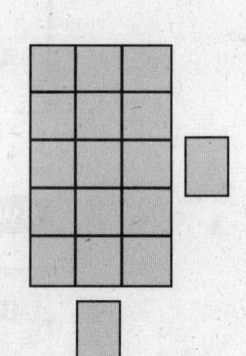

2. Shade ☐ of the rectangle.   Select ☐ of the shaded rectangle.

Answer: ☐ of the ☐ squares is selected, so $\frac{1}{5} \times \frac{1}{3} =$ ☐.

So, ☐ of a 24-hour day is spent in REM sleep.

Guided Practice Draw a model to find the product.

1. $\frac{1}{2} \times \frac{1}{3}$

2. $\frac{2}{3} \times \frac{1}{5}$

3. $\frac{3}{4} \times \frac{3}{5}$

Multiplying Fractions

Words product of fractions = $\dfrac{\text{product of the } \boxed{}}{\text{product of the } \boxed{}}$

Numbers $\dfrac{1}{3} \times \dfrac{4}{5} = \dfrac{\boxed{} \times \boxed{}}{\boxed{} \times \boxed{}} = \dfrac{\boxed{}}{\boxed{}}$

Algebra $\dfrac{a}{b} \cdot \dfrac{c}{d} = \dfrac{\boxed{} \cdot \boxed{}}{\boxed{} \cdot \boxed{}}$ ($b, d \neq 0$)

EXAMPLE 2 Multiplying Two Fractions

$\dfrac{5}{8} \times \dfrac{3}{2} = \dfrac{\boxed{} \times \boxed{}}{\boxed{} \times \boxed{}}$ Use the rule for multiplying fractions.

$= \dfrac{\boxed{}}{\boxed{}}$ Multiply. The product is in simplest form.

EXAMPLE 3 Evaluating an Algebraic Expression

Algebra Evaluate the expression $\frac{1}{4}n$ when $n = \frac{3}{5}$.

$\frac{1}{4}n = \boxed{} \times \boxed{}$ Substitute $\boxed{}$ for n.

$= \dfrac{\boxed{} \times \boxed{}}{\boxed{} \times \boxed{}}$ Use the rule for multiplying fractions.

$= \dfrac{\boxed{}}{\boxed{}}$ Multiply. The product is in simplest form.

> Notice in Example 3 that the product is less than either fraction.

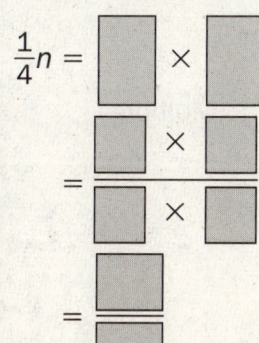

Lesson 7.2 Multiplying Fractions **151**

Guided Practice In Exercises 4–7, find the value.

4. Find the product $\frac{1}{2} \times \frac{3}{8}$.	**5.** Find the product $\frac{1}{5} \times \frac{4}{7}$.
6. Evaluate $\frac{2}{9}n$ when $n = \frac{4}{3}$.	**7.** Evaluate $\frac{4}{5}x$ when $x = \frac{6}{7}$.

8. Is the product in Example 2 less than both fractions?

EXAMPLE 4 — Simplifying Before Multiplying

$\frac{1}{18} \times \frac{4}{15} = \dfrac{\square \times \square}{\square \times \square}$ Use the rule for multiplying fractions.

$= \dfrac{\square \times \square \,\square}{\square \times \square}$ $\square$ is a factor of 4 and $\square$.

Divide 4 and $\square$ by $\square$.

$= \dfrac{\square \times \square}{\square \times \square}$ Rewrite.

$= \dfrac{\square}{\square}$ Multiply.

To simplify in Example 4, find the greatest factor of 4 that is also a factor of 18 or 15.

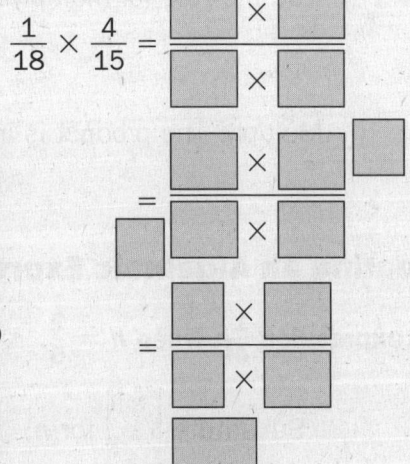

EXAMPLE 5 Multiplying Three Fractions

$\frac{1}{4} \times \frac{3}{5} \times \frac{2}{9} = \frac{\square \times \square \times \square}{\square \times \square \times \square}$ Use the rule for multiplying fractions.

$= \dfrac{\square \times \square \times \square}{\square \times \square \times \square}$ $\square$ is a factor of 3 and $\square$.

$\square$ is a factor of 2 and $\square$.

$= \dfrac{\square \times \square \times \square}{\square \times \square \times \square}$ Rewrite.

$= \dfrac{\square}{\square}$ Multiply.

WATCH OUT!
Rewrite the fraction after dividing out common factors. You will be less likely to make an error when you multiply.

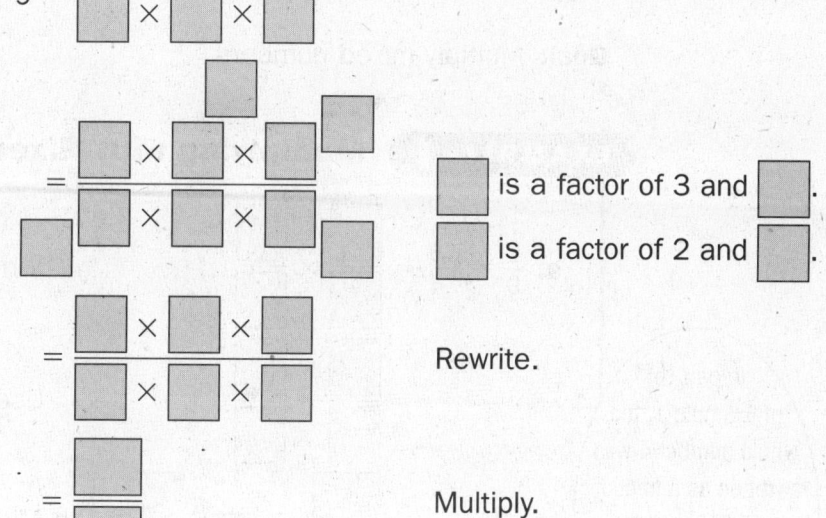

Guided Practice Multiply. Write the answer in simplest form.

9. $\frac{2}{7} \times \frac{5}{8}$	10. $\frac{4}{9} \times \frac{3}{16}$	11. $\frac{5}{24} \times \frac{6}{35}$
12. $\frac{5}{8} \times \frac{2}{3} \times \frac{1}{15}$	13. $\frac{4}{11} \times \frac{3}{8} \times \frac{11}{15}$	14. $\frac{5}{6} \times \frac{1}{10} \times \frac{12}{13}$

15. What do all of the products in Exercises 9–14 have in common?

Lesson 7.2 Multiplying Fractions

7.3 Multiplying Mixed Numbers

Goal: Multiply mixed numbers.

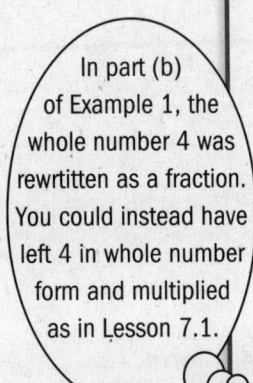

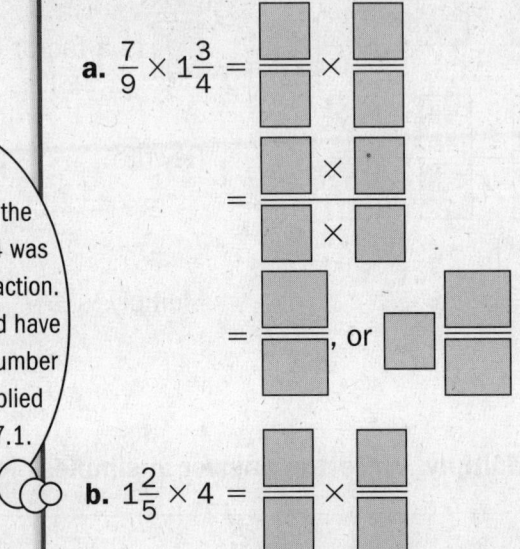

EXAMPLE 1 Multiplying with Mixed Numbers

a. $\dfrac{7}{9} \times 1\dfrac{3}{4} = \dfrac{\square}{\square} \times \dfrac{\square}{\square}$ Write $1\dfrac{3}{4}$ as an improper fraction.

$= \dfrac{\square \times \square}{\square \times \square}$ Use the rule for multiplying fractions.

$= \dfrac{\square}{\square}$, or $\dfrac{\square}{\square}$ Multiply. Write the answer in simplest form.

> In part (b) of Example 1, the whole number 4 was rewrtitten as a fraction. You could instead have left 4 in whole number form and multiplied as in Lesson 7.1.

b. $1\dfrac{2}{5} \times 4 = \dfrac{\square}{\square} \times \dfrac{\square}{\square}$ Write $1\dfrac{2}{5}$ and 4 as improper fractions.

$= \dfrac{\square \times \square}{\square \times \square}$ Use the rule for multiplying fractions.

$= \dfrac{\square}{\square}$, or $\square\dfrac{\square}{\square}$ Multiply. Write the answer in simplest form.

EXAMPLE 2 Simplifying Before Multiplying

$3\frac{3}{8} \times 4\frac{2}{3} = \dfrac{\square}{\square} \times \dfrac{\square}{\square}$ Write $3\frac{3}{8}$ and $4\frac{2}{3}$ as improper fractions.

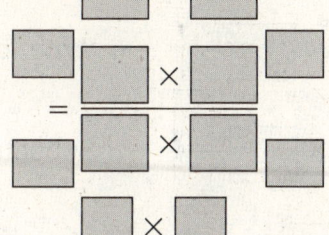

$= \dfrac{\square \; \square \times \square \; \square}{\square \; \square \times \square \; \square}$ Use the rule for multiplying fractions. Divide out common factors.

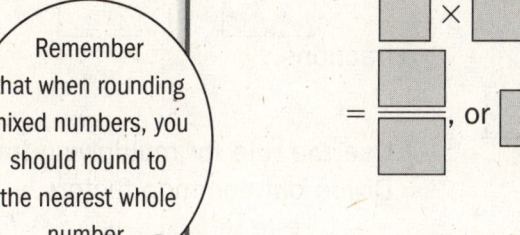

$= \dfrac{\square \times \square}{\square \times \square}$ Rewrite.

$= \dfrac{\square}{\square}$, or $\square \dfrac{\square}{\square}$ Multiply. Write the answer in simplest form.

> Remember that when rounding mixed numbers, you should round to the nearest whole number.

✓ **Check** Round $3\frac{3}{8}$ to $\square$ and $4\frac{2}{3}$ to $\square$. Because $\square \times \square = \square$, the product $\square\dfrac{\square}{\square}$ is reasonable.

Guided Practice   Multiply. Write the answer in simplest form.

1. $4\frac{1}{4} \times \frac{3}{5}$	2. $6 \times 2\frac{5}{6}$	3. $3\frac{3}{4} \times 2\frac{2}{3}$	4. $3\frac{2}{5} \times 2\frac{5}{6}$

Lesson 7.3 Multiplying Mixed Numbers 155

EXAMPLE 3 — Multiplying to Solve Problems

Fields A rectangular field is $42\frac{1}{2}$ feet long and $33\frac{1}{3}$ feet wide. What is the area of the field?

Solution

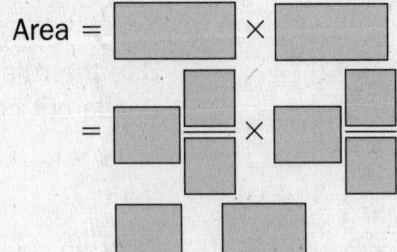

Area = ☐ × ☐   Write formula for area of a rectangle.

= $\dfrac{\square}{\square} \times \dfrac{\square}{\square}$ Substitute for ☐ and ☐.

= $\dfrac{\square}{\square} \times \dfrac{\square}{\square}$ Write ☐ and ☐ as improper fractions.

= $\dfrac{\square \times \square}{\square \times \square}$ Use the rule for multiplying fractions. Divide out common factors.

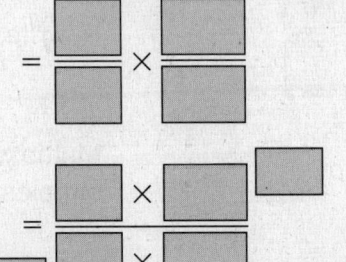

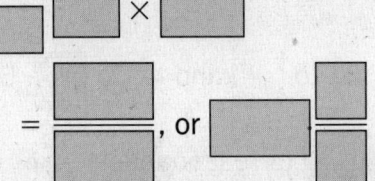

= $\dfrac{\square}{\square}$, or $\dfrac{\square}{\square}$ Multiply. Write the answer in simplest form.

Answer: The area of the field is $\dfrac{\square}{\square}$ square feet.

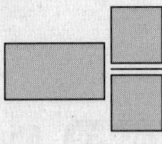

156 | Chapter 7 Notetaking Guide

7.4 Dividing Fractions

Goal: Use reciprocals to divide fractions.

Vocabulary

Reciprocal: _____

EXAMPLE 1 Writing Reciprocals

	Original number	Fraction	Reciprocal	Check
a.	$\frac{2}{9}$	☐/☐ ⤫ ☐/☐		☐/☐ × ☐/☐ = ☐/☐ = ☐
b.	14	☐/☐ ⤫ ☐/☐		☐/☐ × ☐/☐ = ☐/☐ = ☐
c.	$1\frac{3}{5}$	☐/☐ ⤫ ☐/☐		☐/☐ × ☐/☐ = ☐/☐ = ☐

When writing the reciprocal of a mixed number, first write the mixed number as an improper fraction, then find the reciprocal of the improper fraction.

Guided Practice Write the reciprocal of the number.

1. $\frac{1}{6}$	2. 7	3. 20	4. $1\frac{3}{8}$

Lesson 7.4 Dividing Fractions **157**

Dividing Fractions

Words To divide by a fraction, multiply by _____.

Numbers $\dfrac{3}{7} \div \dfrac{4}{5} = \dfrac{\boxed{}}{\boxed{}} \times \dfrac{\boxed{}}{\boxed{}}$

Algebra $\dfrac{\boxed{}}{\boxed{}} \div \dfrac{\boxed{}}{\boxed{}} = \dfrac{a}{b} \cdot \dfrac{d}{c}$ $(b, c, d \neq 0)$

EXAMPLE 2 Dividing Two Fractions

Bees A honey bee is about $\dfrac{2}{3}$ inch long and a yellow jacket is about $\dfrac{1}{2}$ inch long. How many times longer is a honey bee than a yellow jacket?

Solution

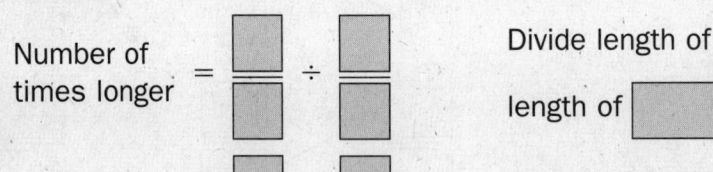

Number of times longer $= \dfrac{\boxed{}}{\boxed{}} \div \dfrac{\boxed{}}{\boxed{}}$ Divide length of _____ by length of _____.

$= \dfrac{\boxed{}}{\boxed{}} \times \dfrac{\boxed{}}{\boxed{}}$ Multiply by the reciprocal of the divisor.

$= \dfrac{\boxed{} \times \boxed{}}{\boxed{} \times \boxed{}}$ Use the rule for multiplying fractions.

$= \dfrac{\boxed{}}{\boxed{}}$, or $\dfrac{\boxed{}}{\boxed{}}$ Multiply.

Answer: The length of a honey bee is $\dfrac{\boxed{}}{\boxed{}}$ times the length of a yellow jacket.

EXAMPLE 3 Dividing a Fraction and a Whole Number

a. If you cut a $\frac{5}{8}$-foot long piece of wood into 10 equally-sized pieces, how long is each of the ten pieces of wood?

b. If you divide a 10-foot long piece of wood into pieces that are each $\frac{5}{8}$ foot long, how many pieces do you have?

WATCH OUT!
When dividing, be sure to take the reciprocal of the divisor, not the dividend. You can multiply to check your work. In Example 3, check part (a) by multiplying your answer by 10 and check part (b) by multiplying your answer by $\frac{5}{8}$.

Solution

a. Divide $\frac{5}{8}$ by 10.

b. Divide 10 by $\frac{5}{8}$.

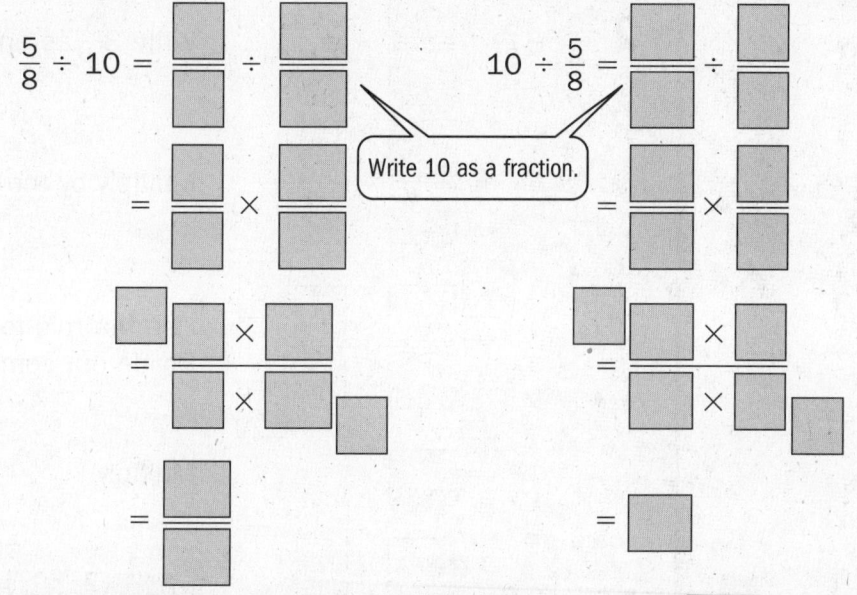

$\frac{5}{8} \div 10 = \frac{\square}{\square} \div \frac{\square}{\square}$

$10 \div \frac{5}{8} = \frac{\square}{\square} \div \frac{\square}{\square}$

Write 10 as a fraction.

$= \frac{\square}{\square} \times \frac{\square}{\square}$

$= \frac{\square}{\square} \times \frac{\square}{\square}$

$= \frac{\square \times \square}{\square \times \square}$

$= \frac{\square \times \square}{\square \times \square}$

$= \frac{\square}{\square}$

$= \square$

Answer: Each piece is $\frac{\square}{\square}$ foot long.

Answer: You have $\square$ pieces.

Guided Practice Divide. Write the answer in simplest form.

| 5. $\frac{7}{9} \div \frac{3}{8}$ | 6. $\frac{5}{6} \div \frac{1}{3}$ | 7. $\frac{8}{15} \div 4$ | 8. $18 \div \frac{3}{4}$ |

Lesson 7.4 Dividing Fractions 159

7.5 Dividing Mixed Numbers

Goal: Divide mixed numbers.

EXAMPLE 1 Dividing a Mixed Number

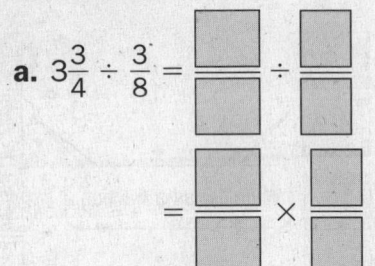

a. $3\dfrac{3}{4} \div \dfrac{3}{8} = \dfrac{\boxed{}}{\boxed{}} \div \dfrac{\boxed{}}{\boxed{}}$ Write $3\dfrac{3}{4}$ as an improper fraction.

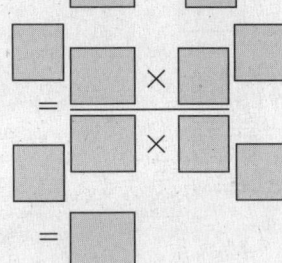

$= \dfrac{\boxed{}}{\boxed{}} \times \dfrac{\boxed{}}{\boxed{}}$ Multiply by the reciprocal of the divisor.

$= \dfrac{\boxed{} \times \boxed{}}{\boxed{} \times \boxed{}}$ Use the rule for multiplying fractions. Divide out common factors.

$= \boxed{}$ Multiply.

b. $2\dfrac{2}{5} \div 8 = \dfrac{\boxed{}}{\boxed{}} \div \dfrac{\boxed{}}{\boxed{}}$ Write $2\dfrac{2}{5}$ and 8 as improper fractions.

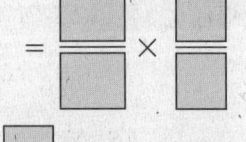

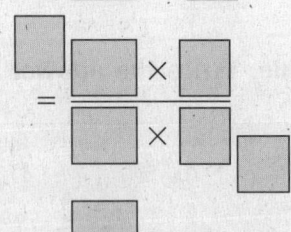

$= \dfrac{\boxed{}}{\boxed{}} \times \dfrac{\boxed{}}{\boxed{}}$ Multiply by the reciprocal of the divisor.

$= \dfrac{\boxed{} \times \boxed{}}{\boxed{} \times \boxed{}}$ Use the rule for multiplying fractions. Divide out common factors.

$= \dfrac{\boxed{}}{\boxed{}}$ Multiply.

160 Chapter 7 Notetaking Guide

EXAMPLE 2 Dividing by a Mixed Number

$6\frac{1}{4} \div 1\frac{1}{9} = \frac{\square}{\square} \div \frac{\square}{\square}$ Write $6\frac{1}{4}$ and $1\frac{1}{9}$ as improper fractions.

$= \frac{\square}{\square} \times \frac{\square}{\square}$ Multiply by the reciprocal of the divisor.

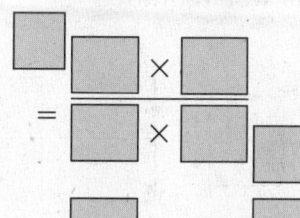

$= \frac{\square \times \square}{\square \times \square}$ Use the rule for multiplying fractions. Divide out common factors.

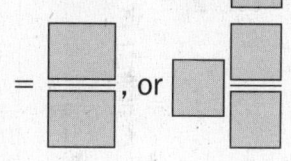

$= \frac{\square}{\square}$, or $\frac{\square}{\square}$ Multiply.

✓ **Check** Round $6\frac{1}{4}$ to $\square$ and replace $1\frac{1}{9}$ with the compatible number $\square$. The answer is reasonable because it is close to the estimate $\square \div \square = \square$.

> **WATCH OUT!**
> When you divide by a mixed number, first you rewrite it as an improper fraction. Then don't forget to multiply by the *reciprocal* of the improper fraction.

Guided Practice Find the quotient. Use estimation to check your answer.

1. $5\frac{1}{4} \div 7$
2. $5\frac{3}{5} \div \frac{14}{15}$
3. $\frac{7}{8} \div 4\frac{2}{3}$
4. $3\frac{1}{8} \div 7\frac{1}{2}$

5. Which quotient in Exercises 1–4 is greater than 1?

Lesson 7.5 Dividing Mixed Numbers

EXAMPLE 3 Choosing an Operation

Peanuts A person working at a natural foods store is packaging peanuts from a 50-pound bag into $1\frac{1}{4}$-pound bags. How many bags will he need?

Solution

1. Choose the operation by thinking about a similar whole number problem: If the peanuts in a 50-pound bag were being packaged into 2 pound bags, you would *divide* ☐ by ☐. So, *divide* ☐ by ☐.

2. Divide. ☐ ÷ ☐ = ☐/☐ ÷ ☐/☐

    = ☐/☐ × ☐/☐

    = ☐/☐×☐ × ☐

    = ☐

Answer: He will need ☐ bags.

> When solving division problems that involve whole numbers and fractions or mixed numbers, rewrite the whole number as an improper fraction.

7.6 Weight and Capacity in Customary Units

Goal: Use customary units of weight and capacity.

Vocabulary

Ounce (oz):

Pound (lb):

Ton (T):

Fluid ounce (fl oz):

Cup (c):

Pint (pt):

Quart (qt):

Gallon (gal):

EXAMPLE 1   Choosing Units of Weight

Complete the statement using an appropriate customary unit.

a. A ball of yarn weighs $2\frac{1}{2}$? .   b. A book weighs $2\frac{1}{2}$? .

Solution

a. A ball of yarn weighs $2\frac{1}{2}$ _____, because it is heavier than _____ and lighter than _____.

b. A book weighs $2\frac{1}{2}$ _____, because it is heavier than _____ and much lighter than _____.

Just as you did in Lesson 4.7 with metric units of mass and capacity, you should use your benchmarks for customary units of weight to choose appropriate units for measurement.

Lesson 7.6 Weight and Capacity in Customary Units 163

Guided Practice Choose an appropriate customary unit to measure the weight.

1. light bulb	2. school bus	3. refrigerator

EXAMPLE 2 Choosing Units of Capacity

Choose an appropriate customary unit to measure the capacity.

a. cereal bowl   b. large flower vase

Solution

a. A cereal bowl holds about as much as _____.

You can use _____ or one of the smaller units, _____.

b. A large flower vase holds about as much as

_____.

You can use _____, but you wouldn't use

_____.

Notice that there are two types of ounces: the fluid ounce (fl oz) used for measuring capacity and the ounce (oz) used for measuring weight.

EXAMPLE 3 Choosing Customary Units

What does each measure describe about an empty sauce pot?

a. 5 quarts   b. 2 pounds

Solution

a. A quart is a measure of _____, so 5 quarts describes

_____.

b. A pound is a measure of _____, so 2 pounds describes

_____.

164 | Chapter 7 Notetaking Guide

Guided Practice Choose an appropriate customary unit to measure.

4. capacity of a bucket	5. capacity of a kitchen garbage can	6. weight of a stapler

Tell whether the measurement is a *weight* or a *capacity*.

7. 4 gallons	8. 10 pounds	9. 10 fluid ounces

EXAMPLE 4 Standardized Test Practice

Water Maria has a full pitcher of water that she wants to divide evenly among 10 equal-sized glasses. Arrange the following problem-solving steps in the correct order for Maria to determine how much water to pour in each glass.

Step X Divide the capacity of the pitcher by 10.

Step Y Estimate the capacities of both the pitcher and one of the glasses.

Step Z Compare the total estimated capacity of all 10 glasses with the capacity of the pitcher.

Ⓐ x, y, z   Ⓑ x, z, y   Ⓒ y, z, x   Ⓓ z, y, x

Solution

First Maria must estimate the capacities of both the pitcher and one of the glasses. Then she must compare the total estimated capacity of all 10 glasses with the capacity of the pitcher. Finally, she should divide the capacity of the pitcher by 10 to determine the amount of water to pour in each glass.

Answer: The correct order of the steps is ☐. The correct answer is ☐.   Ⓐ Ⓑ Ⓒ Ⓓ

Lesson 7.6 Weight and Capacity in Customary Units   165

CHAPTER 7.7 Changing Customary Units

Goal: Change customary units of measure.

EXAMPLE 1 Changing Units Using Multiplication

Change 3 mi 540 yd to yards.

3 mi 540 yd = ☐ + ☐   Write the measurement as a sum.

= (3 ☐ ☐) yd + ☐ yd   Change the miles to yards.

= ☐ yd + ☐ yd   ☐.

= ☐ yd   Add.

EXAMPLE 2 Changing Units Using Division

Change 43 fl oz to cups. Express the answer in two ways.

There are 8 fl oz in a cup, so ☐ 43 by 8.

☐ R ☐
8)43
☐
☐ ⟵ You can interpret the remainder as ☐ fl oz.

⟵ You can also interpret the remainder as ☐ c, because the remaining division ☐ ÷ ☐ can be written as ☐.

Answer: There are ☐ c ☐ fl oz in 43 fl oz. This can also be written as ☐ c.

WATCH OUT!
There should always be more of the smaller unit and fewer of the larger unit. So, you *multiply* by 12 to change feet to inches and you *divide* by 16 to change ounces to pounds.

Guided Practice Copy and complete the statement.

1. 2 ft 9 in. = _?_ in.	**2.** 52 oz = _?_ lb	**3.** $9\frac{1}{4}$ T = _?_ lb

166 | Chapter 7 Notetaking Guide

EXAMPLE 3 — Multiplying by a Form of 1

Change $4\frac{2}{3}$ oz to pounds.

> To get the correct unit in the answer, choose the form of 1 that has the unit you are changing to in the numerator and the unit you are changing from in the denominator.

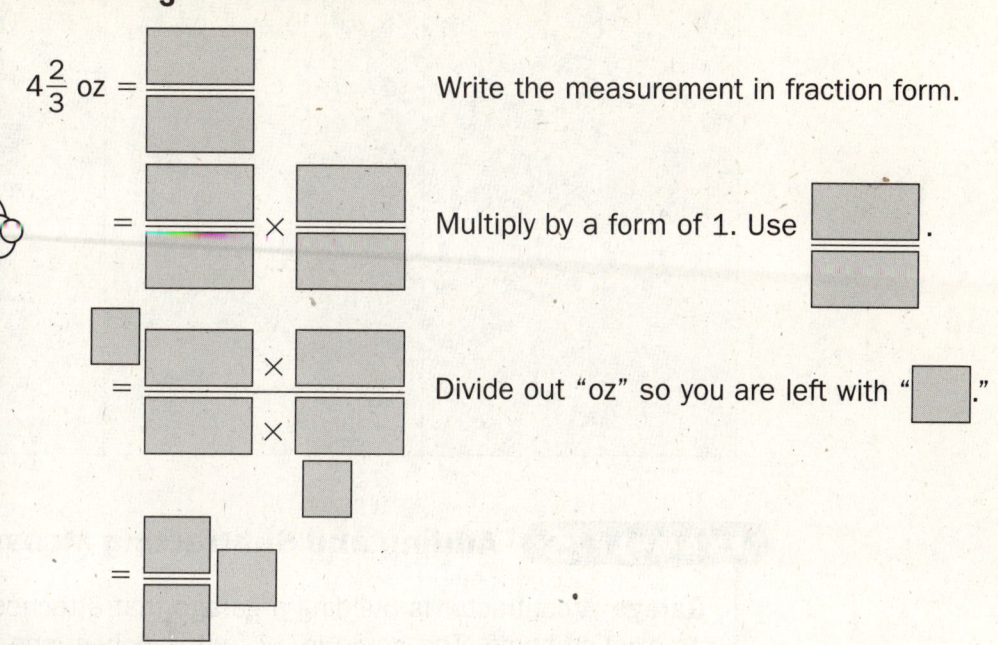

$4\frac{2}{3}$ oz = $\dfrac{\square}{\square}$ Write the measurement in fraction form.

= $\dfrac{\square}{\square} \times \dfrac{\square}{\square}$ Multiply by a form of 1. Use $\dfrac{\square}{\square}$.

= $\dfrac{\square \times \square}{\square \times \square}$ Divide out "oz" so you are left with "$\square$."

= $\dfrac{\square}{\square}$

EXAMPLE 4 — Standardized Test Practice

On a typical day, Sasha drinks 64 fluid ounces of water. How many gallons of water does Sasha drink on a typical day?

Ⓐ 2 gallons   **Ⓑ** 1 gallon   **Ⓒ** $\frac{1}{2}$ gallon   **Ⓓ** $\frac{1}{4}$ gallon

Solution

1. Find the relationship between gallons and fluid ounces. Use the four relationships 1 gal = 4 qt, 1 qt = 2 pt, 1 pt = 2 c, and 1 c = 8 fl oz.

$\dfrac{1\ \square}{4\ \square} \times \dfrac{1\ \square}{2\ \square} \times \dfrac{1\ \square}{2\ \square} \times \dfrac{1\ \square}{8\ \square}$

$= \dfrac{\square \times \square \times \square \times \square}{\square \times \square \times \square \times \square} = \dfrac{\square}{\square}$

So, 1 gallon = $\square$ fluid ounces.

2. Multiply 64 fl oz by a form of 1 that relates gallons and fluid ounces.

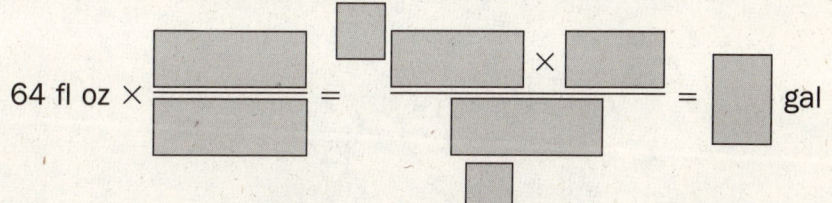

64 fl oz $\times \dfrac{\square}{\square} = \dfrac{\square \times \square}{\square} = \square$ gal

Answer: Sasha drinks $\square$ gallon of water on a typical day. The correct answer is $\square$.   Ⓐ Ⓑ Ⓒ Ⓓ

Lesson 7.7   Changing Customary Units   **167**

Guided Practice Copy and complete the statement.

4. $\frac{7}{10}$ yd = ? in.	5. $5\frac{3}{4}$ lb = ? oz	6. 20 fl oz = ? qt

EXAMPLE 5 Adding and Subtracting Measures

Garage A contractor is building a garage that attaches along the length of an existing home. The home is 24 feet 5 inches long and the garage will be 20 feet 8 inches long.

a. What is the sum of the lengths of the home and the garage?

b. What is the difference in the lengths of the home and the garage?

Solution

a. Add. Then rename the sum.

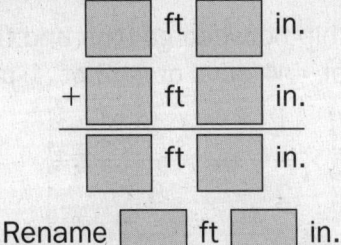

☐ ft ☐ in.
+ ☐ ft ☐ in.
———————
☐ ft ☐ in.

Rename ☐ ft ☐ in. as ☐ ft ☐ in.

Answer: The sum of the lengths is ☐ ft ☐ in.

b. Rename. Then subtract.

Rename one of the feet as ☐ in.

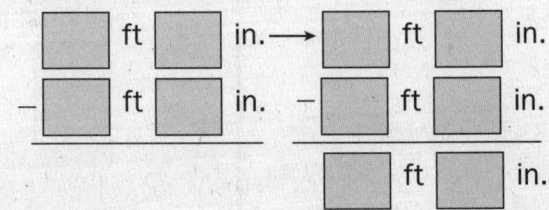

☐ ft ☐ in. ⟶ ☐ ft ☐ in.
− ☐ ft ☐ in.   − ☐ ft ☐ in.
————————   ————————
                                ☐ ft ☐ in.

Answer: The difference in the lengths is ☐ ft ☐ in.

Chapter 7 Words to Review

Give an example of the vocabulary word.

Reciprocal

Ounce

Pound

Ton

Fluid ounce

Cup

Pint

Quart

Gallon

Review your notes and Chapter 7 by using the Chapter Review on pages 387–390 of your textbook.

Lesson 8.1

Ratios

Goal: Write ratios and equivalent ratios.

Vocabulary

Ratio:

Equivalent ratio:

EXAMPLE 1 Writing a Ratio in Different Ways

Baseball A baseball team is made up of nine players: three outfielders, four infielders, one pitcher, and one catcher. Write the ratio of the number of infielders to the total number of players.

Solution

Because four of the nine players are infielders, the ratio of the number of infielders to the total number of players,

$\dfrac{\text{Number of infielders}}{\text{Total number of players}}$, can be written as $\dfrac{\square}{\square}$, as $\square : \square$,

or as $\square$ to $\square$.

EXAMPLE 2 Writing Ratios in Simplest Form

Use the information in Example 1. Write the ratio of the number of outfielders to the total number of players in simplest form.

Solution

$\dfrac{\text{Number of outfielders}}{\text{Total number of players}} = \dfrac{\square}{\square} = \dfrac{\square \times \square}{\square \times \square} = \dfrac{\square}{\square}$

Answer: The ratio is $\dfrac{\square}{\square}$, or $\square$ to $\square$, so there is $\square$ outfielder for every $\square$ players.

Lesson 8.1 Ratios 171

Guided Practice In Exercises 1 and 2, write the ratio in three ways.

1. catchers to infielders	**2.** outfielders to infielders

3. Write the ratio of the number of pitchers and catchers to the number of infielders in simplest form.

EXAMPLE 3 Writing an Equivalent Ratio

Complete the statement $\frac{7}{12} = \frac{?}{48}$ to write equivalent ratios.

Solution

Think about the denominators of the two fractions.

$7 \times \square$

$\frac{7}{12} = \frac{\square}{48}$

You multiplied 12 by $\square$ to get 48, so multiply 7 by $\square$ also.

$12 \times \square$

Answer: $\frac{7}{12} = \frac{\square}{48}$

Need help with equivalent fractions? See page 243 of your textbook.

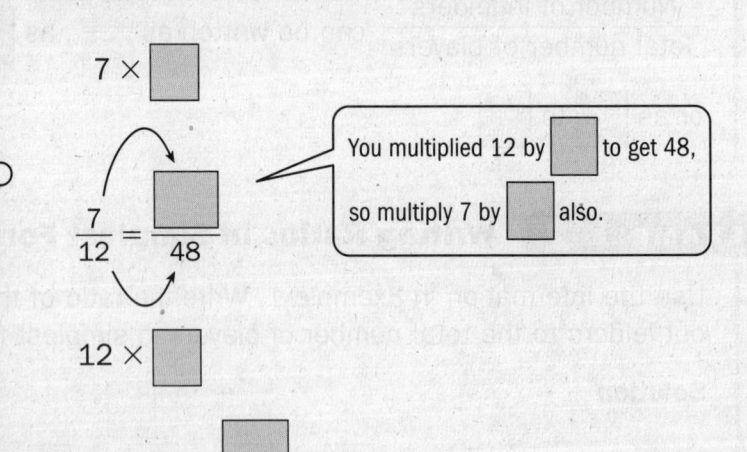

172 | Chapter 8 Notetaking Guide

EXAMPLE 4 Comparing Ratios Using Decimals

Homework Tara has completed $\frac{3}{5}$ of her history problems and 10 out of 16 of her biology problems. Which set of problems is closer to being completed?

Solution

Write each ratio as a decimal. Then compare the decimals.

History: $\frac{3}{5}$ = ____   Biology: 10 out of 16 = ____ = ____

Answer: Because ____ > ____ , Tara is closer to completing her ____ problems.

Need help writing fractions as decimals? See page 271 of your textbook.

Guided Practice Copy and complete the statement.

4. $\frac{3}{4} = \frac{?}{20}$

5. $\frac{8}{?} = \frac{48}{54}$

6. $\frac{20}{35} = \frac{4}{?}$

Copy and complete the statement using <, >, or =.

7. $\frac{11}{30}$ __?__ $\frac{7}{15}$

8. $\frac{3}{7}$ __?__ 12 out of 28

9. 4 : 6 __?__ 5 : 30

Lesson 8.1 Ratios 173

LESSON 8.2 Rates

Goal: Write rates, equivalent rates, and unit rates.

Vocabulary

Rate:

Unit Rate:

EXAMPLE 1   Standardized Test Practice

Swimming Pool A machine that pours concrete used to form the bottom and sides of an inground swimming pool pumps the concrete into the ground at a rate of 540 gallons every 60 minutes. How long will it take to pump 1080 gallons?

A 30 minutes   **B** 120 minutes   **C** 150 minutes   **D** 1080 minutes

Solution

Write an *equivalent rate* that has 1080 gallons in the numerator.

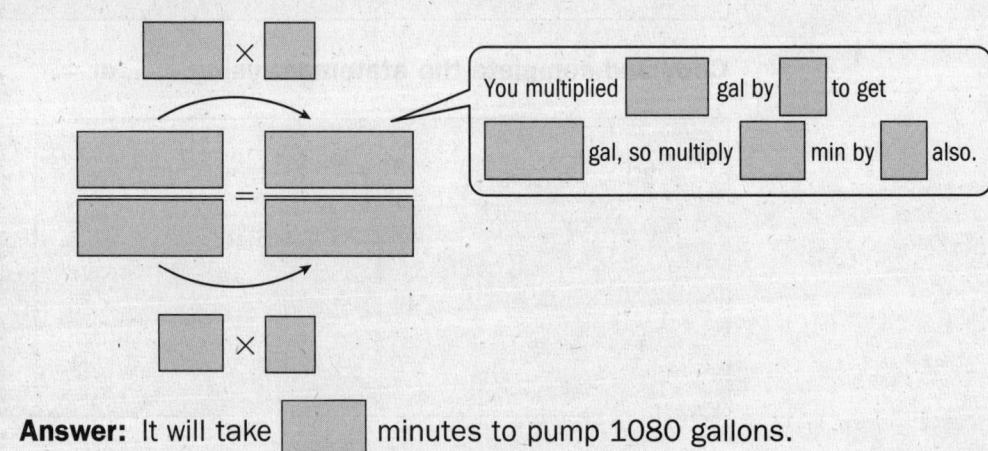

☐ × ☐

☐ / ☐ = ☐ / ☐

You multiplied ☐ gal by ☐ to get ☐ gal, so multiply ☐ min by ☐ also.

☐ × ☐

Answer: It will take ☐ minutes to pump 1080 gallons.

The correct answer is ☐. **A** **B** **C** **D**

EXAMPLE 2 Writing a Unit Rate

Write the machine's pumping rate from Example 1 as a unit rate.

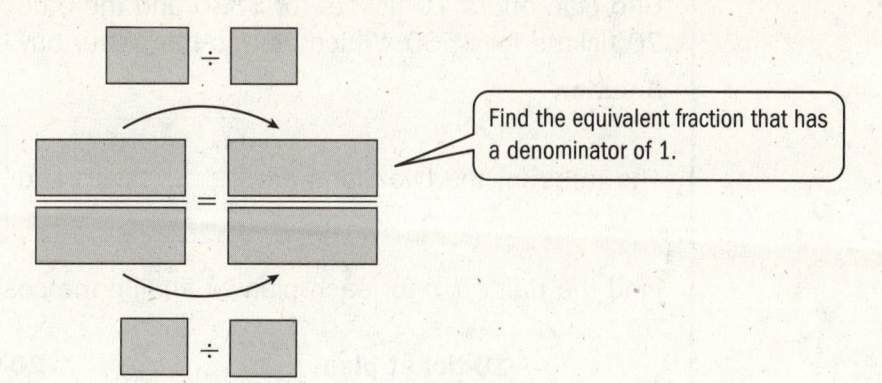

⬜ ÷ ⬜

⬜/⬜ = ⬜/⬜

⬜ ÷ ⬜

> Find the equivalent fraction that has a denominator of 1.

The word per is often used to express division in unit rates, such as gallons per minute.

Answer: The machine's unit rate is ⬜ gallons per minute.

Guided Practice Copy and complete the statement.

1. $\dfrac{3 \text{ in.}}{10 \text{ min}} = \dfrac{18 \text{ in.}}{?}$

2. $\dfrac{\$8}{5 \text{ oz}} = \dfrac{?}{25 \text{ oz}}$

3. $\dfrac{24 \text{ mi}}{3 \text{ h}} = \dfrac{?}{1 \text{ h}}$

EXAMPLE 3 Using a Unit Rate

Measurement There are about 1.609 kilometers in 1 mile. How many kilometers are in 12 miles?

Solution

Write an equivalent rate that has 12 miles in the denominator.

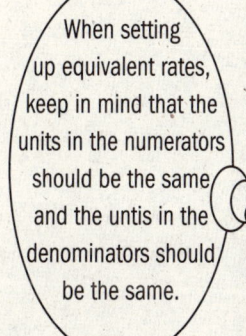

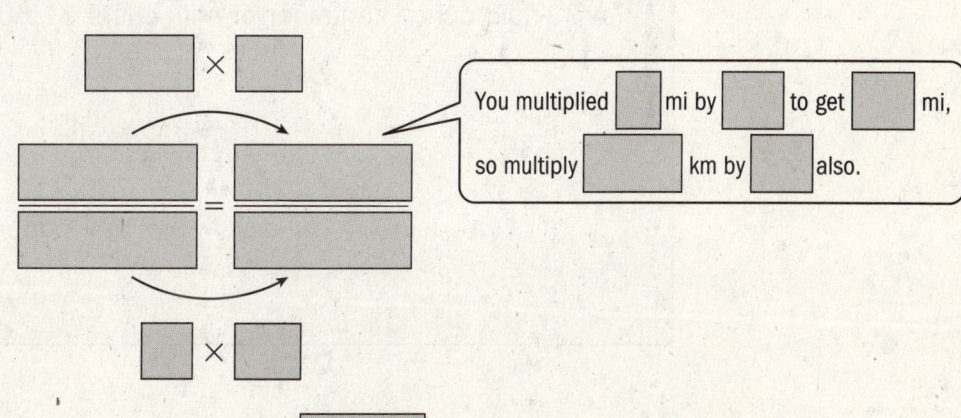

⬜ × ⬜

⬜/⬜ = ⬜/⬜

⬜ × ⬜

> You multiplied ⬜ mi by ⬜ to get ⬜ mi, so multiply ⬜ km by ⬜ also.

When setting up equivalent rates, keep in mind that the units in the numerators should be the same, and the units in the denominators should be the same.

Answer: There are about ⬜ kilometers in 12 miles.

Lesson 8.2 Rates

EXAMPLE 4 Comparing Unit Rates

Hockey A hockey team offers two different plans for buying tickets. One plan offers 10 tickets for $330 and the other plan offers 20 tickets for $560. Which plan is the better buy? Explain.

Solution

The rates for the two plans are ▭/▭ and ▭/▭.

Find the *unit price* for each plan by finding the cost of one ticket.

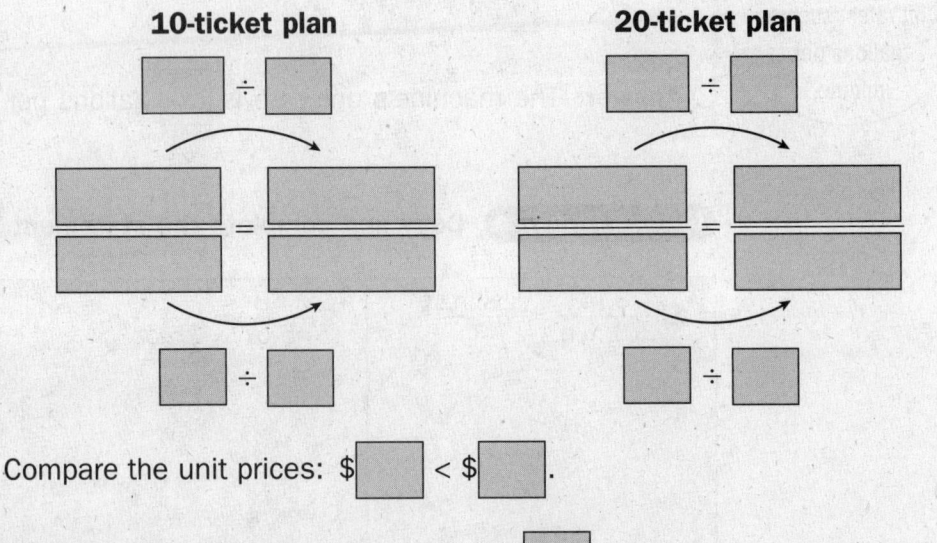

10-ticket plan   **20-ticket plan**

▭ ÷ ▭   ▭ ÷ ▭

▭/▭ = ▭/▭   ▭/▭ = ▭/▭

▭ ÷ ▭   ▭ ÷ ▭

Compare the unit prices: $▭ < $▭ .

Answer: Because the unit price for the ▭-ticket plan is less than the unit price for the ▭-ticket plan, the ▭-ticket plan is the better buy.

Guided Practice Decide which size is the better buy. Explain.

4. A 16-fluid ounce container of milk costs $1.28.
   A 32-fluid ounce container of milk costs $1.60.

Lesson 8.3 Solving Proportions

Goal: Write and solve proportions.

Vocabulary

Proportion: _____

Cross products: _____

Cross Products Property

Words The cross products of a proportion are equal.

Algebra

$\dfrac{p}{q} = \dfrac{r}{s}$, where q and s are nonzero.

☐ · ☐ = ☐ · ☐

Numbers

$\dfrac{2}{3} = \dfrac{8}{12}$

☐ · ☐ = ☐ · ☐

EXAMPLE 1 Checking a Proportion

Use cross products to decide whether the ratios form a proportion.

a. $\dfrac{5}{12} \stackrel{?}{=} \dfrac{20}{48}$

☐ · ☐ $\stackrel{?}{=}$ ☐ · ☐

☐ ☐ ☐

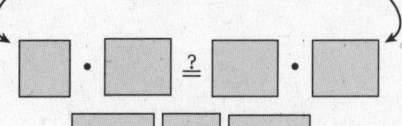

The cross products ☐ equal, so the ratios ☐ form a proportion.

b. $\dfrac{4}{7} \stackrel{?}{=} \dfrac{24}{50}$

☐ · ☐ $\stackrel{?}{=}$ ☐ · ☐

☐ ☐ ☐

The cross products ☐ equal, so the ratios ☐ form a proportion.

The proportion $\dfrac{5}{12} = \dfrac{20}{48}$ in part (a) of Example 1 is read "5 is to 12 as 20 is to 48."

Lesson 8.3 Solving Proportions | 177

EXAMPLE 2 Solving Using Mental Math

Solve the proportion $\frac{3}{15} = \frac{30}{x}$.

Solution

Method 1 Use equivalent ratios.

3 × ☐

$\frac{3}{15} = \frac{30}{\boxed{}}$

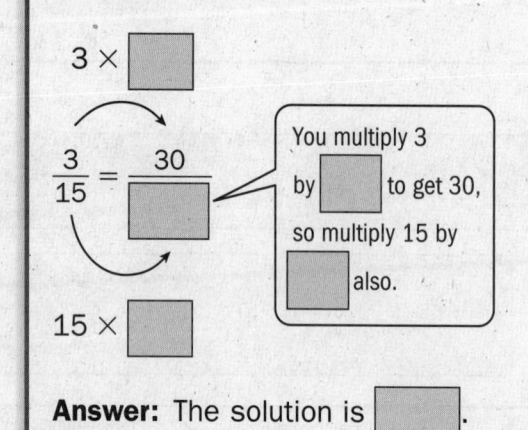

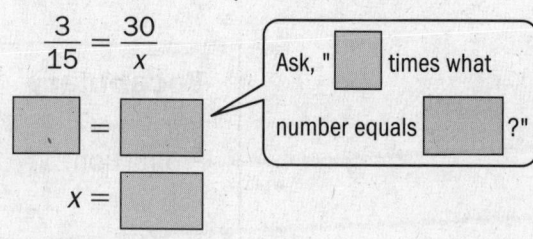

You multiply 3 by ☐ to get 30, so multiply 15 by ☐ also.

15 × ☐

Method 2 Use cross products.

$\frac{3}{15} = \frac{30}{x}$

☐ = ☐

$x = $ ☐

Ask, "☐ times what number equals ☐?"

Answer: The solution is ☐.

Guided Practice   Solve the proportion using mental math.

1. $\dfrac{m}{3} = \dfrac{9}{27}$

2. $\dfrac{16}{12} = \dfrac{4}{c}$

3. $\dfrac{42}{y} = \dfrac{7}{10}$

4. $\dfrac{22}{5} = \dfrac{t}{40}$

EXAMPLE 3 Solving Using a Verbal Model

Trains A passenger train has traveled 180 miles in 3 hours. At that same rate, how long will it take to travel the total distance of 300 miles?

Solution

Use a proportion. Let t represent the total time it will take to travel 300 miles.

$$\frac{\text{Distance traveled}}{\text{Time traveled}} = \frac{\text{Total distance}}{\text{Total time}}$$ Write a verbal model.

$$\frac{\boxed{}}{\boxed{}} = \frac{\boxed{}}{\boxed{}}$$ Substitute values.

$$\frac{\boxed{}}{\boxed{}} = \frac{\boxed{}}{\boxed{}}$$ Rewrite proportion without units.

$$\boxed{} = \boxed{}$$ Write the cross products. They are equal.

$$\boxed{} = \boxed{}$$ Solve using mental math.

Answer: It will take $\boxed{}$ hours to travel 300 miles.

EXAMPLE 4 Solving Using a Related Equation

Solve the proportion $\frac{35}{10} = \frac{x}{8}$.

Solution

$$\frac{35}{10} = \frac{x}{8}$$ Write original proportion.

$$\boxed{} = \boxed{}$$ Write the cross products. They are equal.

$$\boxed{} \div \boxed{} = \boxed{}$$ Write the related division equation.

$$\boxed{} = \boxed{}$$ Divide.

Need help writing a related equation? See page 740 of your textbook.

Answer: The solution is $\boxed{}$.

Lesson 8.3 Solving Proportions 179

Guided Practice Write the related equation. Use it to solve the proportion.

5. $\dfrac{x}{12} = \dfrac{20}{8}$	6. $\dfrac{18}{y} = \dfrac{30}{50}$	7. $\dfrac{40}{15} = \dfrac{b}{9}$	8. $\dfrac{36}{30} = \dfrac{42}{s}$

Lesson 8.4

Proportions and Scale Drawings

Goal: Use proportions to find measures of objects.

EXAMPLE 1 Using a Scale Drawing

Toy Box You are building a toy box for your brother. In the scale drawing of the toy box, the box has a length of 2.6 inches. What is the actual length of the toy box?

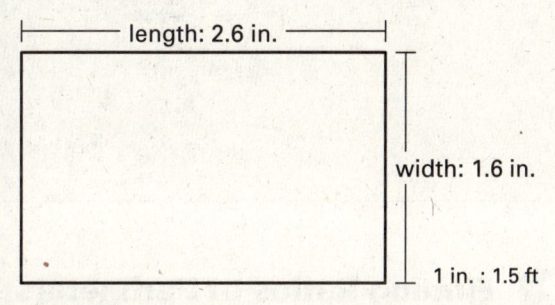

length: 2.6 in.
width: 1.6 in.
1 in. : 1.5 ft

Solution

To solve the problem, write and solve a proportion. Let x represent the actual length of the toy box in feet.

> When setting up a proportion, make sure that the numerators are the scale dimensions and the denominators are the actual dimensions or vice-versa.

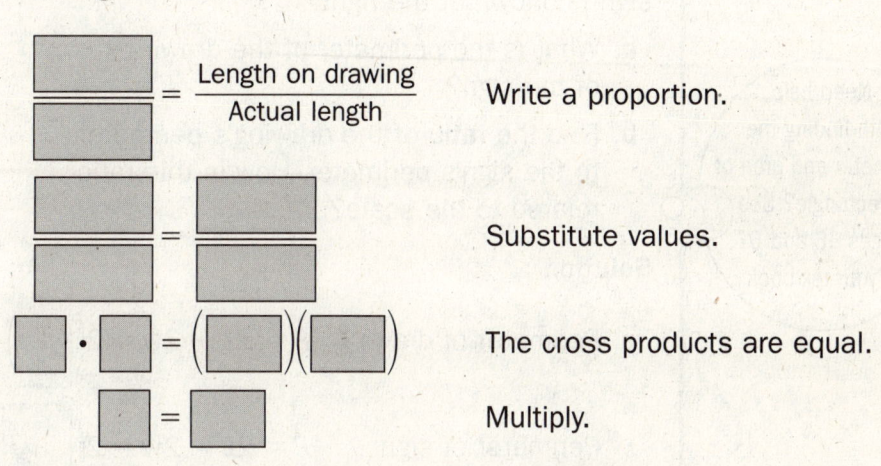

$\dfrac{\Box}{\Box} = \dfrac{\text{Length on drawing}}{\text{Actual length}}$ Write a proportion.

$\dfrac{\Box}{\Box} = \dfrac{\Box}{\Box}$ Substitute values.

$\Box \cdot \Box = (\Box)(\Box)$ The cross products are equal.

$\Box = \Box$ Multiply.

Answer: The actual length of the toy box is $\Box$ feet.

Guided Practice Use the scale drawing shown in Example 1.

1. Find the actual width of the toy box.

2. If the actual height of the toy box is 2.1 feet, what would be the height of the toy box in the drawing?

EXAMPLE 2 Finding Ratios of Perimeters

Road Sign A speed limit sign is to be 1 foot wide and $1\frac{1}{2}$ feet long. A scale drawing of the sign is shown at the right.

  a. What is the perimeter of the drawing? of the sign?

  b. Find the ratio of the drawing's perimeter to the sign's perimeter. How is this ratio related to the scale?

Need help with finding the perimeter and area of a rectangle? See pages 66 and 67 of your textbook.

SPEED LIMIT 50
$\frac{3}{4}$ in.
$\frac{1}{2}$ in.
1 in. : 2 ft

Solution

  a. Perimeter of drawing: $P = 2\ell + 2w = 2(\,\_\,) + 2(\,\_\,) = \_\,$ in.

  Perimeter of sign: $P = 2\ell + 2w = 2(\,\_\,) + 2(\,\_\,) = \_\,$ ft

  b. $\dfrac{\text{Perimeter of drawing}}{\text{Perimeter of sign}} = \dfrac{\_\_}{\_\_} = \dfrac{\_\_}{\_\_}$

Answer: The ratio of the perimeters is [ ] the scale ratio.
[ ] of perimeter in the drawing represents [ ] of actual perimeter.

EXAMPLE 3 Finding Ratios of Areas

Use the information from Example 2. Find the ratio of the drawing's area to the sign's area. How is this ratio related to the scale?

Solution

Area of drawing: $A = \ell w =$ ☐ · ☐ = ☐ in.²

Area of sign: $A = \ell w =$ ☐ · ☐ = ☐ ft²

$\dfrac{\text{Area of drawing}}{\text{Area of sign}} = \dfrac{\Box}{\Box}$ Substitute values.

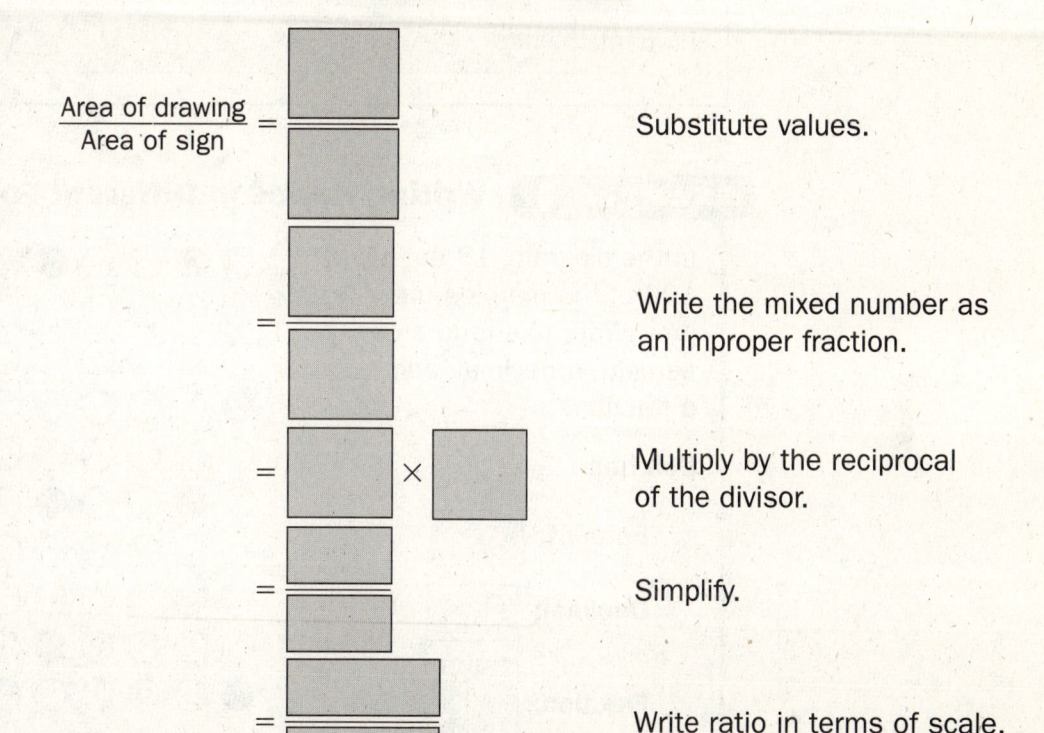

$= \dfrac{\Box}{\Box}$ Write the mixed number as an improper fraction.

$= \Box \times \Box$ Multiply by the reciprocal of the divisor.

$= \dfrac{\Box}{\Box}$ Simplify.

$= \dfrac{\Box}{\Box}$ Write ratio in terms of scale.

Answer: The ratio of the areas, ☐ : ☐ , is ☐ the scale ratio. ☐ of area in the drawing represents ☐ ☐ of actual area.

Guided Practice A rectangular road sign is 120 centimeters long and 90 centimeters wide. A scale drawing of the road sign has a length of 40 millimeters and a width of 30 millimeters. The scale of the drawing is 1 mm : 3 cm.

3. What is the ratio of the perimeters of the drawing and the sign?	4. What is the ratio of the areas of the drawing and the sign?

Lesson 8.4 Proportions and Scale Drawings | 183

Lesson 8.5 Understanding Percent

Goal: Write percents as decimals and fractions.

Vocabulary

Percent:

EXAMPLE 1 Writing Ratios in Different Forms

In the diagram, 13 out of 100 of the marbles are grey. Write this ratio as a percent, a decimal, and a fraction.

Solution

Percent:

Decimal:

Fraction:

EXAMPLE 2 Writing Percents

Write the number in words, and as a percent.

a. $\frac{4}{100}$ b. 0.47   c. $\frac{52.6}{100}$ d. 6, or $\frac{600}{100}$

Solution

a. _____ hundredths, or ___ %   b. _____ hundredths, or ___ %

c. _____ hundredths, or ___ %   d. _____ hundredths, or ___ %

In your notes, you may want to include percents in a concept map about forms of numbers, like the concept map shown on page 400 of your textbook.

Guided Practice Write the number as a percent, a decimal, and a fraction.

1. 71 hundredths	**2.** 1 hundredth	**3.** 200 hundredths

Writing Percents as Decimals and Fractions

To write a percent as a decimal:

☐ the value by ☐.   29% = ☐☐☐ = ☐

To write a percent as a fraction:

Rewrite the percent using a denominator of ☐. Simplify if possible.   84% = ☐/☐ = ☐/☐

EXAMPLE 3 Writing Percents in Different Forms

Remember that when dividing a number by 100, the decimal point in the number moves 2 places to the left.

a. Write 36.5% as a decimal.

36.5% = ☐☐☐ = ☐

b. Write 60% as a fraction.

60% = ☐/☐ = ☐/☐

Lesson 8.5 Understanding Percent

EXAMPLE 4 Circle Graphs with Percents

Survey In a survey, 100 people were asked where they read books at home. The results are shown as percents.

a. What percent of the people responded "Kitchen"?

b. What percent of the people did *not* respond "Family room"?

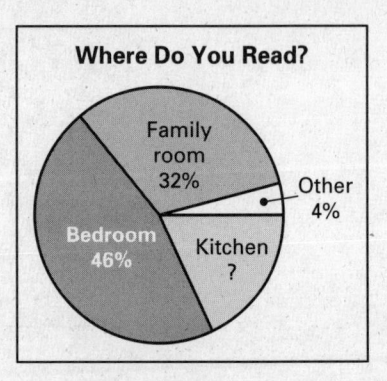

Where Do You Read?
- Family room 32%
- Other 4%
- Bedroom 46%
- Kitchen ?

Solution

a. The circle graph represents ☐%. The sum of the percents shown is ☐% + ☐% + ☐% = ☐%, so the percent of the people who responded "Kitchen" is ☐% − ☐% = ☐%.

b. The percent of people who did *not* respond "Family room" is ☐% − ☐% = ☐%.

Guided Practice Write the percent as a decimal and a fraction.

4. 4%	5. 15%	6. 80%	7. 4.6%

Lesson 8.6 Percents, Decimals, and Fractions

Goal: Write fractions and decimals as percents.

EXAMPLE 1 Writing Fractions as Percents

Restaurants A waitress has been keeping track of the number of items she has sold. She recorded that six of the last ten potato orders were for French fries, and eighteen of the last twenty-five beverage orders were for soft drinks. What percent of the last ten potato orders were for French fries and what percent of the last twenty-five beverage orders were for soft drinks?

Solution

To answer the questions, first write each record as a fraction. Then write an equivalent fraction with a denominator of 100 to find the percent.

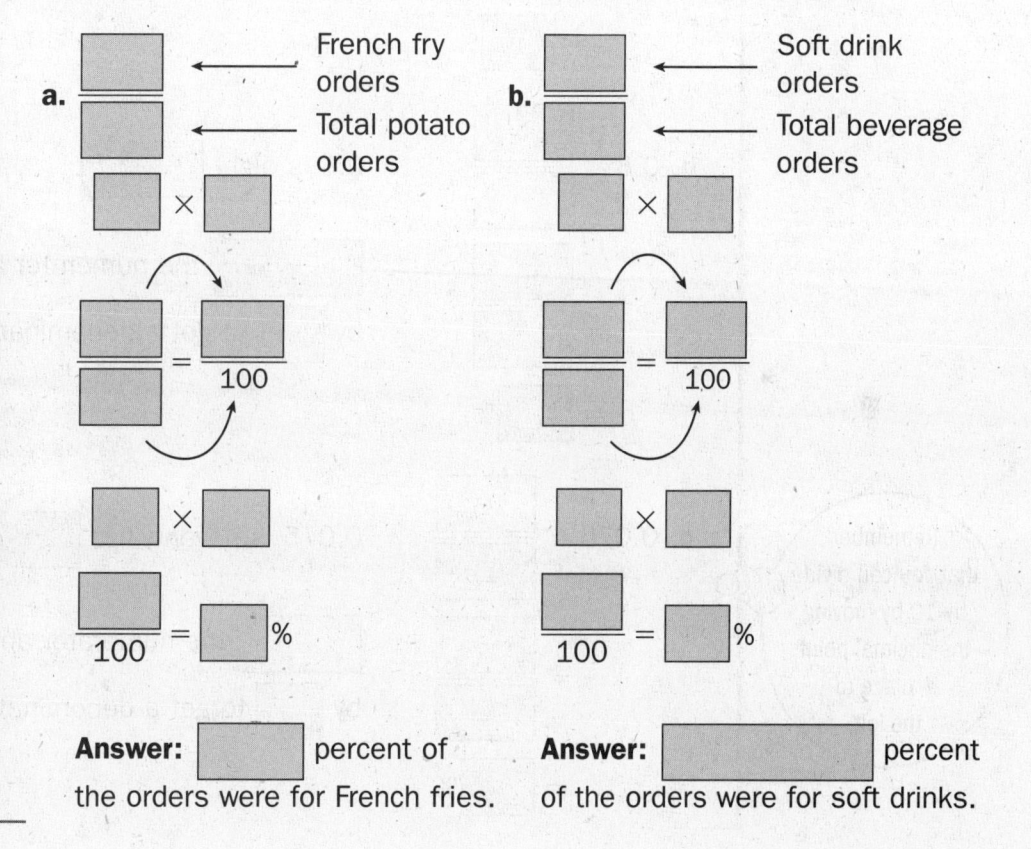

a. ☐/☐ ← French fry orders / Total potato orders

☐ × ☐

☐/☐ = ☐/100

☐ × ☐

☐/100 = ☐ %

b. ☐/☐ ← Soft drink orders / Total beverage orders

☐ × ☐

☐/☐ = ☐/100

☐ × ☐

☐/100 = ☐ %

Answer: ☐ percent of the orders were for French fries.

Answer: ☐ percent of the orders were for soft drinks.

Guided Practice Write the fraction as a percent.

1. $\frac{1}{4}$	2. $\frac{9}{10}$	3. $\frac{11}{20}$	4. $\frac{7}{50}$

EXAMPLE 2 Writing Decimals as Percents

Write the decimal as a percent.

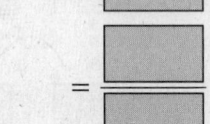

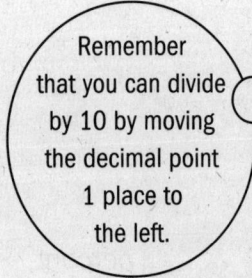

a. $0.08 = \dfrac{\boxed{}}{\boxed{}}$ 0.08 is eight ⬚.

   $= \boxed{}\%$

b. $0.8 = \dfrac{\boxed{}}{\boxed{}}$ 0.8 is eight ⬚.

   $= \dfrac{\boxed{}}{\boxed{}}$ ⬚ the numerator and denominator by ⬚ to get a denominator of ⬚.

   $= \boxed{}\%$

c. $0.075 = \dfrac{\boxed{}}{\boxed{}}$ 0.075 is seventy-five ⬚.

   $= \dfrac{\boxed{}}{\boxed{}}$ ⬚ the numerator and denominator by ⬚ to get a denominator of ⬚.

   $= \boxed{}\%$

Remember that you can divide by 10 by moving the decimal point 1 place to the left.

EXAMPLE 3 Using Decimals to Write Percents

Defective Parts The machine used to manufacture a plastic part occasionally needs to be adjusted. The machine is adjusted when 3% of the parts made contain some kind of defect. During a recent run, 125 parts were made and only 3 were defective. Does the machine need to be adjusted?

Solution

Use decimals to write fractions as percents when you cannot easily write the equivalent form of the fraction with a denominator of 100.

$\dfrac{\boxed{}}{\boxed{}} = \boxed{}$ Divide $\boxed{}$ by $\boxed{}$ to write the fraction as a decimal.

$= \dfrac{\boxed{}}{\boxed{}}$ $\boxed{}$ is $\boxed{}$.

$= \dfrac{\boxed{}}{\boxed{}}$ $\boxed{}$ the numerator and denominator by $\boxed{}$ to get a denominator of $\boxed{}$.

$= \boxed{}\%$

Answer: Because $\boxed{}\%$ $\boxed{}$ 3%, the machine $\boxed{}$ need to be adjusted.

Guided Practice Write the decimal or fraction as a percent.

5. 0.9	**6.** 0.108	**7.** $\dfrac{5}{8}$	**8.** $\dfrac{17}{40}$

Lesson 8.6 Percents, Decimals, and Fractions 189

Common Percents, Decimals, and Fractions

Fifths	Fourths	Thirds
20% = 0.2 = ☐	☐% = 0.25 = $\frac{1}{4}$	$33\frac{1}{3}$% = $0.\overline{3}$ = ☐
☐% = 0.4 = $\frac{2}{5}$	50% = 0.5 = ☐	$66\frac{2}{3}$% = ☐ = $\frac{2}{3}$
60% = ☐ = $\frac{3}{5}$	75% = ☐ = $\frac{3}{4}$	
80% = 0.8 = ☐		

EXAMPLE 4 Using Common Relationships

Order the numbers $\frac{3}{5}$, 40%, and 0.54 from least to greatest.

Write the number as decimals and graph them on a number line.

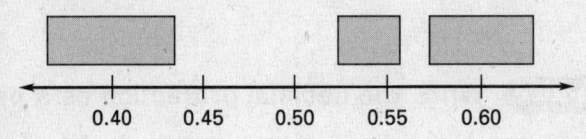

0.40 0.45 0.50 0.55 0.60

Answer: An ordered list of the numbers is ☐ , ☐ , and ☐ .

190 | Chapter 8 Notetaking Guide

Lesson 8.7 Finding a Percent of a Number

Goal: Multiply to find a percent of a number.

Vocabulary

Interest:

Principal:

Annual interest rate:

Simple interest:

> You may want to include Example 1 in your notes to illustrate when a fraction or when a decimal may be the more convenient form of a percent to use. In part (a), the fraction form of 25% is compatible with 80. In part (b), you can multiply by the decimal form of 40% easily using mental math.

EXAMPLE 1 Finding a Percent of a Number

a. Find 25% of 80.
Use a fraction.

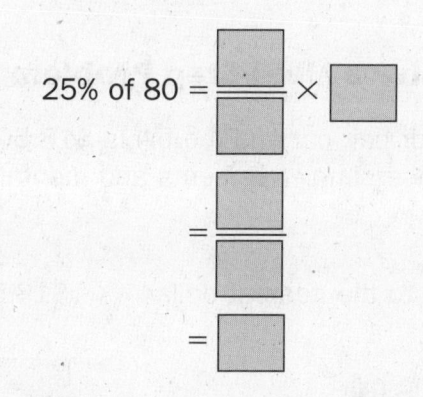

25% of 80 = ▭/▭ × ▭

= ▭/▭

= ▭

Answer: 25% of 80 is ▭.

b. Find 40% of 32.
Use a decimal.

40% of 32 = ▭ × ▭

= ▭

Answer: 40% of 32 is ▭.

Guided Practice   Find the percent of the number. Explain your method.

1. 20% of 48	2. 60% of 75	3. 8% of 30	4. 10% of 97

EXAMPLE 2 Finding a Discount

Inline Skates The regular price of a pair of inline skates is $80. The sale price is 35% off the regular price. What is the sale price?

1. Find the discount. ☐% of $☐ = ☐ × $☐ = $☐

2. Subtract the discount from the regular price. $☐ − $☐ = $☐

Answer: The sale price of the skates is $☐.

EXAMPLE 3 Finding the Sales Tax

Buying a CD You are buying a CD that costs $12. There is a 7% sales tax. What is the total amount of your purchase?

1. Find the sales tax. ☐% of $☐ = ☐ × $☐ = $☐

2. Add the sales tax to the cost of the item. $☐ + $☐ = $☐

Answer: The total amount of your purchase is $☐.

EXAMPLE 4 Solve a Multi-Step Problem

Haircut You get your hair cut and the bill is $18.50. You want to leave a tip of about 15%. Use simpler percents and mental math to estimate the amount of the tip.

1. Round the bill to the nearest dollar. $18.50 ≈ $☐

2. Find 10% of the bill. ☐ × $☐ = $☐

3. Find 5% of the bill. It is half of 10% of the bill. ☐ × $☐ = $☐

4. Add the partial tips. $☐ + $☐ = $☐

Answer: A 15% tip for a $18.50 bill is about $☐.

Guided Practice Find the cost described.

5. A ski jacket's regular price is $110. Find the cost after a 30% discount.

6. The price of a pack of guitar strings is $10.50. Find the cost with a sales tax of 8%.

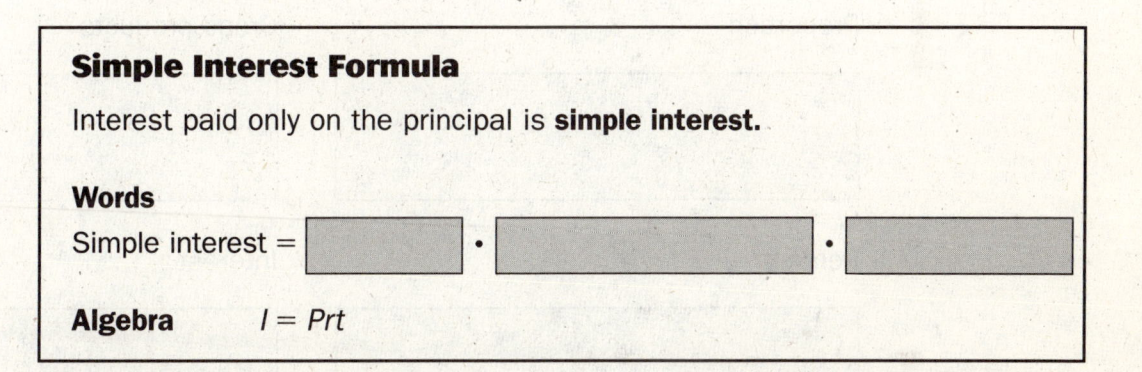

Simple Interest Formula

Interest paid only on the principal is **simple interest.**

Words
Simple interest = ☐ · ☐ · ☐

Algebra $I = Prt$

EXAMPLE 5 Standardized Test Practice

Savings You deposit $55 in an account. The annual interest rate is 2%. How much simple interest will you earn in 3 years?

Ⓐ $1.10   Ⓑ $3.30   Ⓒ $11   Ⓓ $33

Solution

$I = $ ☐   Write the simple interest formula.

= ☐(☐)(☐)   Substitute values. Write 2% as a decimal.

= ☐   Multiply.

Answer: You will earn $☐ in simple interest in 3 years.

The correct answer is ☐.   Ⓐ Ⓑ Ⓒ Ⓓ

Lesson 8.7   Finding a Percent of a Number   193

CHAPTER 8 Words to Review

Give an example of the vocabulary word.

Ratio

Equivalent ratio

Rate

Unit rate

Proportion

Cross products

Percent

Interest

Principal

Annual interest rate

Simple interest

Review your notes and Chapter 8 by using the Chapter Review on pages 443–446 of your textbook.

LESSON 9.1 Introduction to Geometry

Goal: Identify lines, rays, and segments.

Vocabulary

Point:

Line:

Ray:

Endpoint:

Segment:

Plane:

Intersecting lines:

Parallel lines:

EXAMPLE 1 Identifying Lines, Rays, and Segments

From the diagram, identify the *line*, *ray*, or *segment* using words. Then name it using symbols.

a. X———Y

b. S↘↙T

c. U↗V

Solution

a. The figure is a _____ and is represented by _____ or _____.

b. The figure is a _____ and is represented by _____ or _____.

c. The figure is a _____ and is represented by _____.

Lesson 9.1 Introduction to Geometry | 195

Guided Practice Identify and name the *line*, *ray*, or *segment* using words and using symbols.

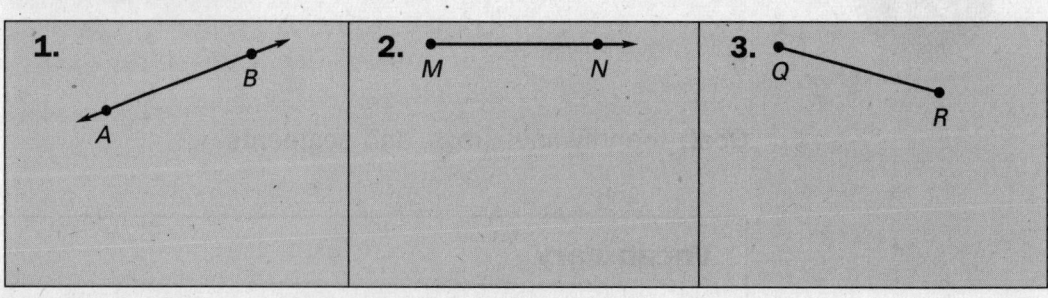

1. [ray with endpoint A through B]
2. [segment/ray from M through N with arrow]
3. [segment Q to R]

EXAMPLE 2 Naming Lines, Rays, and Segments

Use the bookcase at the right.

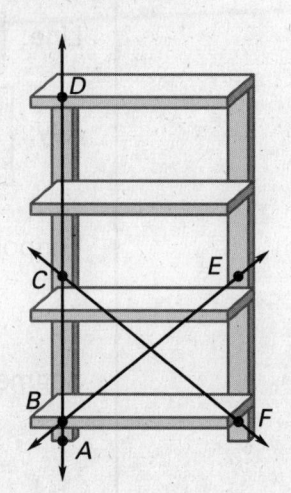

a. Name two rays.
b. Name two segments that have C as an endpoint.
c. Name a line.

WATCH OUT!
When naming a ray, the first letter in the ray's name is the name of the endpoint of the ray.

Solution

a. Two rays are ☐ and ☐.

b. Two segments that have C as an endpoint are ☐ and ☐.

c. One line is ☐.

EXAMPLE 3 Intersecting and Parallel Lines

a. Which lines are intersecting?
b. Which lines are parallel?

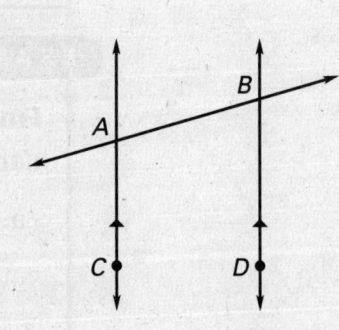

Parallel lines are indicated by special arrows on each line.

Solution

a. ☐ and ☐ intersect at point A.

   ☐ and ☐ intersect at point B.

b. ☐ and ☐ are parallel.

196 | Chapter 9   Notetaking Guide

Guided Practice Use the diagram below.

4. What is another way to write $\overrightarrow{LO}$? $\overrightarrow{PL}$?

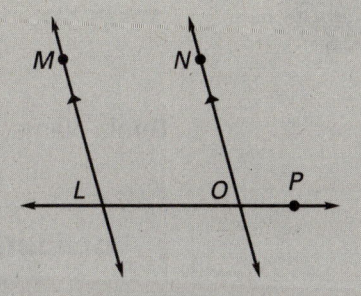

5. Which lines are intersecting? parallel?

Lesson 9.1 Introduction to Geometry

LESSON 9.2

Angles

Goal: Name, measure, and draw angles.

Vocabulary

Angle:

Vertex:

Degrees (°):

EXAMPLE 1 Naming Angles

Lamp The arms of an adjustable lamp form an angle. Name the angle formed by the arms of the lamp in three different ways.

Solution

Name the angle by its vertex alone: _____.

Name the angle by its vertex and two points, with the vertex as the middle point: _____.

Name the angle by its vertex and two points, but switch the order of the two points: _____.

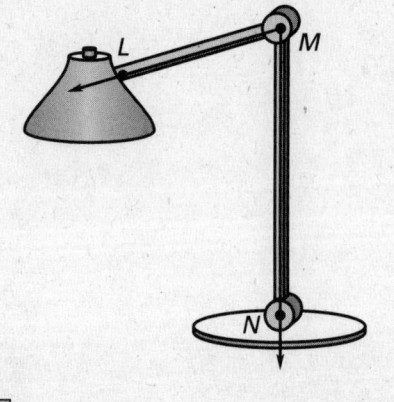

Guided Practice Name the angle in three ways.

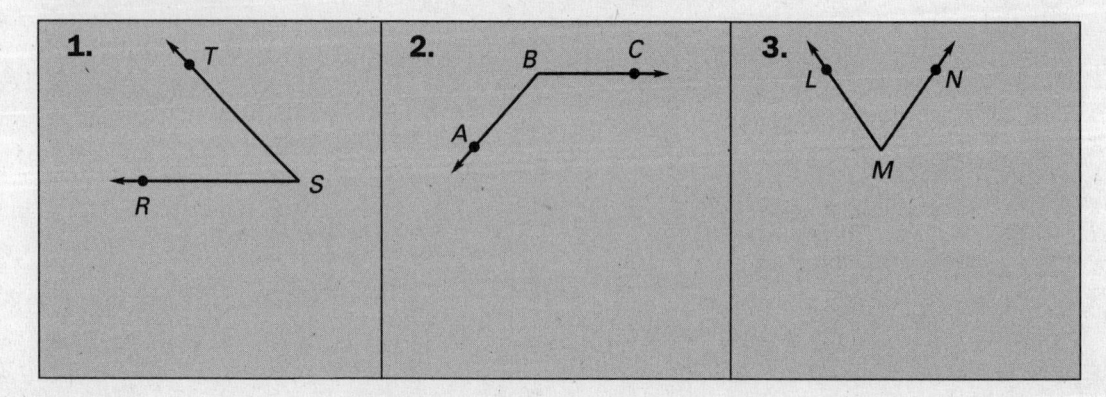

1.

2.

3.

EXAMPLE 2 Standardized Test Practice

Use the protractor shown.
What is the measure of ∠ABC?

Ⓐ 73° Ⓑ 67°
Ⓒ 107° Ⓓ 113°

Solution

Place the center of the protractor on the vertex of the angle. Then line up $\overrightarrow{BC}$ with the 0° mark on one of the scales. In this case, it's the inner scale. Using the same scale, read the measure where the other ray crosses the protractor. $\overrightarrow{BA}$ crosses the inner scale slightly past the ☐ mark. So, the measure of ∠ABC is ☐, which you can write as m∠ABC = ☐. The correct answer is ☐.   Ⓐ Ⓑ Ⓒ Ⓓ

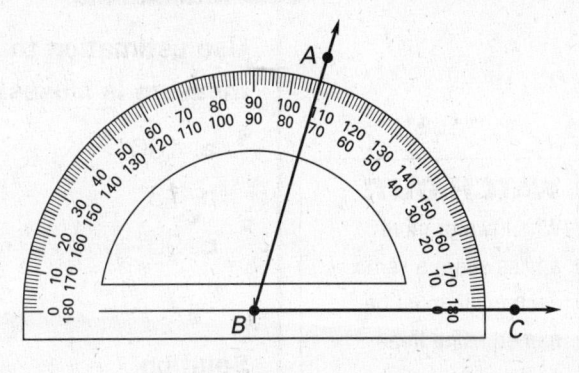

EXAMPLE 3 Drawing Angles

Use a protractor to draw an angle that has a measure of 116°.

Solution

1. Draw and label a ray $\overrightarrow{BC}$.

2. Place the center of the protractor at the endpoint of the ray. Line up the ray with the 0° line. Then draw and label a point at the 116° mark on the ☐ scale.

3. Remove the protractor and draw $\overrightarrow{BA}$ to complete the angle.

> Some protractors have an inner scale and an outer scale. You read one scale when measuring clockwise and the other scale when measuring counterclockwise. Make sure you use the same scale for each ray of the angle.

Guided Practice Use a protractor to draw an angle that has the given measure.

4. 35°	5. 50°	6. 125°	7. 160°

Lesson 9.2 Angles 199

EXAMPLE 4 Estimating Angle Measures

Use estimation to name the angle whose measure is closest to the given measure.

a. 160°
b. 75°
c. 90°

WATCH OUT!
When two or more angles share a vertex, each angle must be named using three points.

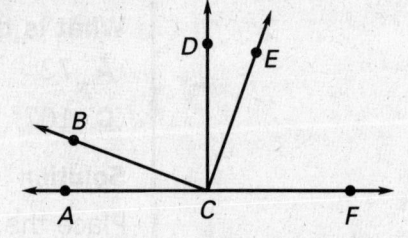

Solution

Imagine that C is at the center and that $\vec{CA}$ and $\vec{CF}$ are on the 0° line.

a. A 160° angle is close to [ ]° and greater than [ ]°, so [ ] has the measure that is closest to 160°.

b. A 75° angle is close to [ ]° and less than [ ]°, so [ ] and [ ] both have measures that are close to 75°.

c. A 90° angle is [ ], so [ ], [ ], and [ ] all have measures that are close to 90°.

200 | Chapter 9 Notetaking Guide

Lesson 9.3

Classifying Angles

Goal: Classify angles and find angle measures.

Vocabulary

Right angle:

Acute angle:

Obtuse angle:

Straight angle:

Vertical angles:

Complementary angles:

Supplementary angles:

Classifying Angles

A _____ **angle** is an angle whose measure is _____.

An _____ **angle** is an angle whose measure is _____.

An _____ **angle** is an angle whose measure is _____.

A _____ **angle** is an angle whose measure is _____.

EXAMPLE 1 Classifying Angles

Classify the angles in the figure as *acute*, *right*, or *obtuse*.

∠R is an ⬚ angle because m∠R is ⬚.

∠S is an ⬚ angle because m∠S is ⬚.

∠T is a ⬚ angle because ∠T is ⬚.

∠U is an ⬚ angle because m∠U is ⬚.

Guided Practice Classify the angle as *acute*, *right*, *obtuse*, or *straight*.

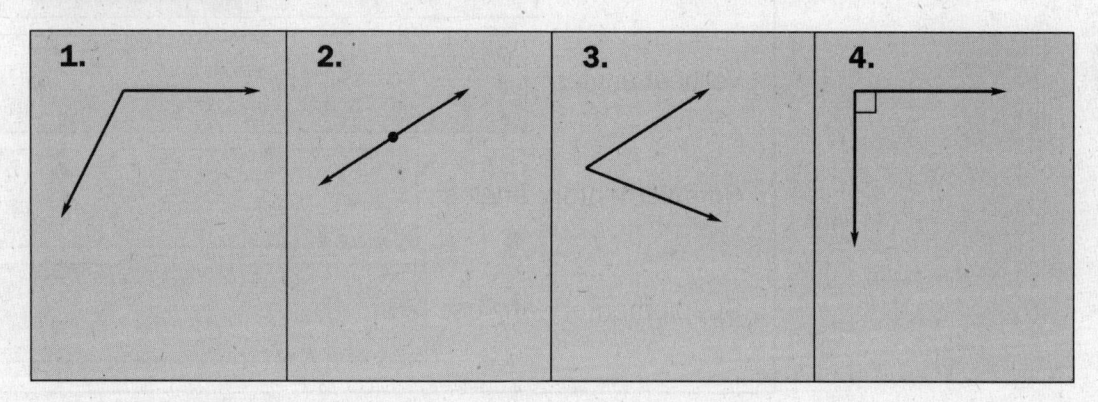

1. 2. 3. 4.

EXAMPLE 2 Using Vertical Angles

Find the measure of ∠CBE.

Because ∠CBE and ⬚ are vertical angles,

m∠CBE = ⬚ = ⬚.

Answer: The measure of ∠CBE is ⬚.

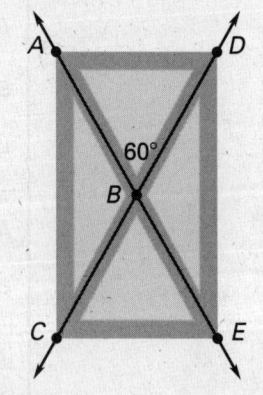

Complementary and Supplementary Angles

Complementary angles Two angles are complementary if the [ ] of their measures is [ ].

m∠1 [ ] m∠2 = [ ]

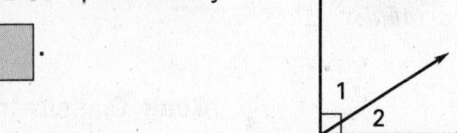

Supplementary angles Two angles are supplementary if the [ ] of their measures is [ ].

m∠3 [ ] m∠4 = [ ]

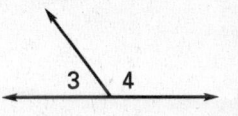

EXAMPLE 3 Classifying Pairs of Angles

Decide whether the angles are *complementary*, *supplementary*, or neither.

a. 35°, 55°

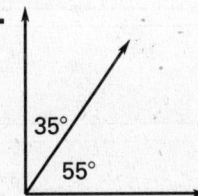

b. 148°, 32°

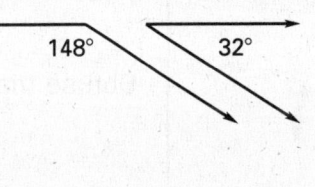

To associate complementary angles with 90° and supplementary angles with 180°, remember that "c" is before "s" in the alphabet and 90 is before 180 on a number line.

Solution

a. The angles are [ ] because [ ] [ ].

b. The angles are [ ] because [ ] [ ].

EXAMPLE 4 Solving for an Unknown Measure

Recliner The back of a recliner can tilt back 125°. What is the angle between the back of the recliner and the floor?

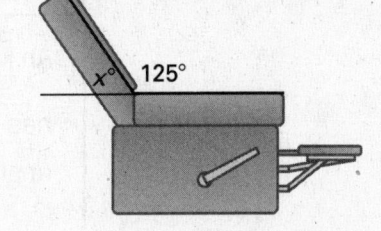

Solution

Start by drawing a diagram. Then find the angle that is [ ] to 125°.

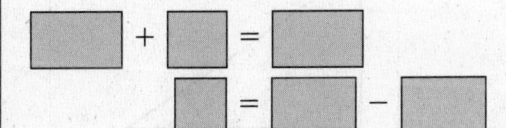

[ ] + [ ] = [ ]   Write an equation that models the situation.

[ ] = [ ] − [ ]   Write a related subtraction equation.

[ ] = [ ]   Subtract.

Answer: The angle between the back of the recliner and the floor is [ ].

Lesson 9.3 Classifying Angles

Lesson 9.4 Classifying Triangles

Goal: Classify triangles by their angles and by their sides.

Vocabulary

Triangle:

Acute triangle:

Right triangle:

Obtuse triangle:

Equilateral triangle:

Isosceles triangle:

Scalene triangle:

Classifying Triangles by Angles

An _____ triangle has _____ angles.

A _____ triangle has _____ angle.

An _____ triangle has _____ angle.

EXAMPLE 1 Classifying Triangles by Angles

Classify the triangle by its angles.

> When classifying a triangle by its angles, it is helpful to identify the largest angle first.

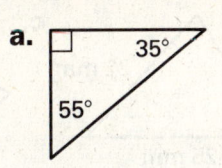

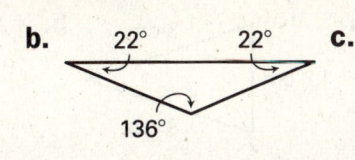

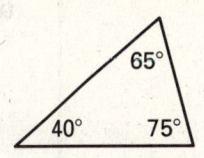

a. (right triangle with 35°, 55°, and right angle)
b. (triangle with 22°, 22°, 136°)
c. (triangle with 65°, 40°, 75°)

Solution

a. The triangle is [   ] because it has [   ] angle(s).

b. The triangle is [   ] because it has [   ] angle(s).

c. The triangle is [   ] because it has [   ] angle(s).

Guided Practice Classify the triangle by its angles.

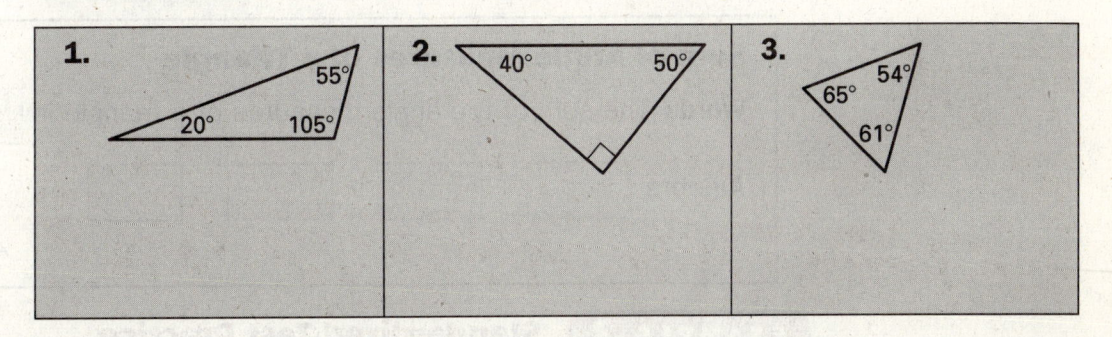

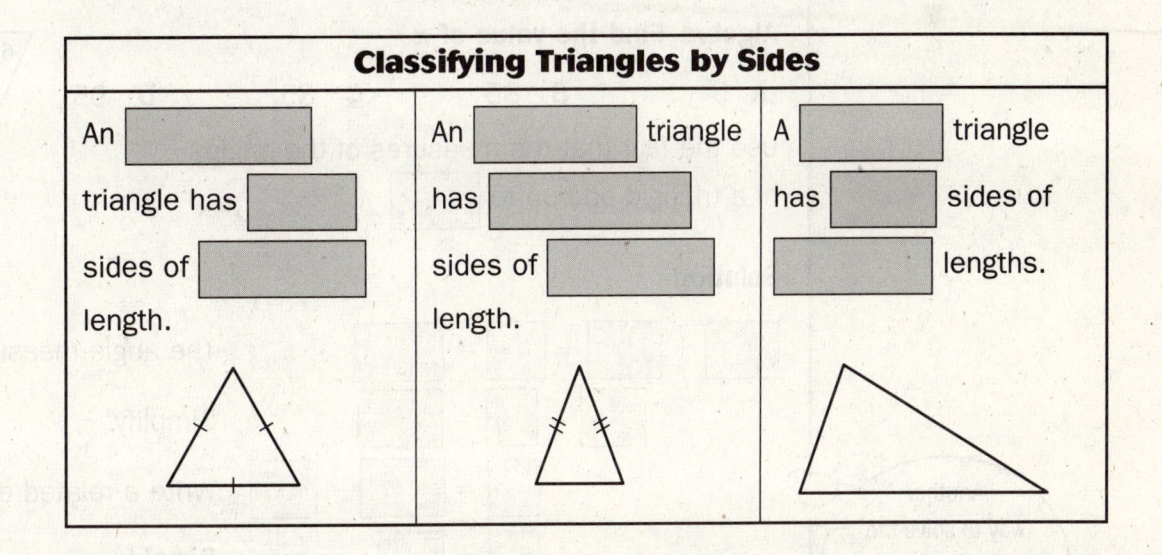

1. (triangle with 55°, 20°, 105°)
2. (triangle with 40°, 50°, right angle)
3. (triangle with 54°, 65°, 61°)

Classifying Triangles by Sides

An [ ] triangle has [ ] sides of [ ] length.	An [ ] triangle has [ ] sides of [ ] length.	A [ ] triangle has [ ] sides of [ ] lengths.

Lesson 9.4 Classifying Triangles 205

EXAMPLE 2 Classifying Triangles by Sides

Classify the triangle by its sides.

a. 3 cm, 1.8 cm, 3 cm
b. 19 mm, 22 mm, 25 mm
c. 4 in., 4 in., 4 in.

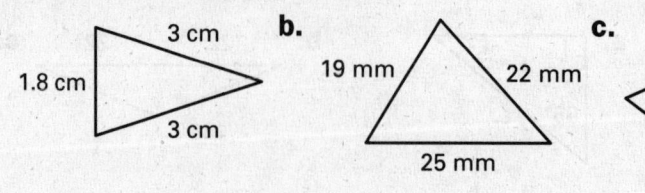

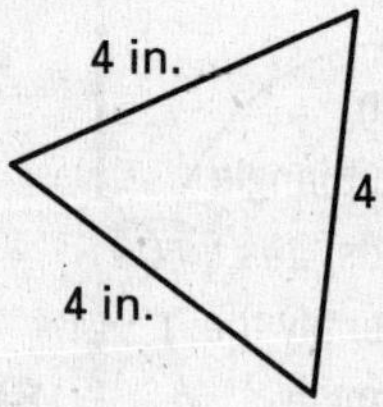

Solution

a. The triangle is ☐ because ☐ of its sides have the same length.

b. The triangle is ☐ because ☐ of its sides have the same length.

c. The triangle is ☐ because ☐ of its sides have the same length.

Sum of Angle Measures of a Triangle

Words The sum of the angle measures of a triangle is ☐.

Algebra ☐ + ☐ + ☐ = ☐

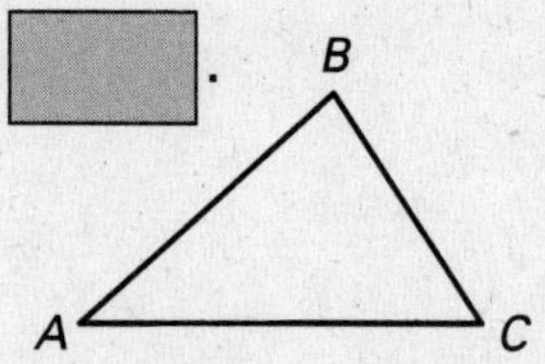

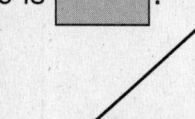

EXAMPLE 3 Standardized Test Practice

Algebra Find the value of x.

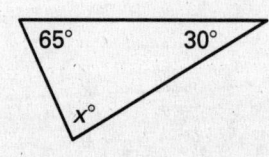

Ⓐ 5   Ⓑ 85   Ⓒ 85   Ⓓ 95

Use the fact that the measures of the angles of a triangle add up to ☐.

Solution

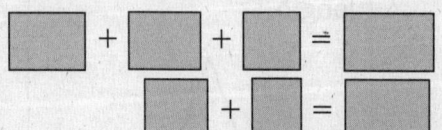

☐ + ☐ + ☐ = ☐   The angle measures add up 180°.

☐ + ☐ = ☐   Simplify.

☐ = ☐ − ☐   Write a related equation.

☐ = ☐   Simplify.

Answer: The value of x is ☐. The correct answer is ☐.

Ⓐ Ⓑ Ⓒ Ⓓ

Another way to solve the equation in Example 3 is by using mental math.

Lesson 9.5 Classifying Quadrilaterals

Goal: Classify quadrilaterals by their angles and sides.

Vocabulary

Quadrilateral:

Parallelogram:

Rectangle:

Rhombus:

Square:

Special Quadrilateral	Diagram
A _____ is a quadrilateral with _____.	
A _____ is a parallelogram with _____.	
A _____ is a parallelogram with _____.	
A _____ is a parallelogram with _____ and _____ _____.	

> Try making a Venn diagram in your notebook to help you organize the different types of quadrilaterals. For help with Venn diagrams, see page 756 of your textbook.

EXAMPLE 1 Classifying Quadrilaterals

Tell whether the statement is *true* or *false*. Explain your reasoning.

a. All rhombuses are squares.

b. Some parallelograms are rectangles.

Solution

a.

b.

EXAMPLE 2 Classifying Parallelograms

Classify the parallelogram in as many ways as possible.

a. 6 in.

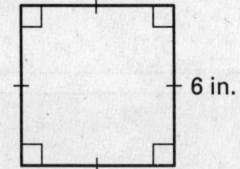

b. 2 m, 2 m, 2 m, 2 m

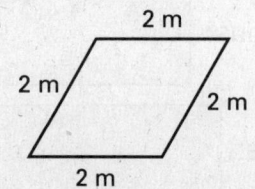

c. 4 ft, 3 ft, 3 ft, 4 ft

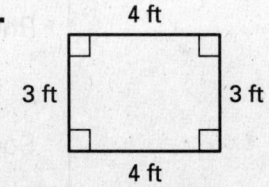

Solution

a. The parallelogram is a _____ because it has _____.

b. The parallelogram is a _____ because it has _____.

c. The parallelogram is a _____ because is has _____.

208 | Chapter 9 Notetaking Guide

EXAMPLE 3 Drawing a Quadrilateral

Before drawing the quadrilateral in Example 3, identify what properties a square has that a rhombus isn't required to have.

Draw a quadrilateral that is a rhombus but not a square.

1. Draw one side.
2. Draw an angle that isn't a [ ] angle. Then draw a side with the [ ] length.
3. Draw the other two sides so they are [ ] to the sides you've already drawn and all the [ ] length.

Guided Practice Classify the quadrilateral in as many ways as possible.

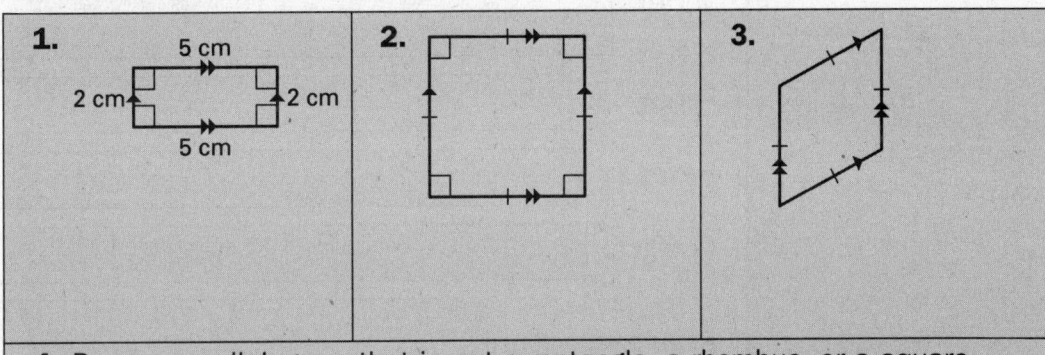

1. 5 cm, 2 cm, 2 cm, 5 cm
2.
3.

4. Draw a parallelogram that is not a rectangle, a rhombus, or a square.

EXAMPLE 4 Standardized Test Practice

Use the diagram of the pattern to determine which number represents the value of x.

Ⓐ 85   Ⓑ 90   Ⓒ 95   Ⓓ 105

Solution

$80° + 124° + 71° + x° = $ [ ]   The measures add up to [ ].

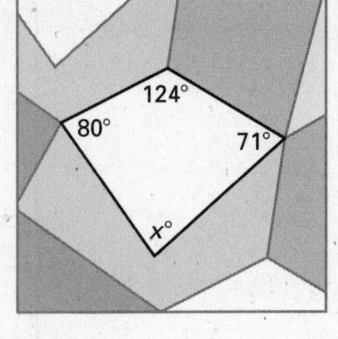

[ ] $+ x = $ [ ]   Simplify.

$x = $ [ ] $-$ [ ]   Write a related equation.

$x = $ [ ]   Simplify.

Answer: The value of x is [ ]. The correct answer is [ ].

Ⓐ Ⓑ Ⓒ Ⓓ

Lesson 9.5 Classifying Quadrilaterals 209

LESSON 9.6

Polygons

Goal: Classify polygons by their sides.

Vocabulary

Polygon:

Vertex:

Pentagon:

Hexagon:

Octagon:

Regular polygon:

Diagonal:

Classifying Polygons

3 sides

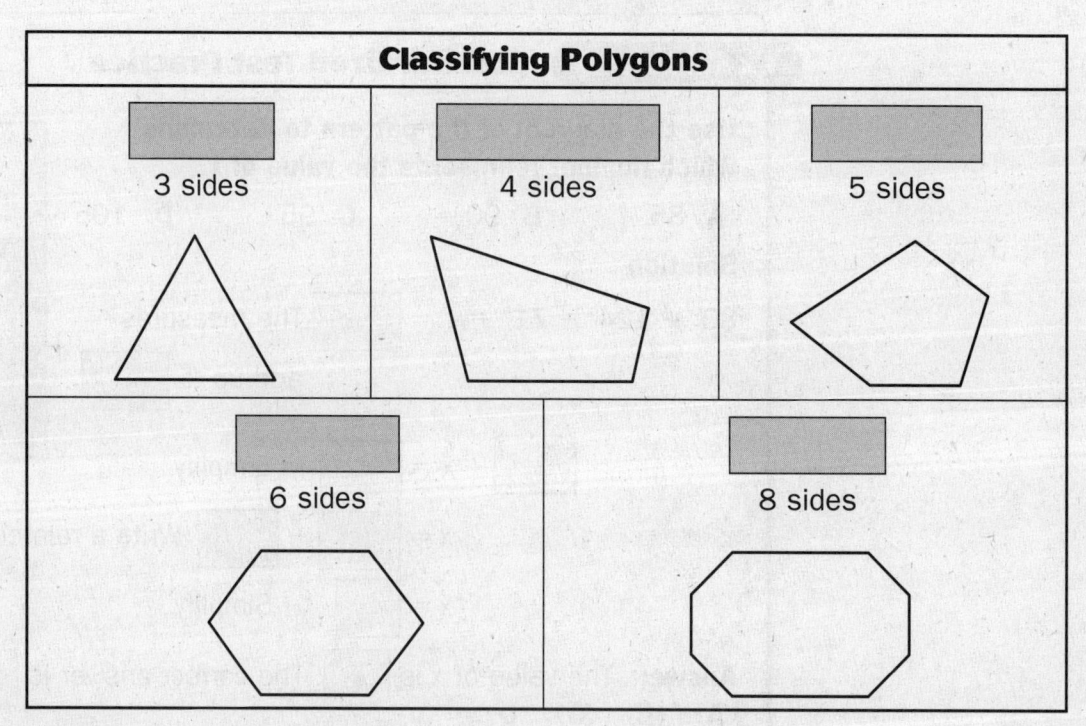

4 sides

5 sides

6 sides

8 sides

EXAMPLE 1 — Classifying Polygons

Patio The pattern for a patio floor is shown. Describe the figures found in the pattern.

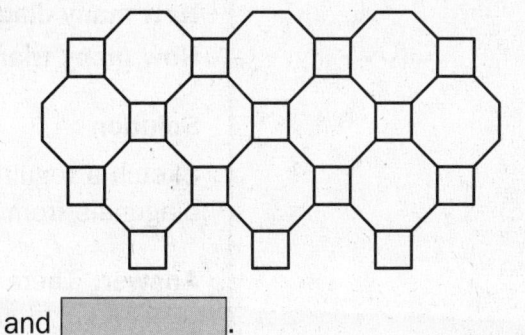

Solution

To describe the figures in the pattern, count the number of sides of each figure.

Answer: The figures are _____ and _____.

> To help remember how many sides a polygon has, use the following.
> "tri" means 3.
> "quad" means 4.
> "penta" means 5.
> "hexa" means 6.
> "octa" means 8.

Guided Practice Classify the polygon.

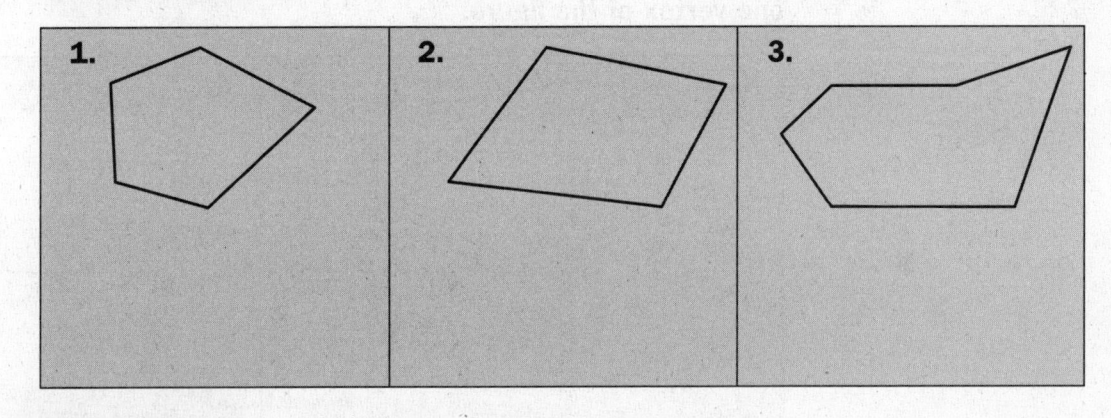

1.
2.
3.

EXAMPLE 2 — Classifying Regular Polygons

Classify the polygon and tell whether it is regular.

a. 12 mm, 12 mm, 12 mm, 12 mm, 12 mm

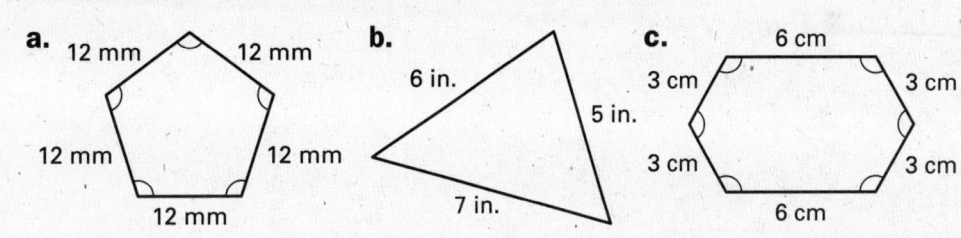

b. 6 in., 5 in., 7 in.

c. 6 cm, 3 cm, 3 cm, 3 cm, 3 cm, 6 cm

> Matching angle marks indicate that the angles have equal measures.

Solution

a. The side lengths of the _____ are _____ and the angle measures are _____, so it _____ a regular _____.

b. The side lengths of the _____ are _____ and the angle measures are _____, so it _____ a regular _____.

c. The side lengths of the _____ are _____, so it _____ a regular _____.

Lesson 9.6 Polygons 211

EXAMPLE 3 **Diagonals of a Regular Polygon**

How many diagonals can be drawn from one vertex of a regular octagon? How many triangles do the diagonals form?

Solution

Sketch a regular octagon and draw all the possible diagonals from one vertex.

Answer: There are ☐ diagonals and ☐ triangles.

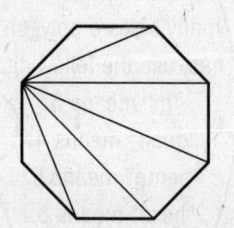

Guided Practice Tell how many triangles are formed by the diagonals from one vertex of the figure.

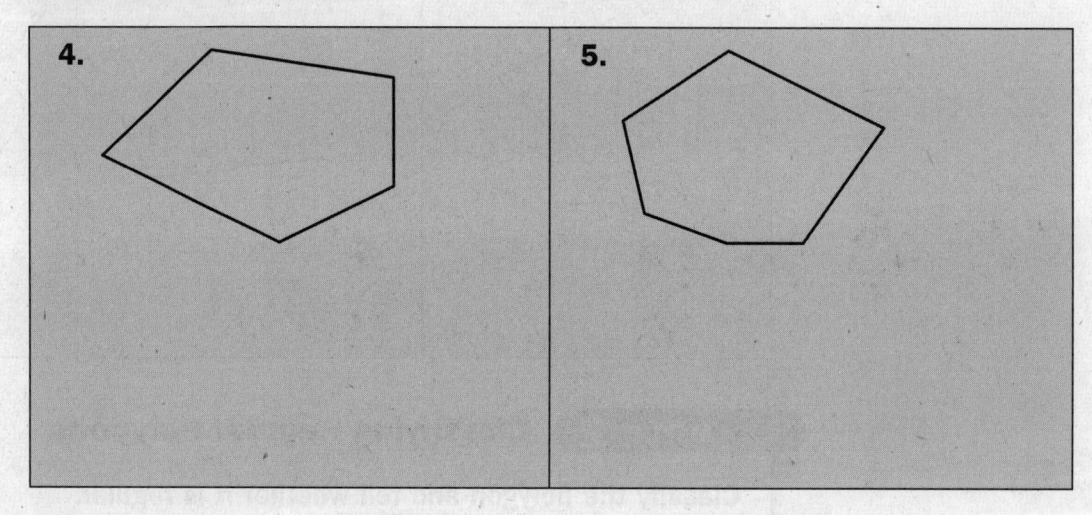

4.

5.

212 | Chapter 9 Notetaking Guide

LESSON 9.7

Congruent and Similar Figures

Goal: Identify similar and congruent figures.

Vocabulary

Congruent:

Similar:

Corresponding parts:

EXAMPLE 1 **Congruent and Similar Triangles**

Tell whether the triangles are *similar*, *congruent*, or *neither*.

Solution

_____ are similar because they have the same _____.

_____ are congruent because they have the same _____.

Lesson 9.7 Congruent and Similar Figures 213

Guided Practice Tell whether the triangles are *similar*, *congruent*, or *neither*.

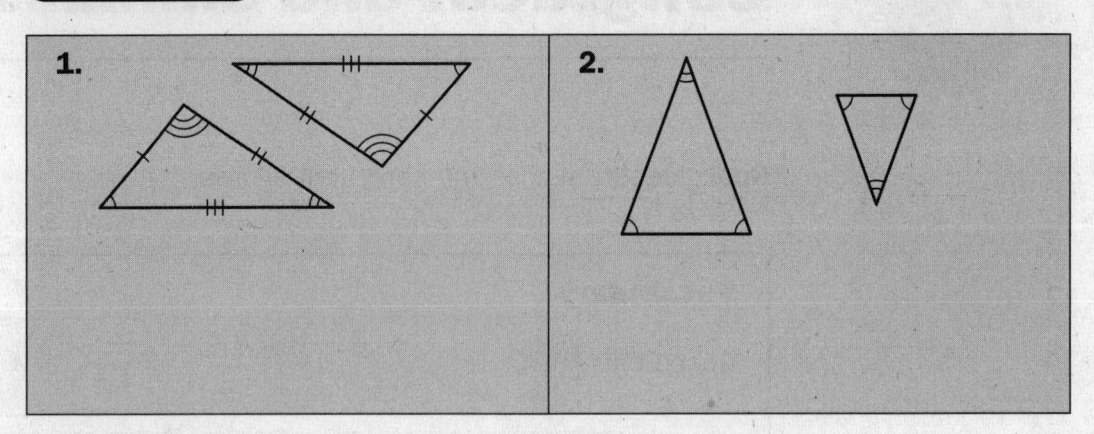

1.

2.

EXAMPLE 2 Listing Corresponding Parts

△DEF and △WXY are congruent. List the corresponding parts.

When identifying corresponding parts of figures, it can be helpful to redraw one of the figures so that it is positioned the same way as the other.

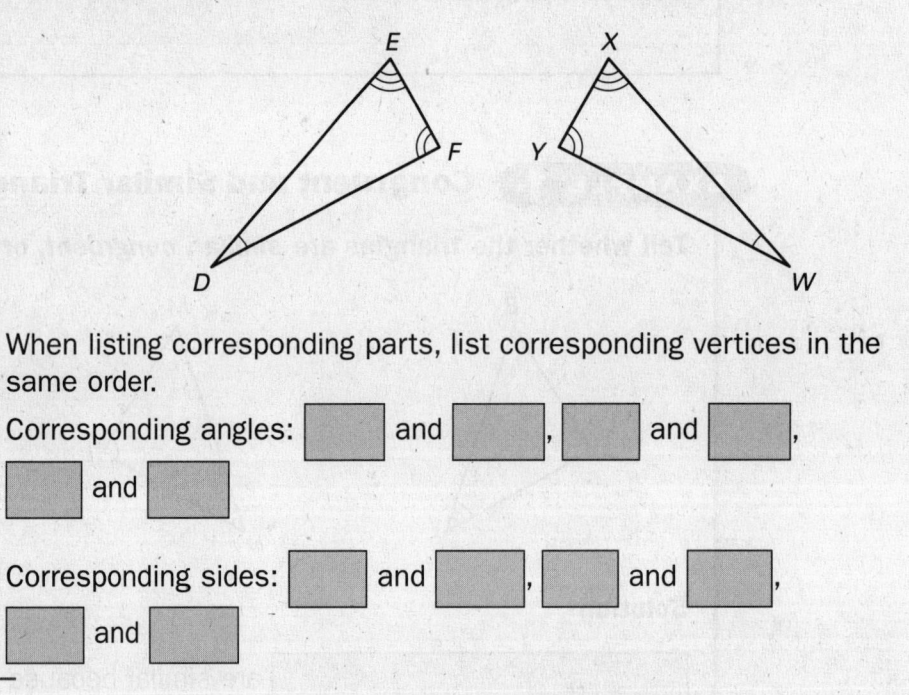

When listing corresponding parts, list corresponding vertices in the same order.

Corresponding angles: ⬚ and ⬚, ⬚ and ⬚, ⬚ and ⬚

Corresponding sides: ⬚ and ⬚, ⬚ and ⬚, ⬚ and ⬚

EXAMPLE 3 Using Corresponding Parts

In Example 3, you may want to draw each parallelogram as a separate figure to help you identify the corresponding parts.

Quilt Pattern In the quilt block shown, ABCD and EFCD are congruent.

a. If $\overline{AD}$ is 5.5 inches long, how long is $\overline{ED}$? Why?

b. If $m\angle CFE = 56°$, what is $m\angle CBA$? Why?

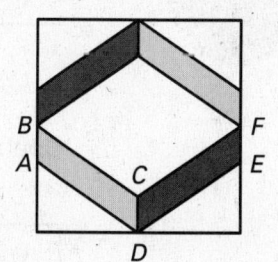

Solution

a. $\overline{ED}$ has a length of ▭ inches because ▭
▭.

b. $m\angle CBA = $ ▭ because ▭
▭.

Guided Practice △ABC and △QRS are similar. List the corresponding parts. Then find $m\angle A$ and $m\angle S$.

3.

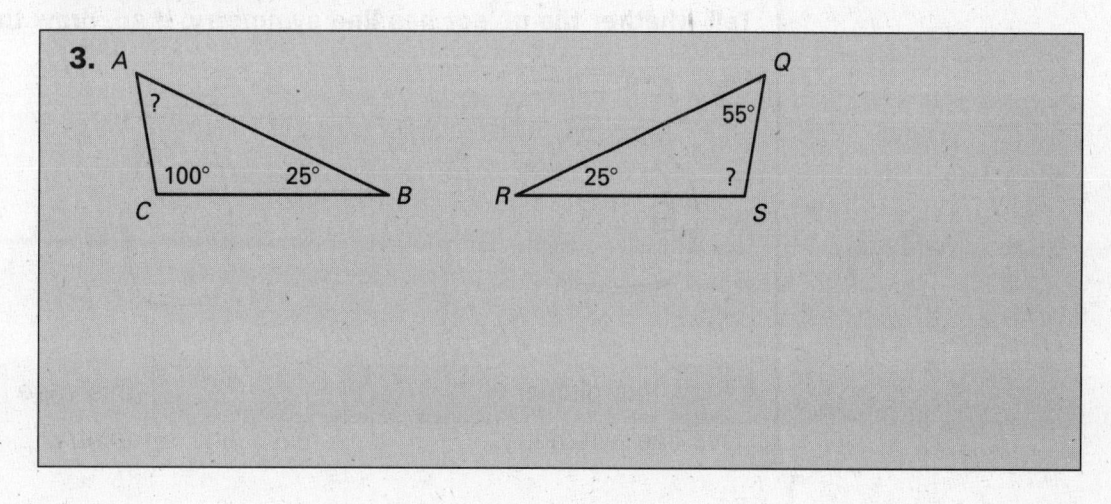

Lesson 9.7 Congruent and Similar Figures | 215

Lesson 9.8 Line Symmetry

Goal: Identify lines of symmetry.

Vocabulary

Line symmetry:

Line of symmetry:

EXAMPLE 1 Identifying Lines of Symmetry

Tell whether the object has line symmetry. If so, draw the line of symmetry.

a.

b.

_____, this pitcher _____ have line symmetry.

_____, this vase _____ have line symmetry.

Guided Practice Tell whether the figure has line symmetry. If so, draw the line(s) of symmetry.

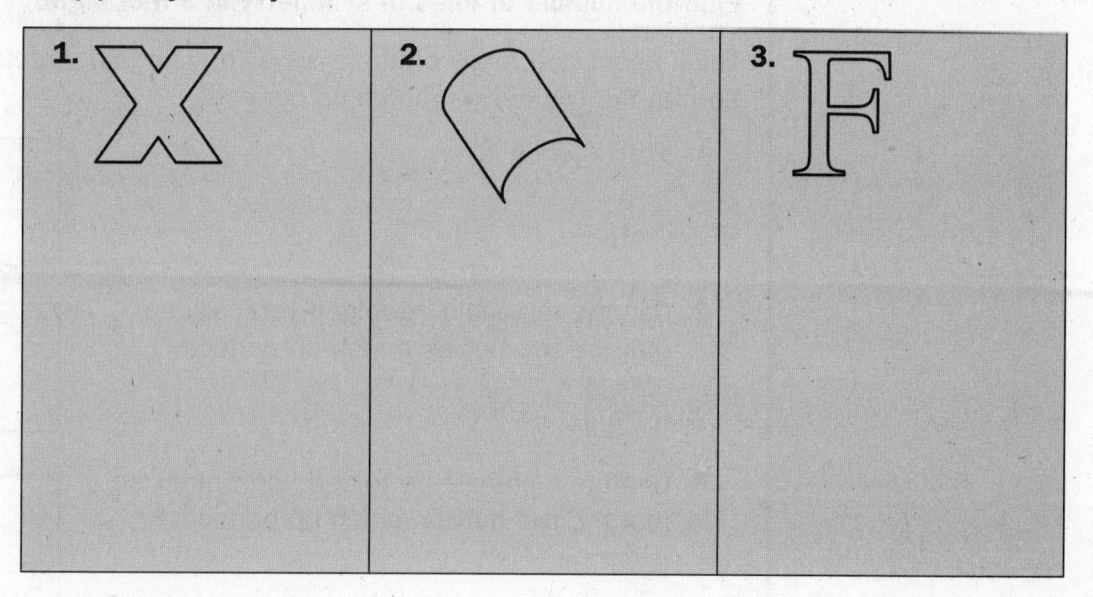

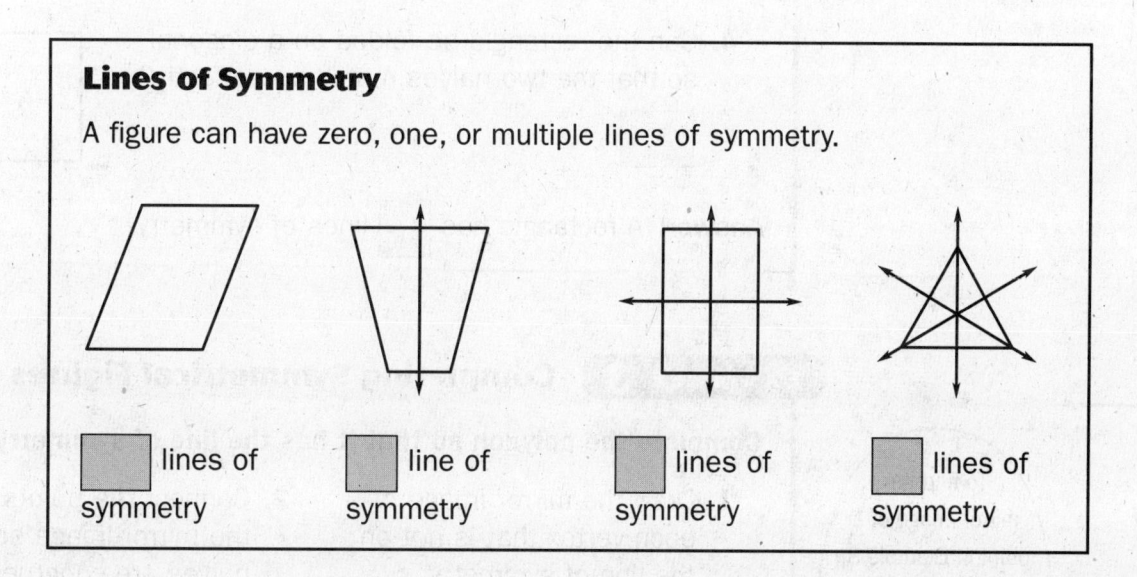

1. X

2. (curved shape)

3. F

Lines of Symmetry

A figure can have zero, one, or multiple lines of symmetry.

☐ lines of symmetry   ☐ line of symmetry   ☐ lines of symmetry   ☐ lines of symmetry

Lesson 9.8 Line Symmetry 217

EXAMPLE 2 Multiple Lines of Symmetry

Find the number of lines of symmetry in a rectangle.

Think about how many different ways you can fold a rectangle in half so that the two halves match up perfectly.

1. Draw a rectangle.

2. Can the rectangle be folded vertically so that the two halves match up perfectly?

3. Can the rectangle be folded horizontally so that the two halves match up perfectly?

4. Can the rectangle be folded on a diagonal so that the two halves match up perfectly?

Answer: A rectangle has ⬜ lines of symmetry.

EXAMPLE 3 Completing Symmetrical Figures

Complete the polygon so that it has the line of symmetry shown.

1. Draw the mirror image of each vertex that is not on the line of symmetry.

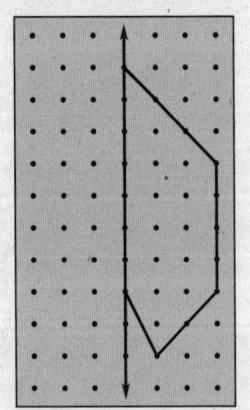

2. Connect the points to complete the mirror image so that the two halves are congruent.

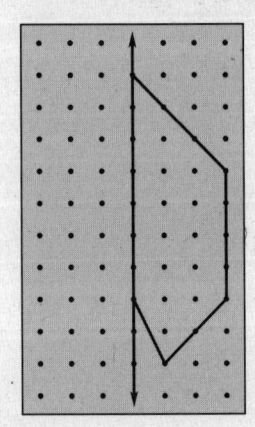

To find the mirror image of a point in Example 3, find the distance between the point and the line of symmetry. Place the mirror image point the same distance from the line of symmetry, but on the opposite side.

218 | Chapter 9 Notetaking Guide

Chapter 9

Words to Review

Give an example of the vocabulary word.

Ray

Endpoint

Segment

Intersecting lines

Parallel lines

Angle

Vertex

Degrees (°)

Acute angle

Right angle

Obtuse angle

Straight angle

Vertical angles

Complementary

Supplementary

Acute triangle

Right triangle

Obtuse triangle

Equilateral triangle

Isosceles triangle

Scalene triangle

Quadrilateral

Parallelogram

Rectangle

Rhombus

Square

Pentagon

Hexagon

Octagon

Regular polygon

Diagonal

Congruent figures

Similar figures

Review your notes and Chapter 9 by using the Chapter Review on pages 500–504 of your textbook.

Lesson 10.1

Area of a Parallelogram

Goal: Find the area of a parallelogram.

Vocabulary

Base of parallelogram: _____

Height of a parallelogram: _____

Perpendicular: _____

Area of a Parallelogram

Words   Area = ⬚ · ⬚

Algebra   A = ⬚

EXAMPLE 1 Finding the Area of a Parallelogram

Find the area of the parallelogram shown.

Solution

A = ⬚   Write the formula for the area of a parallelogram.

= ⬚ · ⬚   Substitute ⬚ for b and ⬚ for h.

= ⬚   Simplify.

Answer: The area of the parallelogram is ⬚ square centimeters.

Include the formula for the area of a parallelogram in your notebook. Include an example like the one shown in Example 1.

3 cm
8 cm

Lesson 10.1 Area of a Parallelogram 223

Guided Practice Find the area of the parallelogram described.

1. base = 4 ft, height = 9 ft	2. base = 11 in., height = 5 in.

EXAMPLE 2 Finding an Unknown Dimension

The area of a parallelogram is 72 square millimeters and the base is 8 millimeters. What is the height?

☐ = ☐   Write the formula for the area of a parallelogram.

☐ = ☐ · ☐   Substitute ☐ for A and ☐ for b.

☐ = ☐ ÷ ☐   Write a related division equation.

☐ = ☐   Simplify.

Instead of writing a related division equation, you could solve the problem in Example 2 by using mental math.

Answer: The height is ☐ millimeters.

224 | Chapter 10   Notetaking Guide

EXAMPLE 3 Estimating Area

Geography The shape of a certain island can be approximated by a parallelogram. Use the map and the scale to estimate the area of the island.

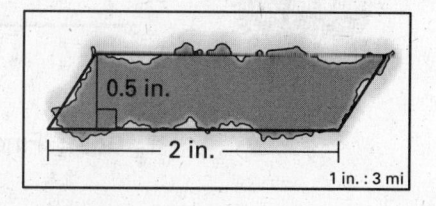

Solution

1. Use the scale to find the base, *b*, and the height, *h*, in miles.

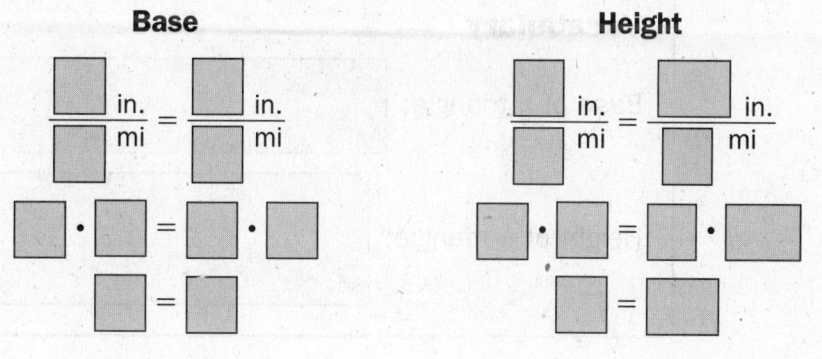

Base

$$\frac{\boxed{}\text{ in.}}{\boxed{}\text{ mi}} = \frac{\boxed{}\text{ in.}}{\boxed{}\text{ mi}}$$

$$\boxed{} \cdot \boxed{} = \boxed{} \cdot \boxed{}$$

$$\boxed{} = \boxed{}$$

Height

$$\frac{\boxed{}\text{ in.}}{\boxed{}\text{ mi}} = \frac{\boxed{}\text{ in.}}{\boxed{}\text{ mi}}$$

$$\boxed{} \cdot \boxed{} = \boxed{} \cdot \boxed{}$$

$$\boxed{} = \boxed{}$$

2. Estimate the island's area.

$A = \boxed{}$ Write the formula for the area of a parallelogram.

$ = \boxed{} \cdot \boxed{}$ Substitute $\boxed{}$ for *b* and $\boxed{}$ for *h*.

$ = \boxed{}$ Simplify.

Answer: The area of the island is about $\boxed{}$ square miles.

Guided Practice Find the unknown dimension.

3. Area of parallelogram = 48 cm², base = __?__, height = 6 cm

4. Area of parallelogram = 18 ft², base = 6 ft, height = __?__

Lesson 10.1 Area of a Parallelogram | 225

Lesson 10.2

Area of a Triangle

Goal: Find the area of a triangle.

Vocabulary

Base of a triangle: _____

Height of a triangle: _____

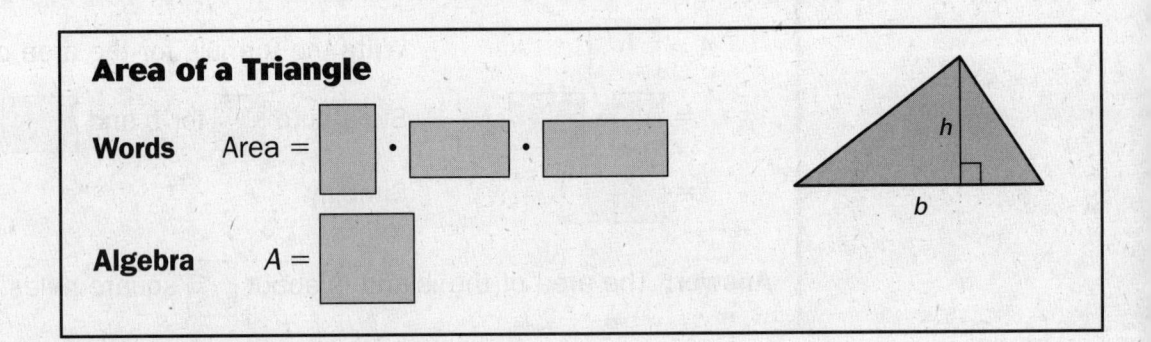

Area of a Triangle

Words Area = ☐ · ☐ · ☐

Algebra A = ☐

EXAMPLE 1 Finding the Area of a Triangle

Find the area of the triangle.

4 in.
7 in.

> As you see in Example 1, the height of an obtuse triangle can be drawn outside the figure.

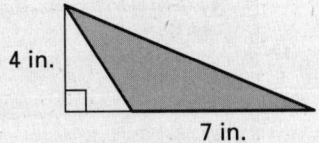

Solution

A = ☐   Write the formula for the area of a triangle.

= ☐ · ☐ · ☐   Substitute ☐ for b and ☐ for h.

= ☐   Simplify.

Answer: The area of the triangle is ☐ square inches.

226 | Chapter 10 Notetaking Guide

Guided Practice Find the area of the triangle described.

1. base = 15 centimeters, height = 6 centimeters

2. base = 8 feet, height = 13 feet

EXAMPLE 2 Standardized Test Practice

Checkout Counter The layout for a checkout counter at a store is shown. How much glass, in square feet, is needed for the countertop?

Ⓐ 15   Ⓑ 20   Ⓒ 35   Ⓓ 41

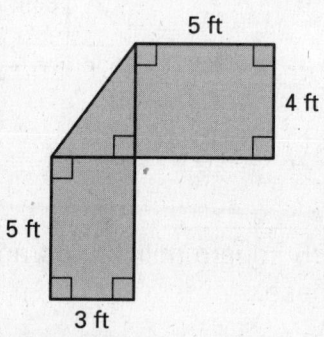

WATCH OUT!
Before finding the area of the triangle, label the lengths of the triangle's legs to make sure you use the correct dimensions.

Solution

1. Find the area of each shape.

   Area of the triangle:

   $A = \square \cdot \square \cdot \square = \square$

   Area of smaller rectangle:

   $A = \square \cdot \square = \square$

   Area of larger rectangle:

   $A = \square \cdot \square = \square$

2. Add the areas to find the total area.

   $\square + \square + \square = \square$

Answer: You will need $\square$ square feet of glass for the countertop.

The correct answer is $\square$.   Ⓐ Ⓑ Ⓒ Ⓓ

Lesson 10.2 Area of a Triangle 227

EXAMPLE 3 **Finding the Height of a Triangle**

The area of a triangle is 54 square meters and the base is 12 meters. What is the height of the triangle?

☐ = ☐   Write the formula for the area of a triangle.

☐ = ☐ · ☐ · ☐   Substitute ☐ for A and ☐ for b.

☐ = ☐ · ☐   Simplify.

☐ = ☐ ÷ ☐   Write a related division equation.

☐ = ☐   Simplify.

Answer: The height of the triangle is ☐ meters.

Guided Practice Solve the problems below.

3. Find the area of the figure at the right.

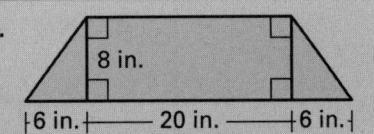

   8 in.
   |6 in.|——— 20 in. ———|6 in.|

4. The area of a triangle is 35 square millimeters and the height is 14 millimeters. Find the base.

Lesson 10.3

Circumference of a Circle

Goal: Find the circumference of a circle.

Vocabulary

Circle: _____

Center: _____

Radius: _____

Diameter: _____

Circumference: _____

Pi (π): _____

Circumference of a Circle

Words

Circumference = ☐ · ☐

Circumference = ☐ · ☐ · ☐

Algebra

$C =$ ☐ d

$C =$ ☐ r

EXAMPLE 1 Finding the Circumference of a Circle

Wall Clock The diameter of the wall clock shown is 15 inches. About how far does the car on the second hand go in one minute? Round your answer to the nearest inch.

Solution

The distance that the car travels in one minute is equal to the circumference of the clock.

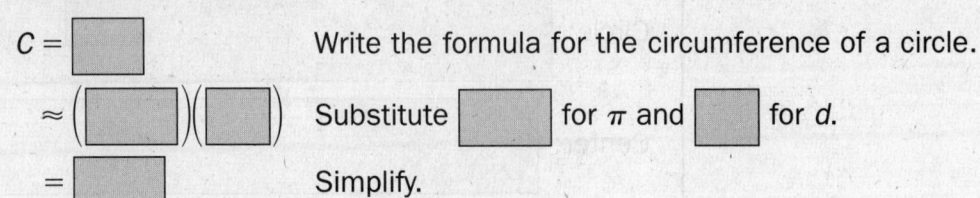

$C = \boxed{}$ Write the formula for the circumference of a circle.

$\approx (\boxed{})(\boxed{})$ Substitute $\boxed{}$ for π and $\boxed{}$ for d.

$= \boxed{}$ Simplify.

Answer: The car will travel about $\boxed{}$ inches in one minute.

EXAMPLE 2 Standardized Test Practice

Find the circumferece of the circle shown.

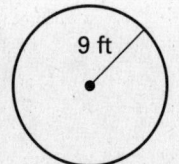

Ⓐ 6.28   Ⓑ 18   Ⓒ 28.26   Ⓓ 56.52

9 ft

The diameter of a circle is twice the radius.

Use $C = \boxed{}$ to find the circumference when you know the radius of a circle.

$C = \boxed{}$ Write the formula for the circumference of a circle.

$\approx \boxed{}(\boxed{})(\boxed{})$ Substitute $\boxed{}$ for π and $\boxed{}$ for r.

$= \boxed{}$ Simplify.

Answer: The circumference of the circle is about $\boxed{}$ feet.

The correct answer is $\boxed{}$. Ⓐ Ⓑ Ⓒ Ⓓ

Guided Practice Find the circumference of the circle.

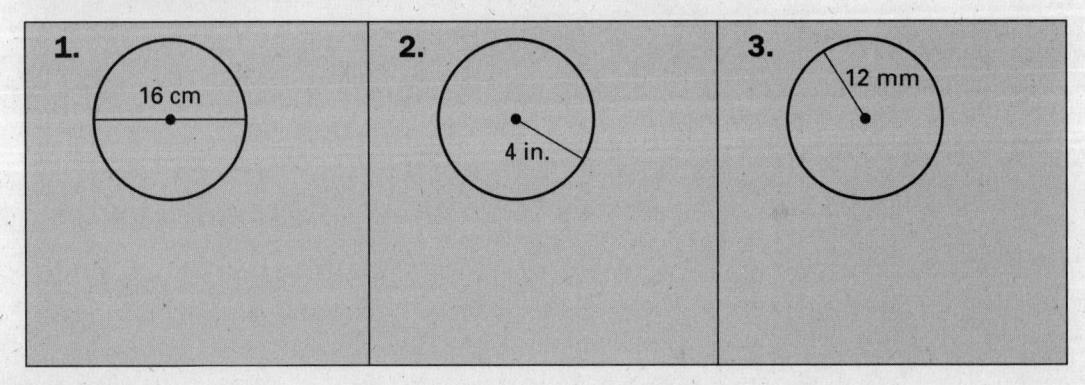

1. 16 cm

2. 4 in.

3. 12 mm

EXAMPLE 3 **Choosing an Approximation of Pi**

Find the circumference of a circle with a diameter of 21 meters.

> When the diameter or radius of a circle is a multiple of 7, use $\frac{22}{7}$ for π.

Because the diameter is a multiple of ☐, use ☐ for π.

$C = $ ☐   Use the formula for the circumference of a circle.

$\approx$ ☐ · ☐   Substitute ☐ for π and ☐ for d.

$= \dfrac{☐ \cdot ☐}{☐}$ Multiply. Divide out the common factor.

$= $ ☐   Simplify.

Answer: The circumference of the circle is about ☐ meters.

Guided Practice Find the circumference of the circle described. Tell what value you used for π. Explain your choice.

4. $d = 18$ in.	5. $d = 28$ mm	6. $r = 56$ cm

Lesson 10.3 Circumference of a Circle 231

EXAMPLE 4 Applying Circumference

Garden You are making the circular garden shown. The garden will be bordered by bricks that are 6 inches long. Estimate how many bricks you will need for the garden.

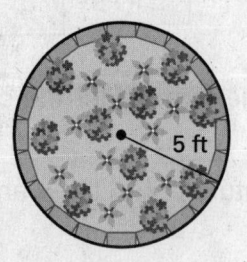

(Diagram: circular garden with radius 5 ft)

WATCH OUT!
Make sure that you are using the correct units when solving a problem. In Example 4, you can convert the length of the brick from inches to feet so that the brick length and the circumference of the garden are in the same units.

Solution

1. Find the circumference of the garden.

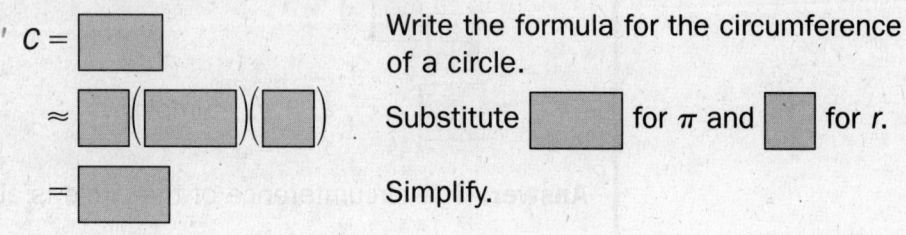

   $C = \boxed{}$ Write the formula for the circumference of a circle.

   $\approx \boxed{}(\boxed{})(\boxed{})$ Substitute $\boxed{}$ for π and $\boxed{}$ for r.

   $= \boxed{}$ Simplify.

2. Estimate the number of bricks that you will need.

   To estimate the number of bricks, divide the circumference by the brick length in feet.

   $\boxed{} \div \boxed{} = \boxed{} \approx \boxed{}$

Answer: You will need about $\boxed{}$ bricks for the garden.

232 | Chapter 10   Notetaking Guide

LESSON 10.4

Area of a Circle

Goal: Find the area of a circle.

Area of a Circle

Words   Area = (☐) · (☐)²

Algebra   A = ☐

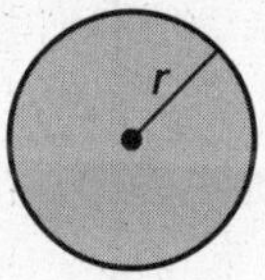

EXAMPLE 1 Finding the Area of a Circle

Swimming Pool A cover is being made for the top of the swimming pool shown. How many square feet of material will you need to cover the pool?

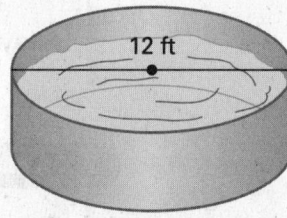

Solution

To answer the question, find the area of a circle with a diameter of 12 feet. Round to the nearest square foot.

Because the diameter is 12 feet, the radius is 12 ☐ 2 = ☐ feet.

A = ☐   Write the formula for the area of a circle.

≈ (☐) · (☐)²   Substitute ☐ for π and ☐ for r.

= ☐   Simplify.

Answer: You will need about ☐ square feet of material to cover the top of the pool.

Guided Practice Find the area of the circle.

1. 22 ft

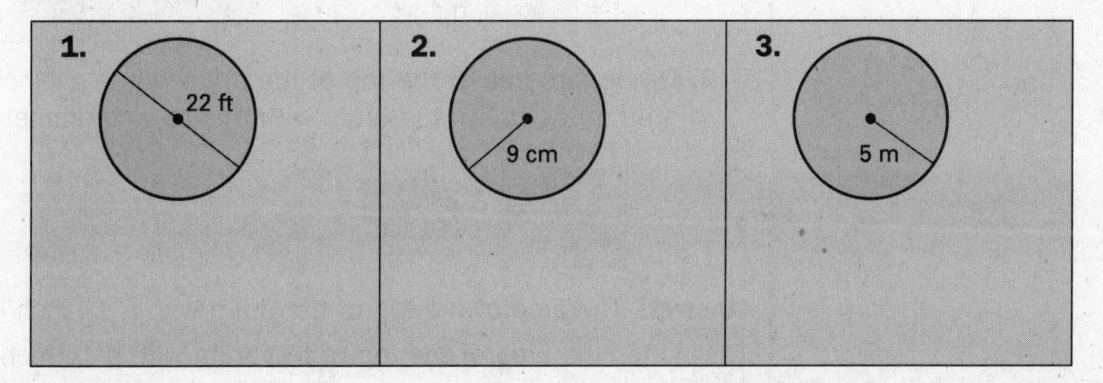

2. 9 cm

3. 5 m

Lesson 10.4   Area of a Circle   233

EXAMPLE 2 **Finding the Area of Combined Figures**

Window Find the area of the window to the nearest square inch.

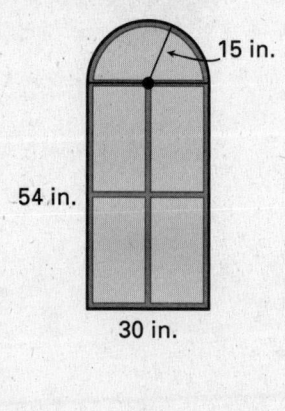

Solution

1. Find the area of each shape.

   Rectangle   **Half-circle**

   $A =$ ▢ $A =$ ▢

   $=$ ▢ · ▢ $\approx$ ▢(▢)(▢)^2

   $=$ ▢ $=$ ▢

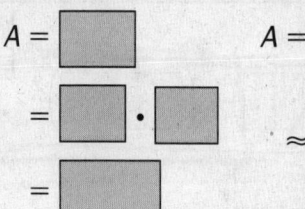

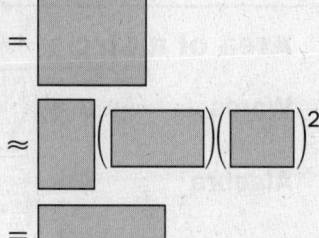

   (Window: 15 in., 54 in., 30 in.)

2. Add the areas to find the total area: ▢ + ▢ = ▢.

Answer: The area of the window is about ▢ square inches.

EXAMPLE 3 **Solve a Multi-Step Problem**

Drums How many times as great as the area of the top of a drum with a 10-inch diameter is the area of the top of a drum with a 14-inch diameter?

Solution

1. Find the area of the top of each drum.

   10-inch diameter   **14-inch diameter** 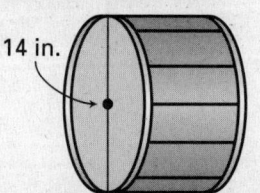
   (10 in.)   (14 in.)

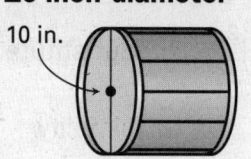

   $A =$ ▢ $A =$ ▢

   $\approx$ (▢)(▢)^2 $\approx$ (▢)(▢)^2

   $=$ ▢ in.^{2} $=$ ▢ in.^{2}

WATCH OUT!
Be sure to read diagrams carefully. The diagrams in Example 3 give the diameters of the drums. To find the area of the top of each drum, you must first find its *radius*.

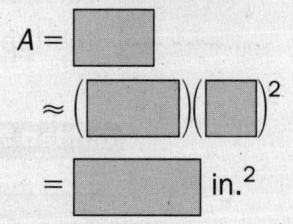

2. Divide the area of the top of the drum with a 14-inch diameter by the area of the top of the drum with the 10-inch diameter.

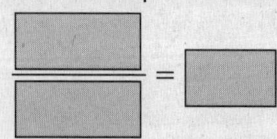

   $\dfrac{▢}{▢} =$ ▢

Answer: The area of the top of the drum with a 14-inch diameter is about ▢ times the area of the top of the drum with a 10-inch diameter.

Guided Practice Find the area of the figure to the nearest square unit.

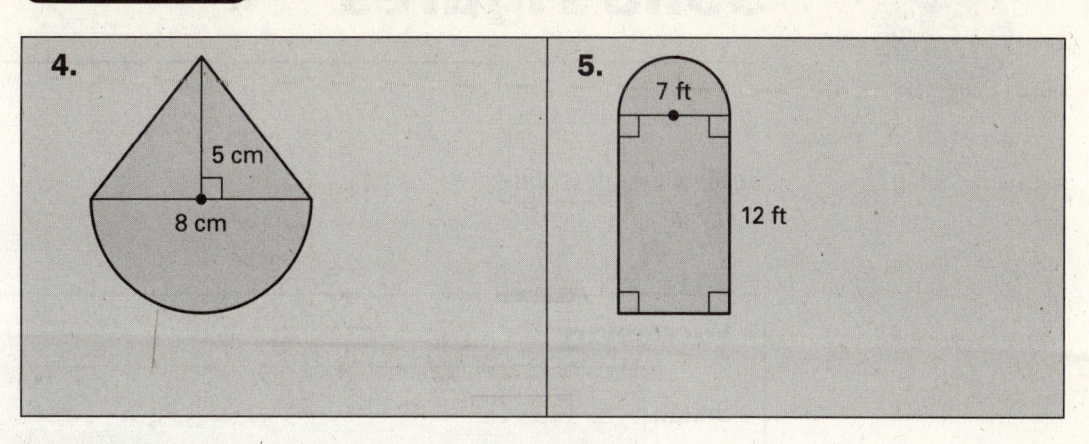

4. [figure: triangle on top of semicircle; triangle height 5 cm, diameter 8 cm]

5. [figure: rectangle with semicircle on top; radius 7 ft, height 12 ft]

EXAMPLE 4 Making a Circle Graph

Arts Fair The table shows what fraction of the booths at an arts fair contain paintings, pottery, and clothing. Make a circle graph to represent the data.

Booth Contents	Paintings	Pottery	Clothing
Fraction of Booths	$\frac{3}{5}$	$\frac{1}{4}$	$\frac{3}{20}$

Solution

1. Find the angle measure of each sector. Each sector's angle measure is a fraction of 360°. Multiply each fraction in the table by 360° to get the angle measure for each sector.

    Paintings

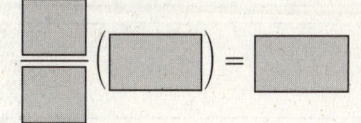

    $\frac{\square}{\square}(\square) = \square$

    Pottery

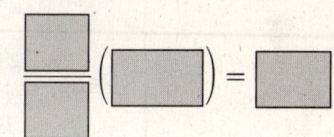

    $\frac{\square}{\square}(\square) = \square$

    Clothing

    $\frac{\square}{\square}(\square) = \square$

    > Need help with reading and interpreting circle graphs? See page 94 of your textbook.

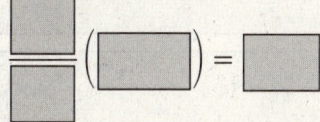

2. Draw the circle graph.

    a. Use a compass to draw a circle.

    b. Use a protractor to draw the angle for each sector.

    c. Label each sector and give your graph a title.

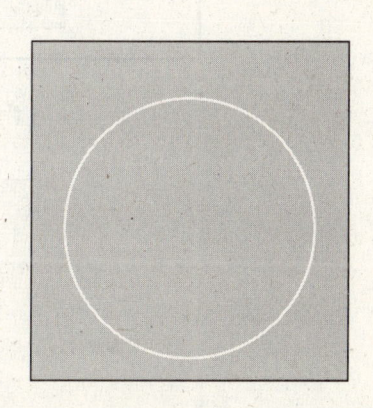

Lesson 10.5

Solid Figures

Goal: Classify solids.

Vocabulary

Solid:

Prism:

Cylinder:

Pyramid:

Cone:

Sphere:

Face:

Edge:

Vertex:

Classifying Solids

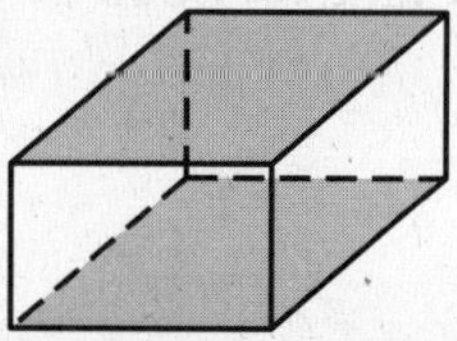

Rectangular prism 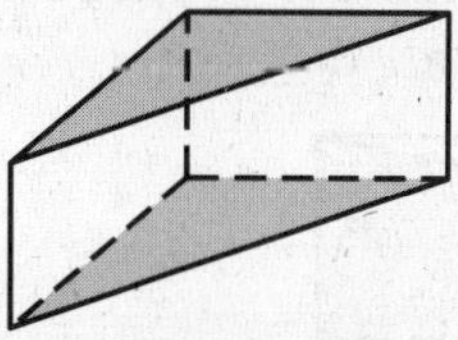   **Triangular prism**

A _____ is a solid with two bases that are _____ polygons.

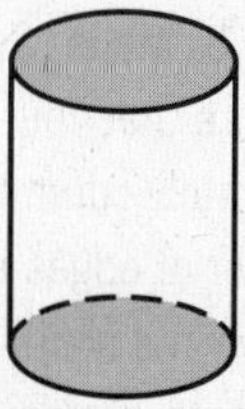

A _____ is a solid with two _____ bases that are _____ circles.

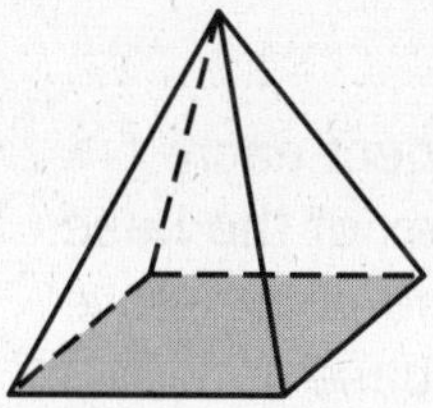

A _____ is a solid made up of _____. The base can be any _____, and the other polygons are _____ that share a common _____.

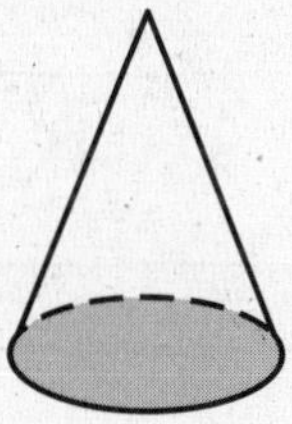

A _____ is a solid that has one _____ base and a _____ that is not in the same plane.

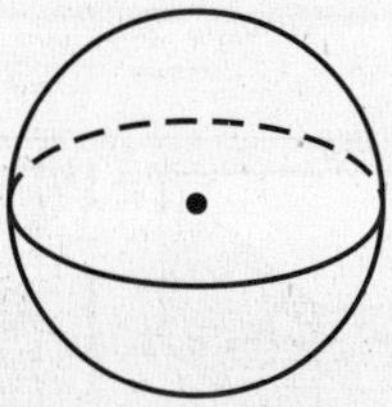

A _____ is the set of all points that are the same _____ from a point called the _____.

EXAMPLE 1 Classifying Solids

Classify the solid.

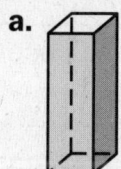

a.   b.   c.

WATCH OUT!
The base(s) of a prism do not have to be on the top or bottom of the solid. They can be on the left- or right-hand side of the solid as in Example 1(c).

Lesson 10.5 Solid Figures **237**

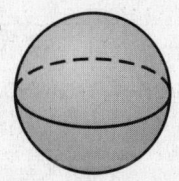

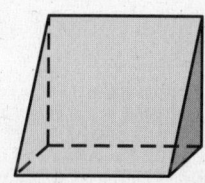

EXAMPLE 2 **Counting Faces, Edges, and Vertices**

Count the number of faces, edges, and vertices of the triangular prism shown.

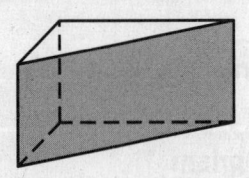

> To make sure that you accurately count the number of edges and vertices in a solid, you can make a mark on each edge and vertex as you are counting.

Answer: There are ☐ rectangular faces and ☐ triangular base(s) for a total of ☐ faces. There are ☐ edges. There are ☐ vertices.

EXAMPLE 3 **Drawing a Solid**

Draw a rectangular pryamid.

1. Draw the base and a point above the base.
2. Connect each vertex of the base to the point above the base.
3. Make hidden lines by partially erasing lines.

Guided Practice Classify the solid and count the number of faces, edges, and vertices.

1. 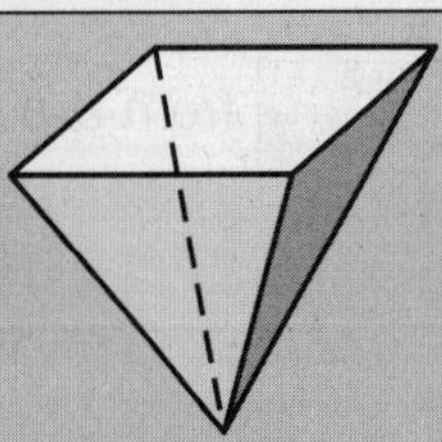
2. 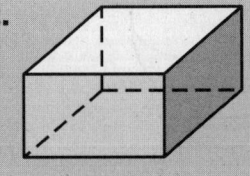
3.

4. A pentagonal pyramid is a pyramid whose base is a pentagon. Draw a pentagonal pyramid.

Lesson 10.6 Surface Area of a Prism

Goal: Find the surface area of a prism.

Vocabulary

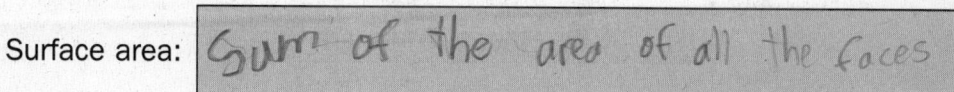

Surface area: Sum of the area of all the faces

EXAMPLE 1 Finding the Surface Area of a Prism

Find the surface area of the rectangular prism.

1. Find the area of each face.

    Area of the top or bottom face:
    $6 \times 4 = 24$ in²

    Area of the front or back face:
    $6 \times 9 = 54$ in²

    Area of the left or right face:
    $9 \times 4 = 36$ in²

2. Add the areas of all six faces to find the surface area.

    $S = 36 + 54 + 24 + 36 + 54 + 24$
    $= 228$ in²

Answer: The surface area is 228 in² square inches.

EXAMPLE 2 Drawing a Diagram

Find the surface area of a rectangular prism that is 11 centimeters by 3 centimeters by 6 centimeters.

1. Draw a diagram of the prism and label the dimensions.

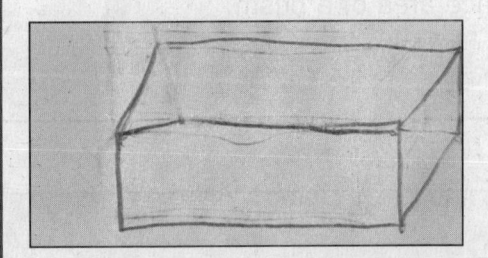

2. Find the area of each face. Then add these areas to find the surface area.

$S = (6 \times 3) + (6 \times 3) + (11 \times 3)$
$ + (11 \times 3) + (11 \times 6) + (11 \times 6)$
$ = 18 + 18 + 33 + 33 + 66 + 66$
$ = 234 \text{ cm}^2$

Answer: The prism has a surface area of 234 cm² square centimeters.

EXAMPLE 3 Using Surface Area

Bookshelf A woodworker is putting a veneer, or a thin piece of expensive wood, on a less expensive board to make the bookshelf shown. The woodworker has 350 square inches of veneer. Is there enough veneer to complete the shelf?

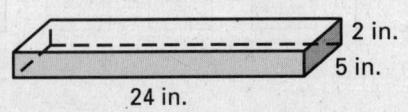

2 in.
5 in.
24 in.

Solution

Find the surface area of the shelf and compare it to the amount of veneer available.

$S = 10 + 10 + 48 + 48 + 120 + 120$
$ = 356 \text{ in}^2$

Answer: The surface area of the shelf is 356 in² square inches. There are 356 in² square inches of veneer available. The woodworker didn't have enough veneer to complete the shelf.

240 | Chapter 10 Notetaking Guide

Guided Practice In Exercises 2 and 3, you may want to draw a diagram.

1. Find the surface area of the rectangular prism shown.

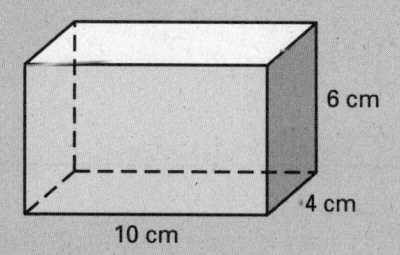

   6 cm
   4 cm
   10 cm

2. A rectangular prism is 2 meters by 5 meters by 5 meters. Find its surface area.

3. You want to paint a door that is 35 inches by 2 inches by 78 inches. The label on the can of paint says the paint covers a total area of 6000 square inches. Do you have enough paint to put 2 coats of paint on the door?

Lesson 10.7

Volume of a Prism

Goal: Find the volume of a rectangular prism.

Vocabulary

Volume: *The volume of a solid is the amount of space*

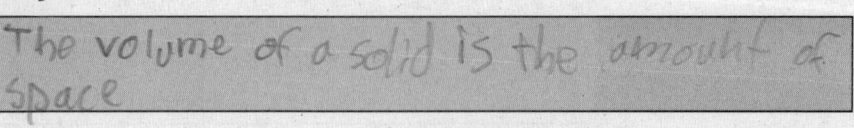

EXAMPLE 1 Counting Cubes in a Stack

Stacking Boxes A grocery store stocker is stacking cube-shaped boxes as shown. How many boxes are stacked?

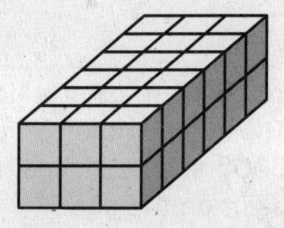

Solution

To find the total number of boxes, multiply the number of boxes in one layer by the number of layers. The boxes are stacked in ☐ layers. Each layer is a rectangle that is ☐ boxes long and ☐ boxes wide.

Boxes in one layer × Number of layers = Number of boxes

(☐ × ☐) × ☐ = ☐

Answer: There are ☐ boxes stacked so far.

If you have small building blocks, build a model of the figure shown in Example 1. Count the number of blocks you used in the model to check your answer.

Volume of a Rectangular Prism

Words   Volume = *height* · *width* · *length*

Algebra   V = *HWL*

EXAMPLE 2 — Finding the Volume of a Prism

Find the volume of the rectangular prism.

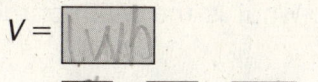

WATCH OUT! Surface area is measured in square units and volume is measured in cubic units.

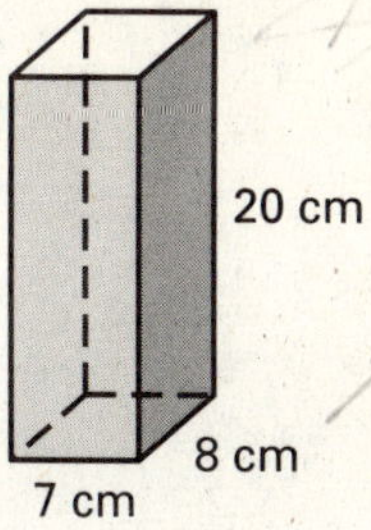

$V =$ [lwh] Write the volume formula.

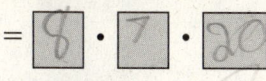

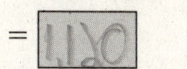

$= 8 \cdot 7 \cdot 20$ Substitute for l, w, and h.

$= 1120$ Simplify.

Answer: The volume is [1120] cubic centimeters.

(Prism: 20 cm height, 7 cm, 8 cm)

Guided Practice — Find the volume of the rectangular prism.

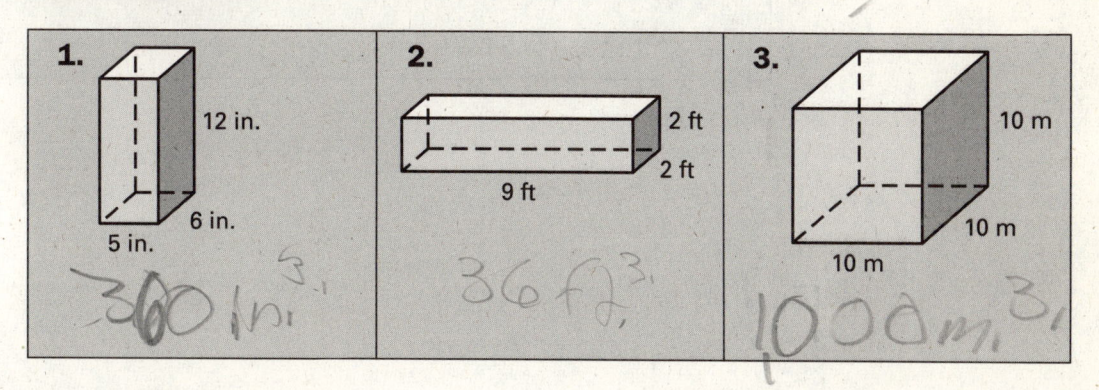

1. 12 in., 5 in., 6 in. — 360 in³
2. 9 ft, 2 ft, 2 ft — 36 ft³
3. 10 m, 10 m, 10 m — 1000 m³

EXAMPLE 3 — Using the Formula for Volume

Fish Hatchery A holding tank at a fish hatchery is 4 feet wide and 18 feet long. The volume of the tank is 576 cubic feet. How deep is the tank?

Solution

☐ = ☐ Write the volume formula.

☐ = ☐ · ☐ · ☐ Substitute for V, l, and w.

☐ = ☐ · ☐ Simplify.

☐ = ☐ ÷ ☐ Write a related division equation.

☐ = ☐ Simplify.

Answer: The depth of the tank is ☐ feet.

Lesson 10.7 Volume of a Prism 243

Guided Practice In Exercises 4 and 5, the solids are rectangular prisms.

4. The volume of a cushion is 2000 cubic inches. The cushion is 20 inches long and 5 inches tall. What is the width of the cushion?

5. The volume of a flower box is 140 cubic feet. The flower box is 5 feet long and 7 feet wide. How deep is the flower box?

Chapter 10 Words to Review

Give an example of the vocabulary word.

Base of a parallelogram

Height of a parallelogram

Perpendicular

Base of a triangle

Height of a triangle

Circle

Center

Radius

Diameter

Circumference

Pi (π)

Solid

Prism

Cylinder

Pyramid

Cone

Sphere

Face

Edge

Vertex

Surface area

Volume

Review your notes and Chapter 10 by using the Chapter Review on pages 559–562 of your textbook.

Lesson 11.1 Comparing Integers

Goal: Compare and order integers.

Vocabulary

Integer: *Any Number -1, 0, 1*

Positive integers: *Any # greater than 0*

Negative integers: *Any # less than zero*

Opposites: *Some distance from zero, but on opposite sides*

EXAMPLE 1 — Standardized Test Practice

A stock's price decreases by $8 on Monday, increases by $12 on Tuesday, increases by $5 on Wednesday, and decreases by $3 on Thursday. What integer represents the change in the stock's price on Thursday?

A) −8　　B) −3　　C) 5　　D) 12

Solution

The stock's price decreased by $3 on Thrusday. The correct answer is *−3*.

Ⓐ **B** Ⓒ Ⓓ

> In your notes, keep a list of words that could indicate a positive integer (increase, profit, above) and a list of words that could indicate a negative integer (loss, decrease, below).

Guided Practice — Write the integer that represents the situation.

1. a $25 loss	2. an increase of 2 inches	3. 17 feet above sea level
−$25	2	17

Lesson 11.1　Comparing Integers　249

EXAMPLE 2 **Identifying Opposites**

Find the opposite of −5.

> The integer −5 is read as "negative 5" or as "the opposite of 5."

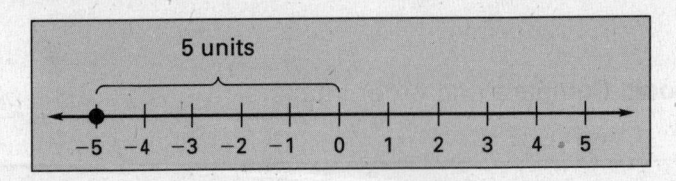

5 units from −5 to 0 on number line

Answer: The opposite of −5 is $\boxed{5}$.

EXAMPLE 3 **Comparing Integers**

Compare −7 and −2.

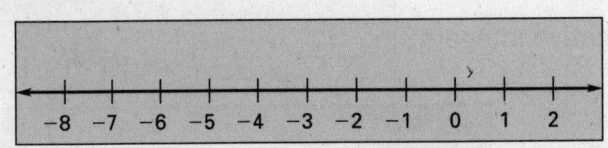

number line from −8 to 2

Answer: Because −7 is to the $\boxed{\text{left}}$ of −2 on the number line, −7 $\boxed{<}$ −2.

Guided Practice Find the opposite of the integer.

4. 2	5. −6	6. −17	7. 1
−2	6	17	−1

Copy and complete the statement using < or >.

8. −8 ? 8	9. 0 ? −10	10. 6 ? −7	11. −3 ? −4
−8 < 8	0 > −10	6 > −7	−4 < −3

250 | Chapter 11 Notetaking Guide

EXAMPLE 4 Ordering Integers

Lakes The table shows the elevations, with respect to sea level, of several natural lakes in the world. Which lake has the lowest elevation?

Lake	Elevation (with respect to sea level)
Caspian Sea	−92 feet
Lagoda	13 feet
Maracaibo	0 feet
Eyre	−52 feet
Nettilling	95 feet

Solution

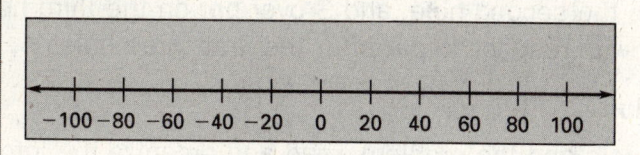

―――|―――|―――|―――|―――|―――|―――|―――|―――|―――|―――
−100 −80 −60 −40 −20 0 20 40 60 80 100

Answer: The [   ] has the lowest elevation.

Lesson 11.1   Comparing Integers   251

Lesson 11.2 Adding Integers

Goal: Add integers.

Vocabulary

Absolute value: A numbers distance from 0 on a number line

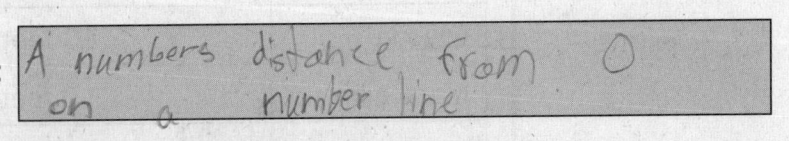

EXAMPLE 1   Modeling Integer Addition

Golf During a game of golf, you score 4 over par on the first hole, 1 under par on the second hole, and 3 over par on the third hole. What is your total score with respect to par after the first three holes?

Solution

To understand the problem, read and organize the information.

First hole: 4 means 4 over par

Second hole: -1 means 1 under par

Third hole: 3 means 3 over par

Start at ___ on a number line. Use arrows to represent over par and under par. Move ___ to add a positive number and ___ to add a negative number.

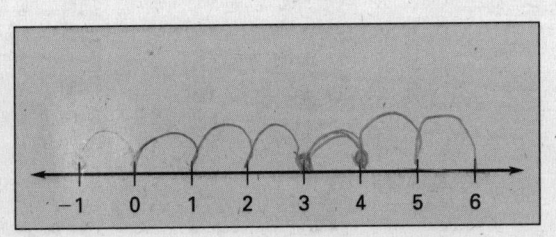

Words like "over" and "under" can be used to indicate positive and negative integers respectively.

First hole: $0 + 4 = 4$

Second hole: $4 + -1 = 3$

Third hole: $3 + 3 = 6$

Answer: Your total score after the first three holes is 6 over par.

Guided Practice Find the sum using a number line.

1. $-7 + (-7) = -14$

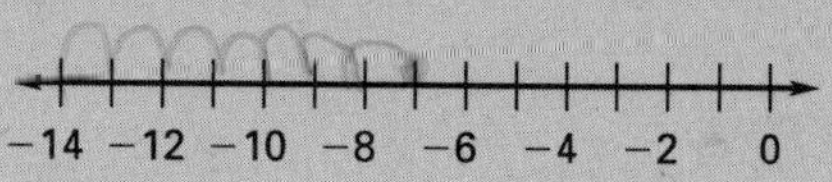

2. $-2 + 2 = 0$

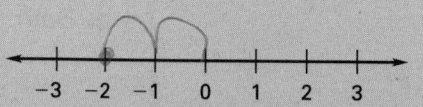

3. $-9 + 13 = 4$

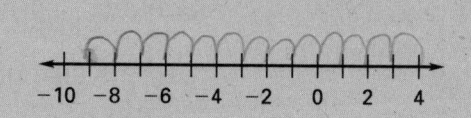

4. $4 + (-6) = -2$

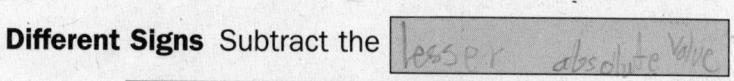

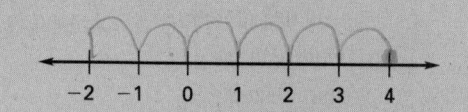

Adding Integers (Absolute value)

Words

Numbers

Same Sign Add the [intergers] and use the [common sign].

$1 + 4 = 5$
$-1 + (-4) = -5$

Different Signs Subtract the [lesser absolute value] from the [greater]. Then use the sign of the number with the [greater value].

$-3 + 11 = 8$
$3 + (-11) = -8$

Opposites The sum of an interger and its opposite is [0]. This property, written as $a + (-a) = $ [0], is called the [invers property of addition]

$-7 + 7 = $ [ ]

Lesson 11.2 Adding Integers | 253

EXAMPLE 2 Adding Integers

Find the sum.

a. $-2 + (-9)$ b. $-5 + 2$ c. $-8 + 15$

a. Both numbers have **same sign**.

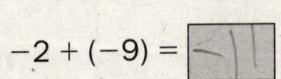

$-2 + (-9) = -11$

Add $|-|$ and $|-|$.
Use the common sign.

> When you find the sum of two numbers with different signs, you first find the number with the greater absolute value.

b. The numbers have **different sign**, and **5** has the **greater** absolute value.

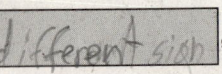

$-5 + 2 = -3$

Subtract $|-|$ from $|+|$.
Use the sign of $-$.

c. The numbers have **different** and **15** has the greater absolute value.

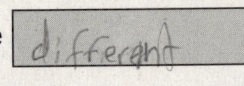

$-8 + 15 = 7$

Subtract $|6|$ from $|15|$.
Use the sign of $+$.

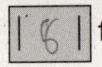

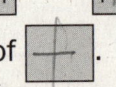

Guided Practice Find the absolute value of each number. Then find the sum.

5. $-12 + (-3)$	6. $-8 + (-1)$	7. $6 + (-11)$	8. $32 + (-32)$
-15	-9	-5	0

LESSON 11.3

Subtracting Integers

Goal: Subtract integers.

EXAMPLE 1 Modeling Integer Subtraction

a. Find the difference 4 − 7.

When you add a positive integer, you move to the ☐ on a number line. When you *subtract* a positive integer, you move to the ☐.

To find 4 − 7, move ☐ 4 units then ☐ 7 units.

Answer: The final position is ☐. So, 4 − 7 = ☐.

b. Find the difference 1 − (−6).

When you add a negative integer, you move to the ☐ on a number line. So to *subtract* a negative integer, you move to the ☐.

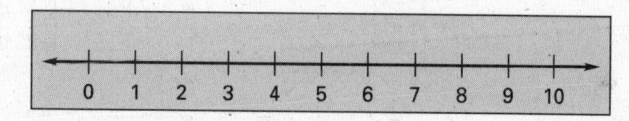

To find 1 − (−6), move ☐ 1 unit then ☐ 6 units.

Answer: The final position is ☐. So, 1 − (−6) = ☐.

In your notes on subtracting integers, you may want to include a number line model as in Example 1 and a numerical example as in Example 2.

Guided Practice Find the difference using a number line.

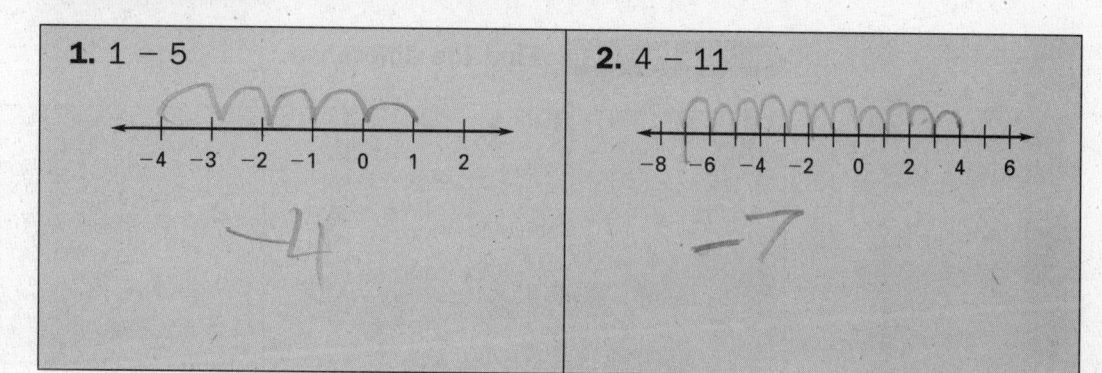

1. 1 − 5

−4

2. 4 − 11

−7

3. $8 - (-2)$

4. $0 - (-6)$

Subtracting Integers

Words To subtract an integer, ☐ its ☐.

Algebra $a - b = a +$ ☐

Numbers $8 - 10 = 8 +$ ☐

$4 - (-9) = 4 +$ ☐

EXAMPLE 2 Subtracting Integers

Find the difference.

a. $-3 - (-6) = -3\ \boxed{+}\ \boxed{6}$

    $= \boxed{3}$

To subtract -6, add its opposite.

Find $|\ \boxed{\ }\ |\boxed{\ }|\ \boxed{\ }\ |$. Use the sign of $\boxed{\ }$.

b. $-2 - 8 = -2\ \boxed{-}\ \boxed{8}$

    $= \boxed{-10}$

To subtract 8, add its opposite.

Find $|\ \boxed{\ }\ |\boxed{\ }|\ \boxed{\ }\ |$. Use the $\boxed{\ }$ sign.

> Recall that when adding integers with different signs, you subtract the lesser absolute value from the greater absolute value, then write the sign of the number with the greater absolute value.

Guided Practice Find the difference.

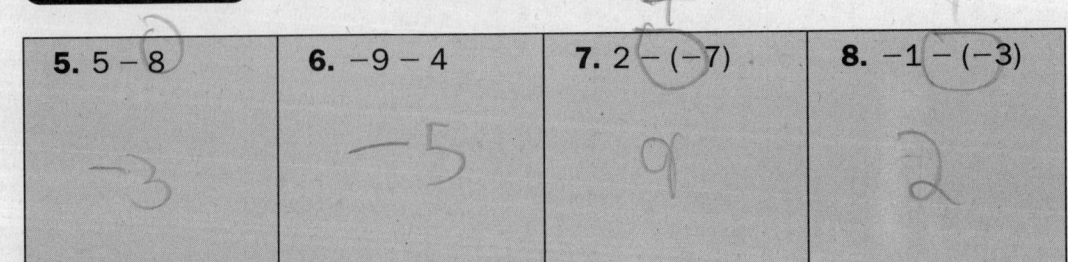

5. $5 - 8$	**6.** $-9 - 4$	**7.** $2 - (-7)$	**8.** $-1 - (-3)$
-3	-5	9	2

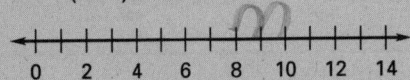

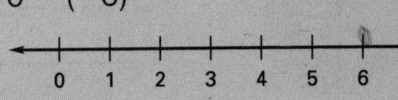

256 | Chapter 11 Notetaking Guide

EXAMPLE 3 Using Integers to Solve Problems

Temperatures In the state of Washington, the highest recorded temperature was 118 degrees Fahrenheit above zero and the lowest recorded temperature was 48 degrees Fahrenheit below zero. What is the difference of the highest recorded temperature and the lowest recorded temperature?

Solution

1. Use integers to represent the two temperatures.

   highest: ☐ °F   lowest: ☐ °F

2. Subtract the lesser temperature from the greater.

   ☐ − ☐ = ☐ + ☐   To subtract ☐, add its opposite.

   = ☐   Simplify.

Answer: The difference of the temperatures is ☐ degrees Fahrenheit.

Lesson 11.4

Multiplying Integers

Goal: Multiply integers.

Multiplying Integers

Words

The product of two positive integers is _____.

The product of two negative integers is _____.

The product of a positive integer and a negative integer is _____.

Numbers

$6(3) =$ _____

$-2(-7) =$ _____

$5(-4) =$ _____

EXAMPLE 1 Multiplying Integers

a. $-9(-3) =$ _____   The product of two negative integers is _____.

b. $6(-5) =$ _____   The product of a positive integer and a negative integer is _____.

c. $-4(20) =$ _____   The product of a negative integer and a positive integer is _____.

Guided Practice Find the product.

1. $6(7)$	2. $-3(-12)$	3. $5(-5)$	4. $-2(8)$

EXAMPLE 2 Applying Integers

Swimming Pool A pump is draining water out of a pool at a rate of 45 gallons per minute. What is the change in the water level of the pool after 4 minutes?

Solution

Change in water level = Rate of change × Number of minutes

= ☐ × ☐

= ☐

Answer: The water level decreases by ☐ gallons after 4 minutes.

> A rate of change can be represented by a positive integer when a rate is causing an increase, or a negative integer when a rate is causing a decrease.

EXAMPLE 3 Evaluating Expressions

Evaluate $-8a$, when $a = -11$.

$-8a = $ ☐(☐)   Substitute ☐ for ☐.

= ☐   The product of two negative integers is ☐.

> Need help with evaluating expressions? See page 29 of your textbook.

Guided Practice Evaluate the expression when $x = 6$ and $y = -9$.

5. $-4x$	6. $7y$	7. $-5y$	8. xy

Lesson 11.4 Multiplying Integers

Lesson 11.5 Dividing Integers

Goal: Divide integers.

EXAMPLE 1 Dividing Integers Using Mental Math

Divide by solving a related multiplication equation.

a. $-25 \div 5 = \boxed{}$ Ask "what number times $\boxed{}$ equals $\boxed{}$?"

b. $36 \div (-4) = \boxed{}$ Ask "what number times $\boxed{}$ equals $\boxed{}$?"

c. $-48 \div 6 = \boxed{}$ Ask, "what number times $\boxed{}$ equals $\boxed{}$?"

Guided Practice Divide by solving a related multiplication equation.

1. $-21 \div 3$	2. $20 \div (-4)$	3. $-40 \div (-5)$	4. $0 \div (-2)$

Dividing Integers

Words

Same Sign The quotient of two integers with the same sign is $\boxed{}$.

Different Signs The quotient of two integers with different signs is $\boxed{}$.

Zero The quotient of 0 and any nonzero integer is $\boxed{}$.

Numbers

$16 \div 4 = \boxed{}$

$-9 \div (-3) = \boxed{}$

$12 \div (-6) = \boxed{}$

$-18 \div 2 = \boxed{}$

$0 \div 8 = \boxed{}$

EXAMPLE 2 Dividing Integers

a. $-72 \div (-8) = \boxed{}$ The quotient of two integers with the same sign is $\boxed{}$.

b. $35 \div (-5) = \boxed{}$ The quotient of two integers with different signs is $\boxed{}$.

c. $-40 \div 4 = \boxed{}$ The quotient of two integers with different signs is $\boxed{}$.

EXAMPLE 3 Standardized Test Practice

Football A football team keeps track of the number of yards gained or lost during the first play of every game. The table shows the number of yards gained or lost during the first plays of the first three games of a season. Find the mean number of yards gained or lost during the first plays.

Game	Yards Gained or Lost During First Play
1	8 yard gain
2	2 yard loss
3	3 yard gain

Ⓐ −3   Ⓑ 3   Ⓒ 9   Ⓓ 13

Need help finding the mean? See page 99 of your textbook.

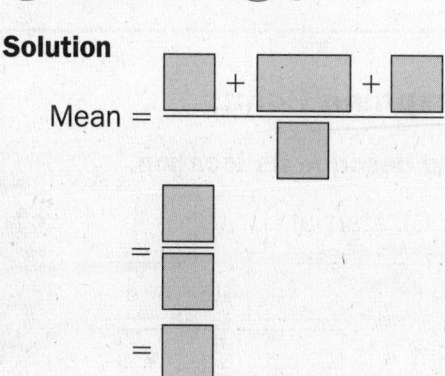

Solution

$$\text{Mean} = \frac{\boxed{} + \boxed{} + \boxed{}}{\boxed{}}$$

$$= \frac{\boxed{}}{\boxed{}}$$

$$= \boxed{}$$

Answer: A mean of $\boxed{}$ yards was gained during the first plays.

The correct answer is $\boxed{}$.   Ⓐ Ⓑ Ⓒ Ⓓ

Guided Practice Find the quotient.

5. $-39 \div 13$ **6.** $26 \div (-2)$ **7.** $8 \div (-8)$ **8.** $-42 \div (-6)$

Lesson 11.5 Dividing Integers

LESSON 11.6

Translations in a Coordinate Plane

Goal: Graph points with negative coordinates.

Vocabulary

Coordinate plane:

Quadrant:

Translation:

Image:

EXAMPLE 1 Graphing Points

Graph the point and describe its location.

a. To graph $A(-4, 0)$, start at ([ ], [ ]).

Move [ ] units [____] and [ ] units [____]. Point A is [_____].

Need help graphing ordered pairs with positive coordinates? See page 88 of your textbook.

b. To graph $B(5, -3)$, start at ([ ], [ ]).

Move [ ] units [_____] and [ ] units [____]. Point B is [_____].

262 Chapter 11 Notetaking Guide

Guided Practice Graph the point and describe its location.

1. A(0, −1)
2. B(−3, −2)
3. C(−4, 1)
4. D(2, −5)

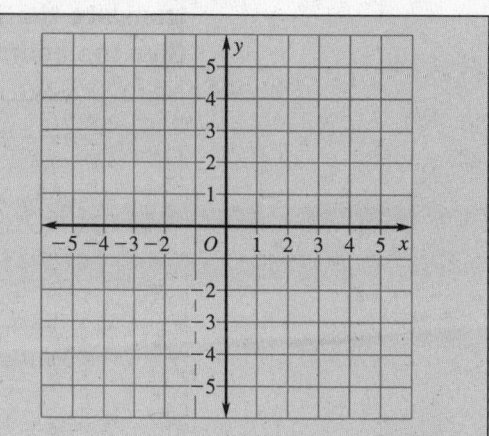

EXAMPLE 2 Translating a Figure

Stenciling You are creating a design on grid paper that will be used to make a stencil. In the design, △ABC will be translated 5 units to the right and 3 units down. The images of points A, B, and C will be points Q, R, and S respectively. Draw the image and give the coordinates of points Q, R, and S.

Solution

To draw the image, think of [   ] the original figure 5 units to the right and 3 units down. You'll get the same image if you [   ] the x-coordinates and [   ] the y-coordinates.

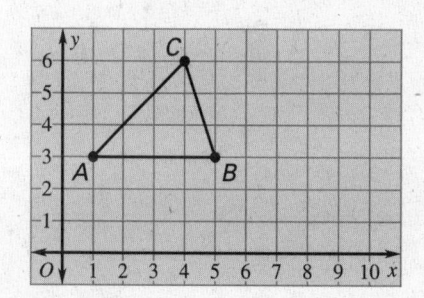

$A(1, 3) \rightarrow (1\ \square\ \square,\ 3\ \square\ \square) \rightarrow Q(\square,\ \square)$

$B(5, 3) \rightarrow (5\ \square\ \square,\ 3\ \square\ \square) \rightarrow R(\square,\ \square)$

$C(4, 6) \rightarrow (4\ \square\ \square,\ 6\ \square\ \square) \rightarrow S(\square,\ \square)$

Answer: The coordinates are Q(☐, ☐), R(☐, ☐), and S(☐, ☐).

Lesson 11.6 Translations in a Coordinate Plane

Guided Practice Graph the points and connect them to form △ABC. Then translate the triangle 4 units to the right and 1 unit down to form △DEF. Give the coordinates of the vertices of △DEF.

5. A(−3, 3), B(−1, −2), C(2, 0)

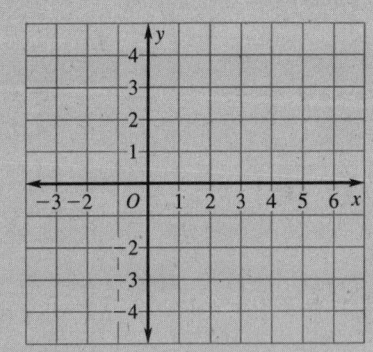

6. A(1, −3), B(4, −2), C(−1, 1)

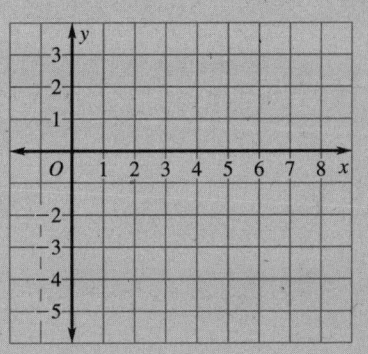

Lesson 11.7

Reflections and Rotations

Goal: Recognize reflections and rotations.

Vocabulary

Reflection:

Line of reflection:

Rotation:

Center of rotation:

Angle of rotation:

Transformation:

EXAMPLE 1 Identifying Reflections

Tell whether the solid figure is a reflection of the dashed figure. If it is a reflection, identify the line of reflection.

In Example 1, you can see that a figure that is not flipped or is not congruent to the original figure cannot be a reflection.

a.

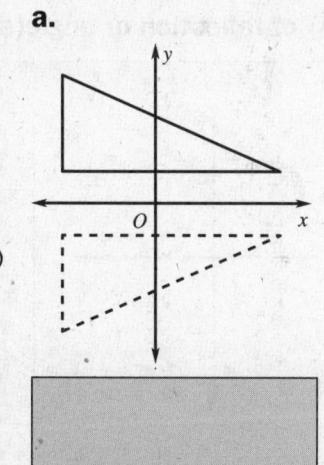

b.

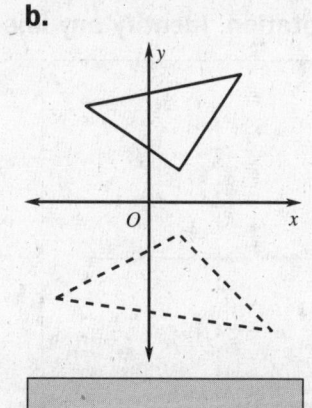

c.

Lesson 11.7 Reflections and Rotations 265

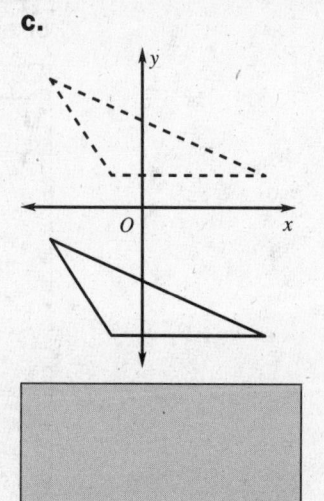

EXAMPLE 2 Identifying Rotations

Tell whether the outlined figure is a rotation of the solid figure about the origin. If it is a rotation, state the angle of rotation.

a.   b.   c.

EXAMPLE 3 Identifying Transformations

Tell whether the transformation is a *translation*, a *reflection*, or a *rotation*.

a.   b.   c.

> You can use tracing paper to help you identify transformations. Trace the original figure, then try to slide, flip, or turn it to produce the image.

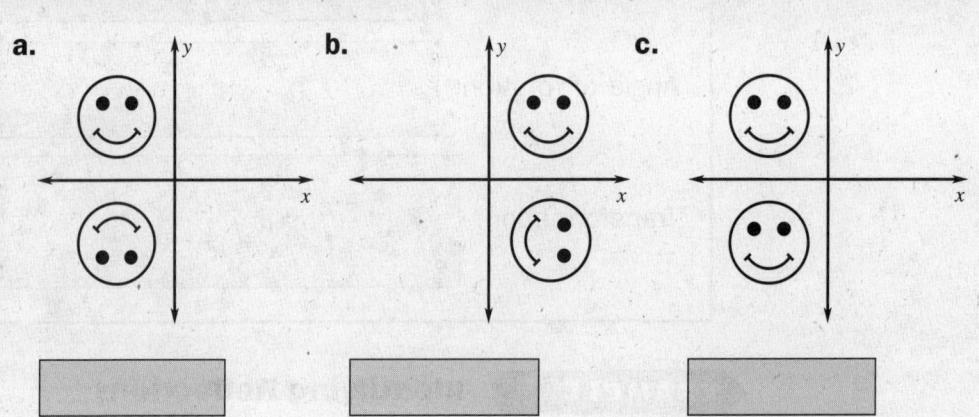

Guided Practice Tell whether the transformation is a translation, a reflection, or a rotation. Identify any line(s) of reflection or angle(s) of rotation.

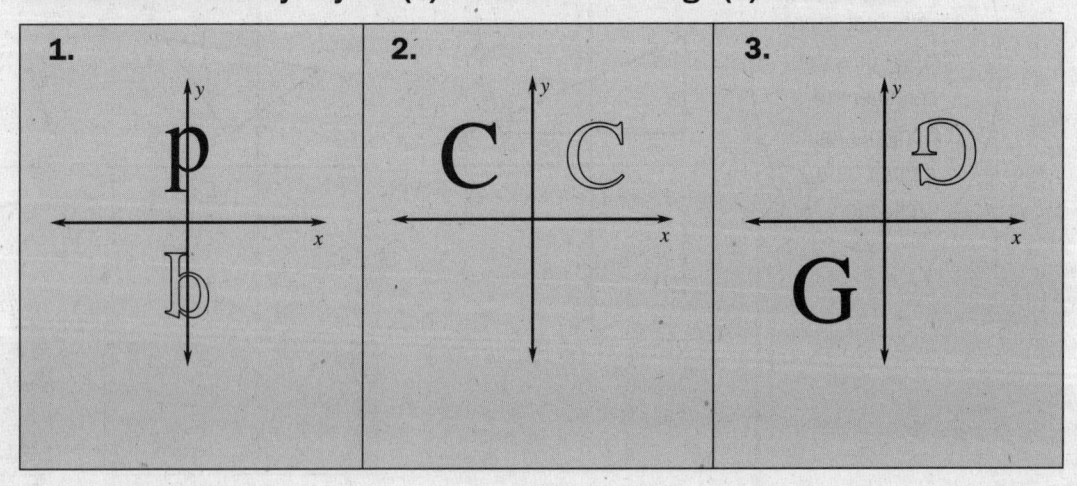

1.   2.   3.

266 | Chapter 11 Notetaking Guide

Chapter 11 Words to Review

Give an example of the vocabulary word.

Integer

Positive integer

Negative integer

Opposites

Absolute value

Coordinate plane

Quadrant

Translation

Image

Reflection

Line of reflection

Rotation

Center of rotation

Angle of rotation

Transformation

Review your notes and Chapter 11 by using the Chapter Review on pages 617–620 of your textbook.

LESSON 12.1

Writing Expressions and Equations

Goal: Write variable expressions and equations.

EXAMPLE 1 **Expressions: Adding and Subtracting**

Write the phrase as an expression. Let x represent the number.

In your notebook, make a table of key words that can indicate addition, subtraction, multiplication, or division, like the one shown on page 629 of your textbook.

Phrase	Expression
x cups of flour **increased by** 5 cups	
The **total** of 8 and a number	
A number **subtracted from** 14	
A number **decreased by** 3	

Guided Practice Write the phrase as a variable expression.

1. A number m increased by 1	2. Seven less than a number t
3. The difference of 6 and a number v	4. Nine added to a number y
5. The sum of 11 and a number b	6. Fifteen fewer than a number n

Lesson 12.1 Writing Expressions and Equations

EXAMPLE 2 **Expressions: Multiplying and Dividing**

Write the phrase as an expression. Let y represent the number.

WATCH OUT!
Order is important with subtraction and division. "The quotient of a number and 6" means $\frac{y}{6}$, not $\frac{6}{y}$.

Phrase	Expression
A number **multiplied by** 9	☐ · ☐ , or ☐
The product of a number and 22	☐ · ☐ , or ☐
12 **divided by** the number of feet	☐ / ☐
The quotient of a number and 17	☐ / ☐

EXAMPLE 3 **Writing Simple Equations**

Write the sentence as an equation.

Sentence	Equation
A number *b* added to 9 **is** 15.	☐
The quotient of 25 and a number *z* **is** 50.	☐

EXAMPLE 4 **Modeling a Situation**

Beach House A family is renting a beach house for a week-long summer vacation. The cost of renting the house is $110 per person per week and the total cost of the house for the week is $1320. Write a multiplication equation that you could use to find the number of people *p* that are going to the beach house.

Solution

The cost per person is ☐ the number of people to get the total cost.

☐ · ☐ = ☐

☐ · ☐ = ☐

270 | Chapter 12 Notetaking Guide

Guided Practice In Exercises 7–10, write the sentence as an equation.

7. The difference of 7 and a number a is 2.

8. A number w times 20 is 160.

9. A number p increased by 4 is 10.

10. The quotient of a number c and 3 is 17.

11. You bought a young tree that is 9 inches tall. According to the label on the tree, the tree will reach a height of 48 inches. Let g be the number of inches the tree will grow. Write an addition equation you could use to find g.

Lesson 12.2

Solving Addition Equations

Goal: Solve one-step addition equations.

EXAMPLE 1 **Solving Equations Using Algebra Tiles**

Use algebra tiles to solve $x + 3 = 4$.

1. Represent the equation using algebra tiles.

2. Take away ☐ 1-tiles from each side.

3. The remaining tiles show that the value of x is ☐.

Answer: The solution is ☐.

Guided Practice Use algebra tiles to solve the equation.

1. $x + 4 = 7$

2. $5 + x = 6$

3. $x + 3 = 3$

4. $8 + x = 10$

Solving Addition Equations

To solve an addition equation, _____ the same number from each side so that the _____ is by itself on one side.

EXAMPLE 2 Solving an Addition Equation

Solve the equation $z + 46 = 130$.

$z + 46 = 130$ Write the original equation.

☐ ☐   ☐ from each side.

☐ = ☐   Simplify.

After solving an equation, you should always check your solution.

✓ Check $z + 46 = 130$ Write the original equation.

☐ $+ 46 \stackrel{?}{=} 130$ Substitute ☐ for z.

☐ = ☐ ✓   Solution checks.

EXAMPLE 3 Using an Addition Equation

Working You work at your job in 8 hour shifts. Today, you've worked 3.5 hours so far. How many hours h do you have left to work?

Solution

Hours worked so far + ☐ = ☐   Write a verbal model.

☐ + ☐ = ☐   Write an equation.

☐   ☐ ☐ from each side.

☐ = ☐   Simplify.

Need help with writing a verbal model? See pages 39 and 40 of your textbook.

Answer: You have ☐ hours left to work.

Guided Practice Solve the equation. Then check the solution.

5. $c + 35 = 96$	**6.** $28 + m = 150$	**7.** $v + 47 = 83$
8. $z + 3.6 = 12.9$	**9.** $14.85 + b = 36.95$	**10.** $x + 2.25 = 60$

Lesson 12.2 Solving Addition Equations

Lesson 12.3 Solving Subtraction Equations

Goal: Solve one-step subtraction equations.

EXAMPLE 1 Working Backward

Shopping You went to a clothing store and bought a shirt for $25. When you got home from the store you had $8 left in your wallet. How much money did you go to the store with? You can find the amount of money m you went to the store with by solving the equation $m - 25 = 8$.

Solution

One way to solve the equation to find the amount of money you went to the store with is to work backward.

After spending $25, you have $8 left. $m - 25 = 8$

To find the amount of money m you had before subtracting 25, you can ☐ to undo the subtraction.   ☐ $= m$

Answer: You went to the store with $☐.

✓ Check $m - 25 = 8$ Write original equation.
          ☐ $- 25 \stackrel{?}{=} 8$ Substitute ☐ for m.
          ☐ $=$ ☐ ✓   Solution checks.

> You can also solve the equation in Example 1 by getting the variable by itself as you did in Lesson 12.2. Instead of subtracting a number from each side of the equation, you add a number to each side of the equation.

Solving Subtraction Equations

To solve a subtraction equation, ☐ the same number to each side so that the ☐ is by itself on one side.

EXAMPLE 2 Solving Subtraction Equations

Solve the equation.

a. $17 = w - 9$

b. $a - 2.4 = 15.75$

Solution

a. In this equation, the variable is on the right side of the equation.

$17 = w - 9$ — Write the original equation.

☐ ☐ — ☐ to each side.
☐ = ☐ — Simplify.

b. $a - 2.4 = 15.75$ — Write the original equation.

☐ ☐ — ☐ to each side.
☐ = ☐ — Simplify.

WATCH OUT!
Line up decimal points correctly before adding decimals.

WRONG	RIGHT
11.95	11.95
+ 3.1	+3.1
12.26	15.05

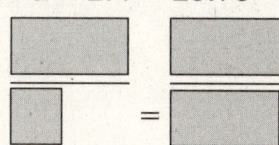

EXAMPLE 3 Using a Subtraction Equation

Weather According to a 5 o'clock news report, the temperature has dropped 6 degrees since noon to 19°F. What was the temperature at noon?

Solution

Let n represent the temperature at noon.

☐ $= 19$ — Write an equation.

☐ ☐ — ☐ to each side.
☐ = ☐ — Simplify.

Answer: The temperature was ☐ °F at noon.

Guided Practice Solve the equation. Then check the solution.

1. $y - 8 = 5$	**2.** $32 = d - 14$	**3.** $7.8 = m - 4.9$

Lesson 12.3 Solving Subtraction Equations

Lesson 12.4 Solving Multiplication and Division Equations

Goal: Solve multiplication and division equations.

EXAMPLE 1 Solving a Multiplication Equation

Solve the equation $7x = 63$.

$7x = 63$ — Write the original equation.

$\dfrac{\square}{\square} = \dfrac{\square}{\square}$ — ☐ each side by ☐.

$\square = \square$ — Simplify.

Guided Practice Solve the equation. Then check the solution.

1. $6m = 42$

2. $4y = 60$

3. $27 = 3c$

4. $88 = 8p$

Solving Multiplication and Division Equations

To solve an equation, try to set the variable by itself on one side of the equation. You can use multiplication and division to undo each other.

Multiplication Equations To solve a multiplication equation, ☐ each side by the number the ☐ is multiplied by.

Division Equations To solve a division equation, ☐ each side by the ☐.

EXAMPLE 2 Solving a Division Equation

Solve the equation $\frac{x}{6} = 10$.

Check your solution to Example 2 by dividing your answer by 6. The result should be 10.

$\frac{x}{6} = 10$ Write the original equation.

☐ = ☐   ☐ each side by ☐.

☐ = ☐   Simplify.

EXAMPLE 3 Using an Equation

Balloons A bag of 75 balloons is split up into bunches of balloons. Each bunch is made up of three balloons. Write and solve a multiplication equation to find b, the number of bunches of balloons.

Solution

☐ = ☐   Write an equation.

☐ = ☐   ☐ each side by ☐.

☐ = b Simplify.

Answer: There are ☐ bunches.

Guided Practice Solve the equation. Then check the solution.

5. $\frac{m}{3} = 12$

6. $\frac{d}{8} = 5$

7. $24 = \frac{v}{4}$

8. $15 = \frac{y}{6}$

Lesson 12.4 Solving Multiplication and Division Equations

LESSON 12.5 Functions

Goal: Evaluate functions and write function rules.

Vocabulary

Function: _____

Input: _____

Output: _____

EXAMPLE 1 Evaluating a Function

Lasagna A cook at a school cafeteria is making pans of lasagna. To make one pan of lasagna, the cook uses 12 ounces of tomato paste. How many ounces of tomato paste does the cook need for 2 pans? for 3 pans? for 4 pans?

Solution

To solve the problem, you can make an *input-output table*. Use the function rule $t = 12p$, where p is the number of pans (input) and t is the number of ounces of tomato paste (output).

Input Pans, p	Substitute in the function $t = 12p$	Output Ounces tomato paste, t
1	$t = 12(1)$	12
2	$t =$	
3	$t =$	
4	$t =$	

Answer: The cook needs ____ ounces of tomato paste for 2 pans, ____ ounces for 3 pans, and ____ ounces for 4 pans.

278 | Chapter 12 Notetaking Guide

Guided Practice Make an input-output table using the function rule and the input values x = 0, 1, 2, 3, 4, and 5.

1. $y = x + 2$

2. $y = 5 - x$

3. $y = 4x$

4. $y = 2x + 1$

EXAMPLE 2 **Standardized Test Practice**

A function rule is written so that it tells you what to do to the input to get the output.

Write a function rule for the input-output table.

Input, x	Output, y
10	13
11	14
12	15
13	16

A $y = x + 13$ **B** $y = x + 10$
C $y = x - 3$ **D** $y = x + 3$

Solution

Each output y is _____.

A function rule is _____.

The correct answer is ____. **A** **B** **C** **D**

Lesson 12.5 Functions 279

EXAMPLE 3 Making A Table to Write a Rule

Pattern Make an input-output table using the number of squares *s* in the figure as the input and the area *a* of the figure as the output. Then write a function rule that relates *s* and *a*. Each square has a side length of two units.

> It can be helpful to choose letters that remind you of what the variables stand for. Example 3 uses *s* and *a*, the first letters of the words *squares* and *area*.

Solution

Each output value is ⬚ the input value. The area is ⬚ the number of squares in the figure.

Squares, s	Area, a (square units)
⬚	⬚
⬚	⬚
⬚	⬚
⬚	⬚

Answer: A function rule for this pattern is ⬚.

Guided Practice Write a function rule for the relationship.

5. First make an input-output table. Use the number of dots *n* in the bottom row as the input and the total number of dots *t* as the output.

6. Use the input-output table shown.

Input, x	0	8	16	24	32	40
Output, y	0	1	2	3	4	5

Lesson 12.6 — Graphing Functions

Goal: Graph linear functions in a coordinate plane.

Vocabulary

Linear function: _____

EXAMPLE 1 Graphing a Function

Costumes You are purchasing fabric at a store so that you can make costumes for a school play. You find fabric that costs $3 per yard. The number of yards x of fabric you buy and the amount y you spend on fabric are related by the rule $y = 3x$. Graph the function $y = 3x$.

Solution

1. Make an input-output table for the function $y = 3x$.

2. Write the input and output values as ordered pairs: (input, output).

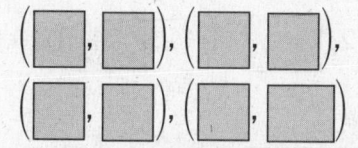

   (☐ , ☐), (☐ , ☐),
   (☐ , ☐), (☐ , ☐)

Input, x	Output, y
1	☐
2	☐
3	☐
4	☐

3. Graph the ordered pairs. Notice that the points all lie along a straight line. If you chose other input values for your table, the points you would graph would also lie along that same line.

4. Draw a line through the points. That line represents the complete graph of the function $y = 3x$.

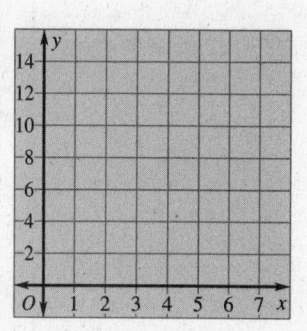

Guided Practice Evaluate the function from Example 1, for the given input. Graph the ordered pair to check whether the point is on the line.

1. $x = 5$

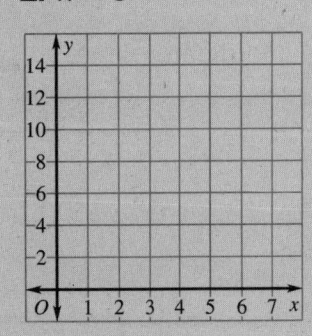

2. $x = 4.5$

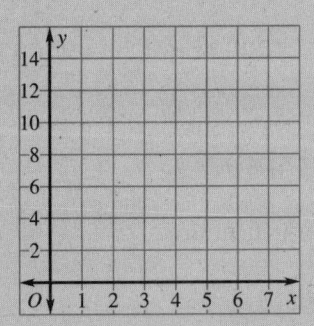

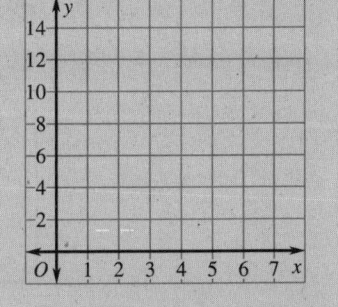

3. $x = \dfrac{1}{4}$

Representing Functions

There are many ways to represent the same function.

Words A number is the difference of another number and two.

Algebra $y = \boxed{}$

Ordered Pairs $\left(-2, \boxed{}\right), \left(-1, \boxed{}\right), \left(0, \boxed{}\right), \left(1, \boxed{}\right), \left(2, \boxed{}\right)$

Input-Output Table

Input, x	Output, y
−2	
−1	
0	
1	
2	

Graph

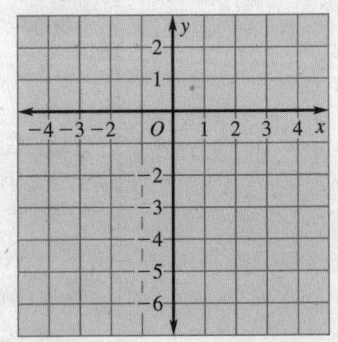

282 | Chapter 12 Notetaking Guide

EXAMPLE 2 Identifying Linear Functions

Tell whether the function is *linear* or *not linear*. Explain.

It may be helpful to include a flow chart in your notes on identifying linear functions. Your flow chart should include steps for graphing ordered pairs, as in Example 1, and a step for deciding whether you can draw a line through the points.

a. [graph of $y = x^2 - 1$]

b. [graph of $y = -x$]

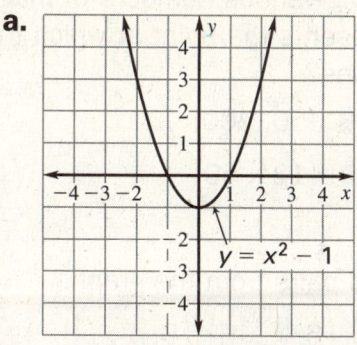

The function ☐ linear, because the graph ☐ a straight line.

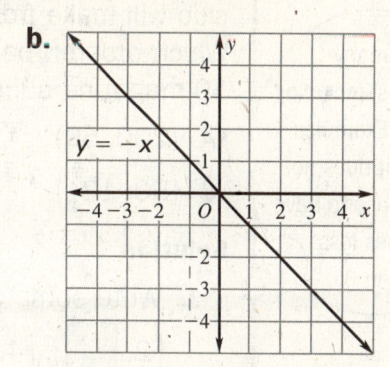

The function ☐ linear, because the graph ☐ a straight line.

Guided Practice Graph the function using the input values $x = -2, -1, 0, 1,$ and 2. Tell whether the function is *linear* or *not linear*. Explain.

4. $y = x + 2$

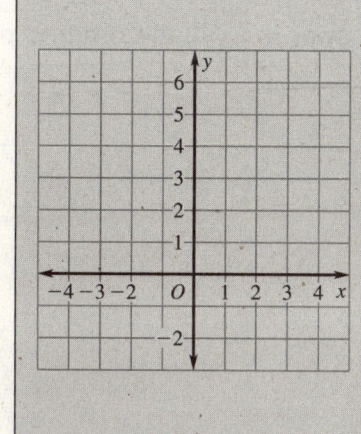

5. $y = 2 - x$

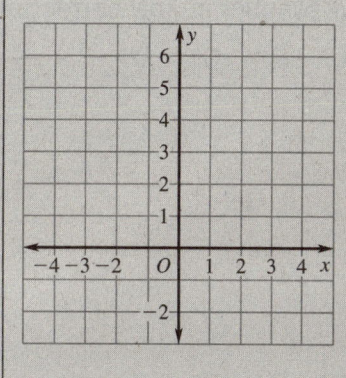

6. $y = 3x + 1$

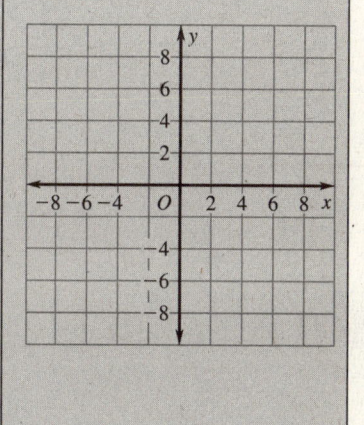

7. Does the graph shown represent a linear function? Explain.

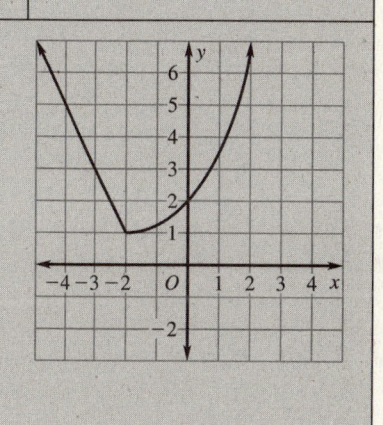

Lesson 12.6 Graphing Functions 283

EXAMPLE 3 **Standardized Test Practice**

Magazine Subscriptions The graph shows the amount of money a school club will make from selling various numbers of magazine subscriptions. Which ordered pair represents the point at which the club has sold 50 magazine subscriptions?

Ⓐ (200, 50) Ⓑ (50, 200)
Ⓒ (50, 12½) Ⓓ (12½, 50)

> In many situations, including those in Examples 1 and 3, it does not make sense to have values less than 0.

Solution

1. Write some ordered pairs from the graph.

   $(2, \square), (4, \square), (6, \square), (8, \square)$

2. Write a function rule.

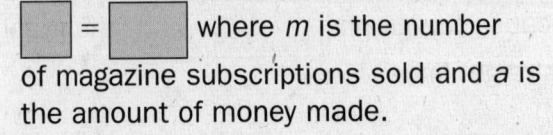

   $\square = \square$ where m is the number of magazine subscriptions sold and a is the amount of money made.

3. Evaluate the function when $m = \square$.

   $\square = \square = \square$

Answer: The club will make $\square$ from selling $\square$ magazine subscriptions. The correct answer is $\square$, the ordered pair $(\square, \square)$.

Ⓐ Ⓑ Ⓒ Ⓓ

284 | Chapter 12   Notetaking Guide

Chapter 12 Words to Review

Give an example of the vocabulary word.

Function

Input

Output

Linear function

Review your notes and Chapter 12 by using the Chapter Review on pages 669–672 of your textbook.

Lesson 13.1 Introduction to Probability

Goal: Write probabilities.

Vocabulary

Outcome:

Event:

Favorable outcomes:

Probability:

Complementary events:

Finding Probabilities

The **probability** of an event is a measure of the likelihood that the event will occur. When all outcomes are equally likely, the probability is found as follows.

$$\text{Probability of event} = \frac{\text{Number of } \rule{2cm}{0.15mm}}{\text{Number of } \rule{2cm}{0.15mm}}$$

EXAMPLE 1 Standardized Test Practice

Board Game A board game has the spinner shown that is used to determine your next move. What is the probability that you will spin the spinner and land on "Move forward 2 spaces?"

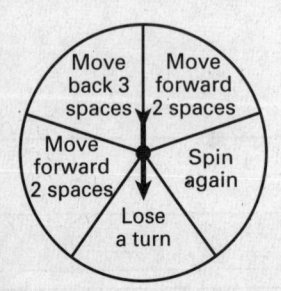

(A) $\frac{1}{3}$ (B) $\frac{2}{5}$ (C) $\frac{3}{5}$ (D) $\frac{2}{3}$

Solution

There are ☐ favorable outcomes, which are _____. The ☐ possible outcomes are _____.

Probability of landing on "Move forward 2 spaces" = $\dfrac{\text{Number of } \boxed{} \text{ outcomes}}{\text{Number of } \boxed{} \text{ outcomes}}$

$= \dfrac{\boxed{}}{\boxed{}}$

Answer: The probability that you will spin the spinner and land on "Move forward 2 spaces" is $\dfrac{\boxed{}}{\boxed{}}$. The correct answer is ☐.

(A) (B) (C) (D)

288 | Chapter 13 Notetaking Guide

EXAMPLE 2 Describing Probabilities

You randomly choose a tile from a bag of lettered tiles. The tiles are shown below. Find and describe the probability of the event.

R E S T L U
A S I S N O

> When you flip a coin, roll a number cube, or randomly choose objects from a bag, you are assuming all the outcomes are equally likely to occur.

a. You choose a vowel.

Because there are ☐ letters in the bag and ☐ of them are vowels,

$P = \dfrac{\Box}{\Box} = \Box = \Box$ %.

Answer: You are likely to choose a vowel ☐.

b. You choose an M.

Because there are ☐ letters in the bag and ☐ of them are M,

$P = \dfrac{\Box}{\Box} = \Box = \Box$ %.

Answer: ☐ to choose an M.

c. You choose an S.

Because there are ☐ letters in the bag and ☐ of them are S,

$P = \dfrac{\Box}{\Box} = \Box = \Box$ %.

Answer: ☐ to choose an S.

d. You choose a letter between A and V.

Because there are ☐ letters in the bag and ☐ of them are between A and V,

$P = \dfrac{\Box}{\Box} = \Box = \Box$ %.

Answer: ☐ to choose a letter between A and V.

Guided Practice Find and describe the probability of the event.

1. Each of the letters in the word CINCINNATI is placed on a separate piece of paper in a bag. You randomly choose a vowel.

2. You roll an even number on a number cube.

EXAMPLE 3 Complementary Events

You roll a number cube.

a. Find the probability of rolling a number less than or equal to 4.

b. Describe the complement of the event in part (a) and find its probability.

Solution

a. Because ☐ of the ☐ numbers are less than or equal to 4, $P = \frac{\Box}{\Box}$.

b. The complement of rolling a number less than or equal to 4 is rolling a number _____. Because ☐ of the ☐ numbers are _____, $P = \frac{\Box}{\Box}$.

The sum of the probabilities of complementary events is always 1. So another way to find the probability in part (b) is to subtract the probability you found in part (a) from 1.

Lesson 13.2

Finding Outcomes

Goal: Use diagrams, tables, and lists to find outcomes.

Vocabulary

Tree diagram:

Combination:

Permutation:

EXAMPLE 1 Using Tree Diagrams

Rugs You are choosing a rug for the floor of your room. You can choose a square rug or a rectangular rug that can be made of wool or cotton. The rug can either have a pattern or be a solid color. What are the different kinds of rugs you can choose?

Solution

To find all possible outcomes, use a tree diagram.

1. List the rug shapes.
2. List the material for each shape.
3. List the appearance for each material.

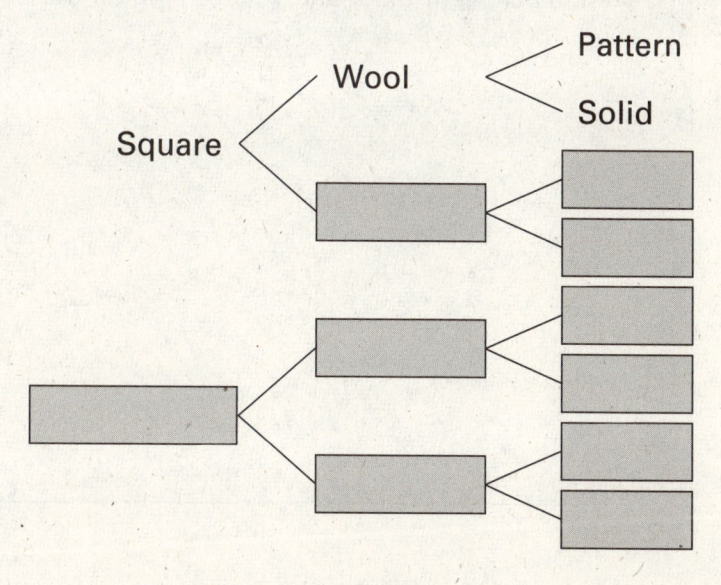

Square — Wool — Pattern
              — Solid

Lesson 13.2 Finding Outcomes 291

4. Find the outcomes.

Guided Practice Use a tree diagram to list all the possible outcomes.

1. You can buy notebooks that are separated into one subject or three subjects. The notebooks come with yellow, red, blue, green, or silver covers. Find all the possible notebook choices.

2. A sporting goods store stocks running, aerobic, basketball, and walking sneakers. The store also stocks each sneaker in the following colors: red, black, light blue, and yellow. Find all the possible sneaker choices.

EXAMPLE 2 Finding Combinations

Music You can choose 2 CDs from a list of 5 CDs. Find all possible pairs of CDs.

Solution

Each outcome is a combination because it doesn't matter which CD you chose first. Use a table to show all the possible pairs of CDs.

CD 1	CD 2	CD 3	CD 4	CD 5	Outcome

If you prefer, you could use a tree diagram instead of a table to answer Example 2.

Lesson 13.2 Finding Outcomes

EXAMPLE 3 **Finding Permutations**

Find all the ways three letters can be arranged using three different letters from A, B, T, E, and S.

Solution

Each outcome is a permutation because the order of the letters matters. You can use an organized list to arrange all the possible outcomes.

Starts with A:

Starts with B:

Starts with T:

Starts with E:

Starts with S:

> **WATCH OUT!**
> Always read the problem statement carefully. In Example 3, all of the letters must be different, but other problems may allow for letters (or other items) to be reused.

Guided Practice Find all possible outcomes.

3. At a restaurant, you can choose two side dishes from the following: French fries, vegetables, applesauce, soup, and tossed salad. Find all the possible different pairs of side dishes.

4. You are scheduling your classes for the upcoming school year. You will be taking English, math, history, and science. Find all the possible ways you can order your classes.

Lesson 13.2 Finding Outcomes

Probability of Independent Events

Goal: Find the probability of two independent events.

Vocabulary

Independent events:

EXAMPLE 1   **Two Independent Events**

Book Store You and your brother like science fiction, mystery, and biography books. At the bookstore you each buy a book. Assuming that you both will choose one of the three book types and that each of you are equally likely to choose each type, what is the probability that you both choose mystery?

Solution

To find the probability, first make a tree diagram of the possible outcomes.

Your choice   Brother's choice   Outcome

☐ of the ☐ outcomes is favorable.

Answer: The probability that both of you choose mystery is ☐/☐.

Guided Practice Use the situation in Example 1.

1. What is the probability that you both choose the same kind of book?

2. What is the probability that at least one of you chooses science fiction?

EXAMPLE 2 Probability of a Sum

You randomly choose a tile from each bag shown below. Find the probability that the sum of the tiles is at most 6.

Another way to state the problem is to say "Find the probability that the sum is less than or equal to 6."

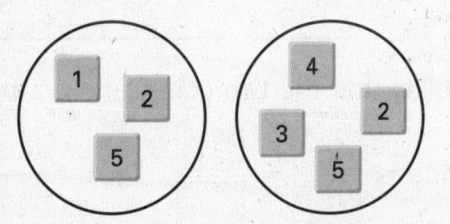

Bag 1: 1, 2, 5
Bag 2: 4, 2, 3, 5

Solution

You can use a table of sums to list all the possible outcomes.

	2	3	4	5
1				
2				
5				

☐ of the ☐ sums are at most 6.

Answer: The probability that the sum is at most 6 is ☐/☐.

Lesson 13.3 Probability of Independent Events | 297

EXAMPLE 3 **Three Independent Events**

Games You are playing a game in which two coins are tossed and a spinner is spun. Find the probability that the two coins land on the same side and the spinner lands on the white section.

Solution

You can use a tree diagram to find all the possible outcomes.

First coin   Second coin   Spinner   Outcome

Whenever you use a letter to represent an item in a tree diagram, you should provide some sort of key to indicate the meaning of the letter.

Answer: The probability that the two coins land on the same side and the spinner lands on white is $\frac{\Box}{\Box} = \frac{\Box}{\Box}$.

Guided Practice Find the probability of the event.

3. The sum in Example 2 is at least 5.

4. Exactly one of the coins in Example 3 lands on tails.

LESSON 13.4

Misleading Statistics

Goal: Recognize how statistics can be misleading.

EXAMPLE 1 Potentially Misleading Graphs

Lakes The bar graph shows the areas of three of the five Great Lakes. Without using the scale, about how many times greater does the area of Lake Superior appear to be than the area of Lake Michigan? Then compare the areas using the scale.

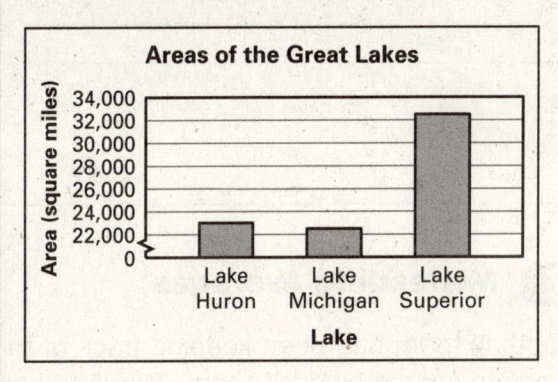

Areas of the Great Lakes

(bar graph with y-axis "Area (square miles)" showing values 22,000 to 34,000 with a break; bars for Lake Huron, Lake Michigan, and Lake Superior)

Solution

The area of Lake Superior appears to be about ⬚ the area of Lake Michigan, because the bar for Lake Superior is about ⬚ as high as the bar for Lake Michigan.

The area of Lake Superior is actually about ⬚% of the area of Lake Michigan, because

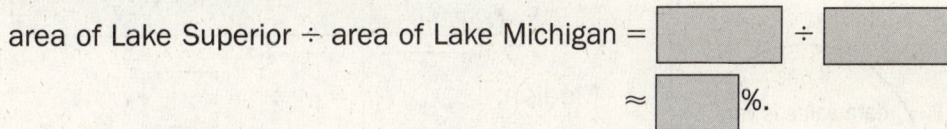

area of Lake Superior ÷ area of Lake Michigan = ⬚ ÷ ⬚

≈ ⬚%.

The break in the scale distorts the ⬚ of the bars.

Guided Practice Solve the problem below.

1. Tell which line graph makes the population of Akron, Ohio appear to decrease more dramatically. Explain.

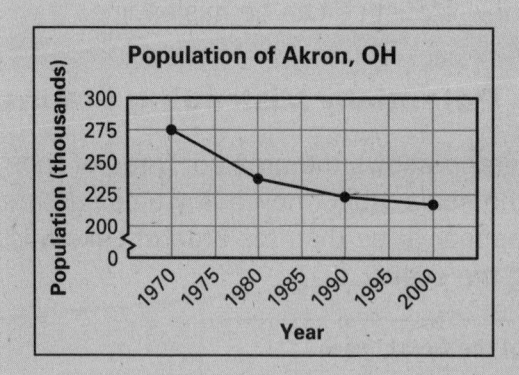

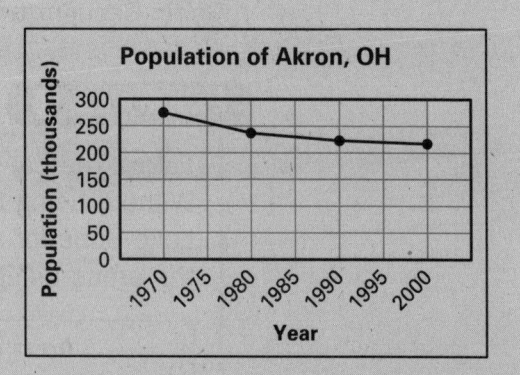

EXAMPLE 2 Misleading Averages

Football A football team has been keeping track of the differences in the numbers of points scored by each team. The differences in the numbers of points for the games the team has won is shown.

   3, 21, 3, 2, 2, 14, 1, 2

Does 6 points describe well the differences in the points for the games won? Why might a team use this number?

Solution

Mean: ▭ / ▭ = ▭ / ▭ = ▭

Median: ▭ = ▭ = ▭

Mode: ▭

> Need help with finding the mean, median, and mode? See page 99 of your textbook.

> If one data value is very small or very large compared to the other data values, then the mean could be distorted.

The ▭, 6, ▭ describe the data well because it is ▭ the numbers. A team might use this number to convince people that ▭.

300 | Chapter 13 Notetaking Guide

Guided Practice The numbers of hours students in your class spent watching television in one week are listed below. Use this data in Exercises 2 and 3.

23, 12, 22, 24, 13, 25, 21, 12

2. Does 12 describe the numbers of hours well? Why or why not?

3. Why might a student use 12 as the average number of hours of television watched?

Lesson 13.4 Misleading Statistics

Lesson 13.5 Stem-and-Leaf Plots

Goal: Organize data using stem-and-leaf plots.

Vocabulary

Stem-and-leaf plot:

Leaf:

Stem:

EXAMPLE 1 Making a Stem-and-Leaf Plot

Computer Printers You are shopping for black and white laser printers. The prices of the models you are looking at are listed below. Organize the prices in a stem-and-leaf plot.

$699, $644, $699, $678, $619, $687, $657, $632, $699, $668, $647, $660, $639, $618

Solution

1. Order the stems from least to greatest.

2. Write the leaves next to their stems.

3. Order the leaves from least to greatest.

Key: 61 | 9 = 619   Key: 61 | 9 = 619

WATCH OUT! Be sure to include all of the stems between the least and greatest. In Example 1, 62 is a stem even though none of the data values have a 6 in the hundreds' place and a 2 in the tens' place.

Guided Practice Make a stem-and-leaf plot of the data.

1. 56, 38, 44, 62, 50, 48, 65, 39, 56, 34, 69, 50, 47

EXAMPLE 2 Interpreting Stem-and-Leaf Plots

Pumpkins The stem-and-leaf plot shows the weights, in pounds, of pumpkins at a grocery store.

```
1 | 3 5 6 7
2 | 0 5 6 8 9
3 | 5 6 8
4 | 2 5 7 8    Key: 1 | 3 = 1.3
```

a. What is the range of the weights?

b. Describe the weight group with the least number of pumpkins.

WATCH OUT!
Read the key in a stem-and-leaf plot carefully. In Example 1, the key indicates that the data are whole numbers. In Example 2, the key indicates that the data are decimals.

Solution

a. The lightest pumpkin weighs ☐ pounds, because the least data value is ☐. The heaviest pumpkin weighs ☐ pounds, because the greatest data value is ☐. The range is ☐ pounds, because ☐ − ☐ = ☐.

b. The least number of pumpkins is between ☐ and ☐ pounds, because the stem of ☐ has the least number of data values.

Lesson 13.5 Stem-and-Leaf Plots 303

EXAMPLE 3 Finding the Mean, Median, and Mode

Use the stem-and-leaf plot.

a. Find the mean.
b. Find the median.
c. Find the mode.

```
1 | 5 7
2 | 0 5
3 | 2 3 3     Key: 2 | 5 = 25
```

Solution

Make an ordered list of the ☐ values in the stem-and-leaf plot.

☐, ☐, ☐, ☐, ☐, ☐, ☐

a. Mean: ⎯⎯⎯⎯⎯⎯⎯⎯ = ☐/☐ = ☐

b. The median is ☐, because ⎯⎯⎯⎯⎯⎯⎯⎯.

c. The mode is ☐, because ⎯⎯⎯⎯⎯⎯⎯⎯.

Guided Practice Use the stem-and-leaf plot in Example 2.

2. Describe the weights of the pumpkins that are in the most common weight group.

3. Find the mean, median, and mode(s) of the data.

Lesson 13.6

Box-and-Whisker Plots

Goal: Represent data using box-and-whisker plots.

Vocabulary

Box-and-whisker plot: _____

Lower quartile: _____

Upper quartile: _____

Lower extreme: _____

Upper extreme: _____

EXAMPLE 1 Making a Box-and-Whisker Plot

Volleyball The heights, in inches, of players on a volleyball team are shown below. Make a box-and-whisker plot of the data.

70, 65, 68, 72, 69, 72, 68, 70, 71, 74

Solution

1. Order the data to find the median, the quartiles, and the extremes.

   Lower half   Upper half

   ☐ ☐ ☐ ☐ ☐ ☐ ☐ ☐ ☐ ☐

   The median is (☐ + ☐) ÷ ☐ = ☐, the lower quartile is ☐, the upper quartile is ☐, the lower extreme is ☐, and the upper extreme is ☐.

If a data set has an odd number of data values, then the median is not included in either half of the data.

2. Plot the five values below a number line.

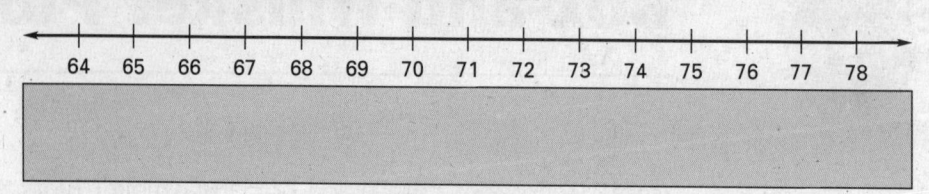

|64|65|66|67|68|69|70|71|72|73|74|75|76|77|78|

3. Draw a box with sides at both quartiles.

4. Draw a vertical line through the median.

5. Draw "whiskers" from the box to both extremes.

Guided Practice Make a box-and-whisker plot of the data.

1. 46, 37, 39, 52, 48, 45, 57, 32, 61

|30|35|40|45|50|55|60|65|

2. 28, 15, 21, 24, 16, 19, 11, 20, 29, 13

|9|12|15|18|21|24|27|30|

EXAMPLE 2 **Reading a Box-and-Whisker Plot**

Identify the median, the lower and upper quartiles, and the lower and upper extremes in the box-and-whisker plot below.

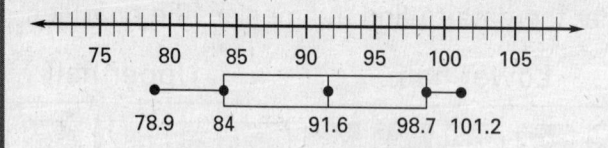

75 80 85 90 95 100 105
   78.9 84 91.6 98.7 101.2

Answer: The median is ☐. The lower quartile is ☐. The upper quartile is ☐. The lower extreme is ☐. The upper extreme is ☐.

306 | Chapter 13 Notetaking Guide

EXAMPLE 3 Interpreting Box-and-Whisker Plots

Horses The box-and-whisker plots below represent the heights, in inches, of two different breeds of horses at a horse farm.

   a. Find the ranges of the heights.

   b. Compare the heights of the two breeds of horses.

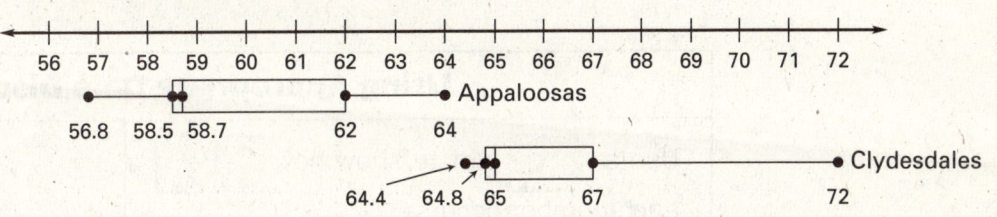

Appaloosas: 56.8, 58.5, 58.7, 62, 64

Clydesdales: 64.4, 64.8, 65, 67, 72

Solution

   a. The range is the difference between the ☐.

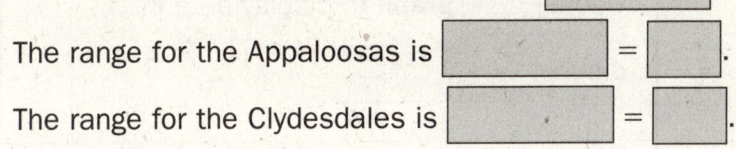

   The range for the Appaloosas is ☐ = ☐.

   The range for the Clydesdales is ☐ = ☐.

   b. ☐

Guided Practice Use the box-and-whisker plots in Examples 2 and 3.

3. Find the range of the data in Example 2.

4. Identify the median, the lower and upper quartiles, and the lower and upper extremes for the heights of the Appaloosas in Example 3.

Lesson 13.6 Box-and-Whisker Plots | 307

Lesson 13.7 Choosing an Appropriate Data Display

Goal: Choose appropriate data displays.

Using Appropriate Data Displays	
Use a ____ **plot** to show how ____ each number occurs.	(line plot with X's)
Use a ____ **graph** to display data in distinct ____.	(bar graph)
Use a ____ **graph** to display data over ____.	(line graph)
Use a ____ **graph** to represent data as ____.	(circle graph)
Use a ____ **plot** to ____ a data set.	1 | 3 5 6 7 2 | 0 5 6 8 9 3 | 5 6 8 4 | 2 5 7 8 Key: 1|3 = 13
Use a ____ **plot** to show the data's distribution in quarters, using the ____, ____, and ____.	(box-and-whisker plot)

308 | Chapter 13 Notetaking Guide

EXAMPLE 1 Choosing an Effective Display

> You can use either graph to find the median of the data in Example 1. The question is, in which graph is it easier to find the median?

CDs Which plot is more effective in finding the median number of CDs bought by a group of people in a month?

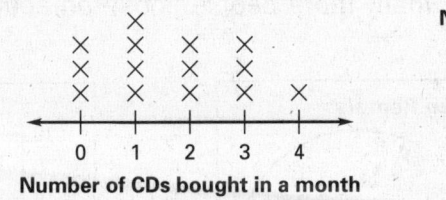

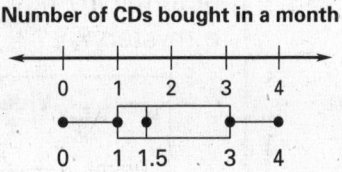

Number of CDs bought in a month

Answer: The _____ plot is more effective in finding the median number of CDs because _____.

EXAMPLE 2 Making an Appropriate Display

Bus Ride You ask 15 people on a bus how long their ride is to their destination. The list below shows their responses, in minutes. Make a data display that shows all of the data values.

15, 12, 12, 5, 8, 19, 10, 20, 18, 5, 17, 24, 6, 5, 15

Solution

You can use a _____ or a _____ to show all of the data values.

Lesson 13.7 Choosing an Appropriate Data Display

EXAMPLE 3 **Choosing an Appropriate Display**

Videos The data displays show the kinds of videos rented by people in a video store during a recent weekday. Which display is appropriate for determining how many more people chose an action/adventure movie than a mystery?

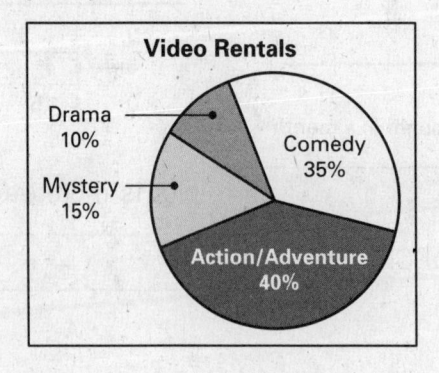

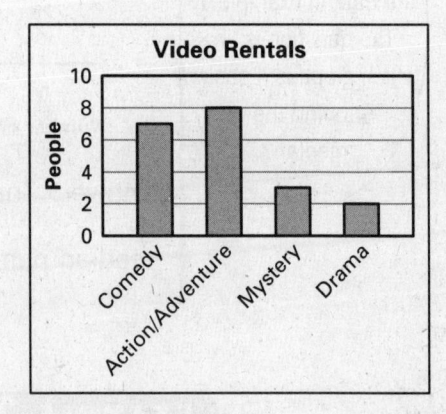

Video Rentals
- Drama 10%
- Mystery 15%
- Comedy 35%
- Action/Adventure 40%

Video Rentals (bar graph)
- Comedy: 7
- Action/Adventure: 8
- Mystery: 3
- Drama: 2

Solution

The [____] graph is appropriate for finding the difference because the [____] graph shows the [____] of people that chose each movie type while the [____] graph shows the [____] of people that chose each movie type.

[____] more people chose an action/adventure movie than a mystery.

For each type of data display you studied in you textbook, you may want to include an example in your notebook along with a summary of the information that you can read from the display.

Guided Practice Choose an appropriate display for the given situation.

1. You record the height, in inches, of a plant every day at 4:00 P.M. for a week. The data are listed below. Which data display would you use to show how the height changed during that time?

   0.5 in.   0.8 in.   1.5 in.   1.7 in.   2.4 in.   2.8 in.   3.1 in.

310 | Chapter 13   Notetaking Guide

CHAPTER 13

Words to Review

Give an example of the vocabulary word.

Outcome

Event

Favorable outcomes

Probability

Complementary events

Tree diagram

Combination

Permutation

Independent events

Stem-and-leaf plot

Leaf

Stem

Box-and-whisker plot

Lower quartile

Upper quartile

Lower extreme

Upper extreme

Review your notes and Chapter 13 by using the Chapter Review on pages 725–728 of your textbook.

ADDITIONAL LESSON A

Estimation and Precision of Measurement

Goal • Choosing the most precise measurement.

Your Notes

VOCABULARY

Estimation

When to Estimate

Precision:

Calculation Of Error

Example 1 — Estimate a reasonable solution

Estimate: $\sqrt{53}$

Find the perfect square just less than 53 and the perfect square just greater than 53.

The perfect squares on either side of 53 are 49 . . . 53 . . . 64. Therefore $\sqrt{53}$ is between $\sqrt{49}$ and $\sqrt{64}$ which means the $\sqrt{53}$ is between 7 and 8.

The difference between 49 and 53 is 4, the difference between 49 and 64 is 15, the difference between 7 and $\sqrt{53}$ is "x" and the difference between 7 and 8 is 1.
Solve the following proportion.

$$\frac{4}{15} = \frac{x}{1}$$

$$15x = 4$$

$$x = \frac{4}{15}$$

$$x = .266$$

Therefore $\sqrt{53} = 7.3$, with accuracy to the tenths place.

Additional Lesson A • **Math Course 1 Lesson Plan**   A1

Example 2 — Estimate and determine a reasonable amount of error

Estimate the measure of ∠ABC and ∠FBC in the drawing.

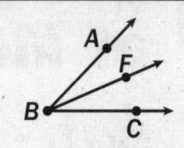

Compare ∠ABC with an angle of known measure such as a right angle or a straight angle.

If ∠DBC is a right angle, and ∠ABC appears to be approximately $\frac{1}{2}$ of ∠DBC, then ∠ABC is approximately 45°.

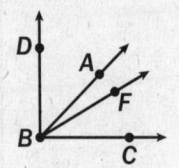

∠FBC is approximately $\frac{1}{3}$ of the right angle ∠DBC, or approximately 30°. Depending on your estimation skills, the error of the measure of the angle could be as much as 10° on either side of 30°.

Example 3 — Using tools to measure line segments and angles

What is the measure of line segment $\overline{AB}$?

If the ruler being used has increments of eighths of an inch, the measure is approximately $1\frac{5}{8}$ inches with an error of $\frac{1}{8}$ inch in either direction. If the ruler is incremented in sixteenths of an inch, the measure is $1\frac{11}{16}$ inches with an error of $\frac{1}{16}$ of an inch in either direction.

What is the measure of ∠CAB?

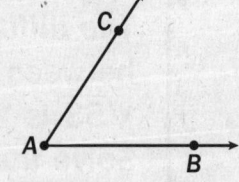

If the protractor that is being used has increments in degrees, the measure of the angle is approximately 56° with an error of 1° greater or less than 56°.

If the protractor is incremented every 5°, the angle is still approximately 56° with an error range of 5° greater or less than 56°.

Your Notes

✓ **Checkpoint** Complete the following exercises.

1. Estimate the $\sqrt{94}$.

2. Estimate the measure of ∠CAT.

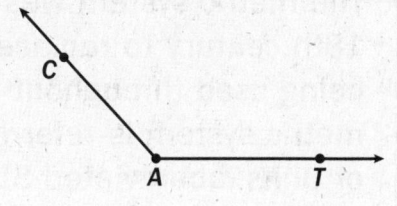

3. Measure ∠CAT.

4. Measure line segment $\overline{ME}$.

ADDITIONAL LESSON B

Metric/Customary Conversions

Goal • Use the Metric to Customary Conversion Tables to understand how one unit of measure relates to the other.

Your Notes

HISTORY

The metric system was developed in France in the late 18th century to replace the various systems that were being used throughout the world at that time. Today, the metric system is referred to as the International System of Units, abbreviated SI. Customary Systems grew out of the customs of the area. The system presently used in the United States is the English System and the United States is the only industrial nation using it.

ABBREVIATIONS

Customary	Metric
inch = in.	centimeter = cm
foot = ft.	meter = m
mile = mi.	kilometer = km
quart = qt.	liter = l or L
gallon = gal.	Celsius = C
Fahrenheit = F	

CONVERSION TABLES

Into Metric   **Into Customary**

Length

From	multiply by	To	From	multiply by	To
in.	2.54	cm	m	39.36	in.
ft.	30.48	cm	cm	0.39	in.
mi.	1.61	km	km	0.62	mi.

Mass (Weight)

From	multiply by	To	From	multiply by	To
qt.	.95	L	L	1.06	qt.
gal.	3.79	L	L	0.26	gal.

Temperature

From		To	From		To
F	subtract 32 then multiply by $\frac{5}{9}$	C	C	multiply by $\frac{9}{5}$ then add 32	F

A4 Math Course 1 Lesson Plan • Additional Lesson B

Example 1 — Convert from Customary into Metric Units

Convert 4.56 in. to centimeters.

$$4.56 \times 2.54 = 11.58 \text{ cm}$$

Convert 5 miles to kilometers

$$5 \times 1.61 = 8.05 \text{ km}$$

Example 2 — Convert from Metric into Customary Units

The Smith family is driving a rental car in Europe. They stop and put 52 liters of gas into the car. They are surprised at such a large number for the amount of gas. Determine the number of gallons they used.

$$52 \times 0.26 = 13.52 \text{ gallons}$$

Example 3 — Convert from Celsius (C) to Fahrenheit (F)

As they were driving through a small town, they noticed a sign at the bank indicating that the temperature was 10°. Knowing that Celsius is the unit used in Europe for temperature, what is the Fahrenheit equivalent?

$$10 \times \frac{9}{5} = 18.0, \; 18.0 + 32 = 50.0°F$$

Additional Lesson B • Math Course 1 Lesson Plan

Your Notes

✓ **Checkpoint** Complete the following exercises.

> You are planning on taking a trip to Canada and driving through the country for two weeks. In order to budget enough money for the trip, you need to determine the cost of gas. You have found out that the average cost of gas in Canada is $0.78 per liter (Canadian Dollars). What is the cost of gas in gallons (in Canadian dollars)? You have also calculated that you will be driving approximately 1890 kilometers on your trip. How many miles will you be driving?
>
>
>
> The average temperature in Canada at the time of your trip is 23°C. Are you going to dress for warm or cold weather? Determine the temperature in Fahrenheit.
>
>
>
> You may want to bring shorts.

A6 Math Course 1 Lesson Plan • Additional Lesson B

ADDITIONAL LESSON C

Expressing Place Value Using Exponents

Goal • Express place value patterns using exponents to write powers of ten.

Your Notes

VOCABULARY

Whole numbers:

Digit:

Place Value:

Exponent:

Example 1 Convert to Expanded Form

Write the number 385,109 in expanded form.

The zero in the tens' position is a placeholder

385,109 = 300,000 + 80,000 + 5000 + 100 + 9

= (3 × 100,000) + (8 × 10,000) + (5 × 1000) + (1 × 100) + (9 × 1)

= (3 × 10^5) + (8 × 10^4) + (5 × 10^3) + (1 × 10^2) + (9 × 10^0)

Additional Lesson C • **Math Course 1 Lesson Plan** A7

Example 2 — Convert to Standard Form

a. Write $(9 \times 10^{12}) + (5 \times 10^2) + (4 \times 10^0)$ in standard form.

$(9 \times 10^{12}) + (5 \times 10^2) + (4 \times 10^0)$

$= (9 \times 1{,}000{,}000{,}000{,}000) + (5 \times 100) + (4 \times 1)$

$= 9{,}000{,}000{,}000{,}000 + 500 + 4$

$= 9{,}000{,}000{,}000{,}504$

b. Write "four hundred billion, twenty" in standard form and expanded exponential form.

Standard form: Write 4 in the hundred billions' place and 2 in the tens' place. Use zeros as placeholders in all other places. The answer is 400,000,000,020.

Expanded exponential form:

$400{,}000{,}000{,}020 = (4 \times 100{,}000{,}000{,}000) + (2 \times 10)$

$= (4 \times 10^{11}) + (2 \times 10^1)$

Your Notes

✓ **Checkpoint** Complete the following exercises.

Write the number in expanded exponential form and in words.

1. 4,001,000,345,000

2. 870,000,000,609

3. 1,000,900,430

4. 55,600,001,900

5. 2,600,050,000,000

6. 794,000,001

Write the number in standard form.

7. $(4 \times 10^{12}) + (9 \times 10^5) + (5 \times 10^2) + (7 \times 10^1) + (1 \times 10^0)$

8. four hundred fifty billion, three

9. Eight trillion, seven hundred

ADDITIONAL LESSON D

Solving Two-Step Equations

Goal • Solve two-step equations.

Example 1 Solving a Two-Step Equation

Solve $2m - 7 = -19$.

$2m - 7 = -19$	Write original equation.
$2m - 7 + 7 = -19 + 7$	Add 7 to each side.
$2m = -12$	Simplify.
$\dfrac{2m}{2} = \dfrac{-12}{2}$	Divide each side by 2.
$m = -6$	Simplify.

Don't forget to check your solution by substituting back into the original equation.

Example 2 Solving a Two-Step Equation

Solve $\dfrac{p}{5} + 7 = -2$.

$\dfrac{p}{5} + 7 = -2$	Write original equation.
$\dfrac{p}{5} + 7 - 7 = -2 - 7$	Subtract 7 from each side.
$\dfrac{p}{5} = -9$	Simplify.
$5\left(\dfrac{p}{5}\right) = 5(-9)$	Multiply each side by 5.
$p = -45$	Simplify.

Your Notes

✓ **Checkpoint** Complete the following exercises.

1. $7q - 4 = 10$

2. $\frac{j}{6} + 2 = 0$

3. $\frac{y}{5} - 6 = -6$

Example 3 — Writing and Solving a Two-Step Equation

Long Distance Calls A long distance phone company charges customers a $5 monthly fee plus $3 per hour for long distance phone calls. One customer's bill was $23. How many hours of long distance calls did the customer make?

Solution

Write a verbal model. Let h represent the number of hours of long distance the customer used.

$$\begin{array}{c}\text{Monthly} \\ \text{fee}\end{array} + \begin{array}{c}\text{Hourly cost of} \\ \text{long distance}\end{array} \cdot \begin{array}{c}\text{Hours of} \\ \text{long distance}\end{array} = \begin{array}{c}\text{Total} \\ \text{cost}\end{array}$$

$$5 + 3 \cdot h = 23$$

$5 + 3h = 23$	Write original equation.
$5 - 5 + 3h = 23 - 5$	Subtract 5 from each side.
$3h = 18$	Simplify.
$\frac{3h}{3} = \frac{18}{3}$	Divide each side by 3.
$h = 6$	Simplify.

Answer: The customer made 6 hours of long distance phone calls.

ADDITIONAL LESSON E

Slope

Goal • Find the Slope of a Line.

Your Notes

VOCABULARY

Slope:

Example 1 Finding the Slope of a Line

To find the slope of a line, find the ratio of the rise to the run between two points on the line.

a.

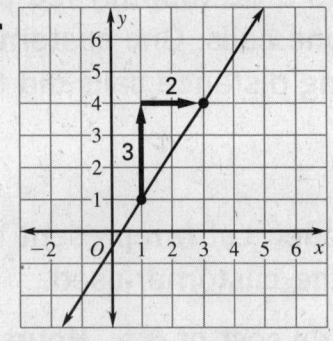

slope = $\frac{rise}{run} = \frac{3}{2}$

b.

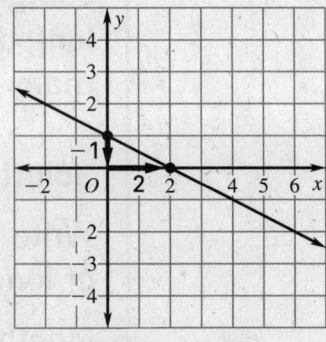

slope = $\frac{rise}{run} = \frac{-1}{2} = -\frac{1}{2}$

Rise is positive when moving up and negative when moving down.

Example 2 Interpreting Slope as a Rate

Lemonade Stand The graph represents the cups of lemonade sold over time. To find the rate of sales, find the slope of the line.

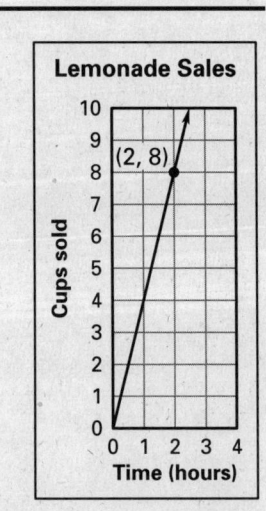

slope = $\frac{rise}{run} = \frac{8}{2}$ Write rise over run.

$= \frac{4}{1}$ Find unit rate.

Lemonade Sales (graph showing point (2, 8), Cups sold vs Time (hours))

Answer: The lemonade sold at a rate of 4 cups per hour.

Your Notes

✓ **Checkpoint** Complete the following exercises.

1. Plot the points (1, 5) and (0, 8). Then find the slope of the line that passes through the points.

2. In Example 2, suppose the line starts at the origin and passes through the point (2, 7). Find the rate of lemonade sales.

Example 3 Using Slope to Draw a Line

Draw the line that has a slope of 4 and passes through (2, 1).

1. Plot (2, 1).
2. Write the slope as a fraction.
   slope = $\frac{rise}{run}$ = $\frac{4}{1}$
3. Move 1 unit to the right and 4 units up to plot the second point.
4. Draw a line through the two points.

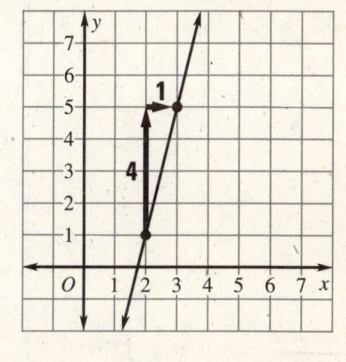

Your Notes

✓ **Checkpoint** Refer to Example 3.

3. Draw the line that has a slope of $-\frac{2}{3}$ and passes through (5, 4).

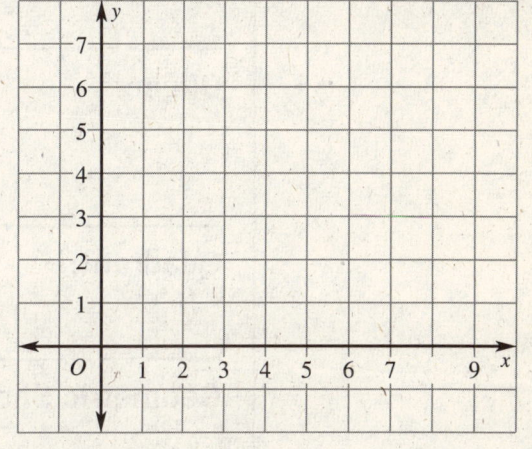

Additional Lesson E • **Math Course 1 Lesson Plan**   A13

ADDITIONAL LESSON F

Coordinate Geometry and Geometric Figures

Goal • Use coordinate geometry to draw and identify a geometric shape including determining a missing coordinate point.

Your Notes

VOCABULARY

Coordinate Plane:

Axes:

Ordered Pair:

Coordinates:

x coordinate:

y coordinate:

Origin:

Quadrant:

Geometric Shapes:

A14   Math Course 1 Lesson Plan • Additional Lesson F

Example 1   Use coordinate geometry to construct geometric shapes

Plot the given ordered pairs on graph paper. Then, connect them to form a geometric figure. Finally, identify what type of figure is formed.

a. $A(1, 3), B(4, 1), C(2, 0)$

The figure formed is a triangle.

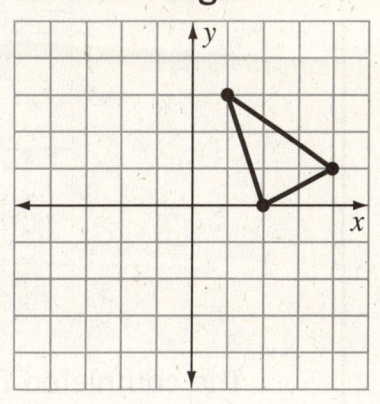

b. $A(-5, -1), B-5, -3), C(-2, -1), D(-2, -3)$

The figure formed is a rectangle.

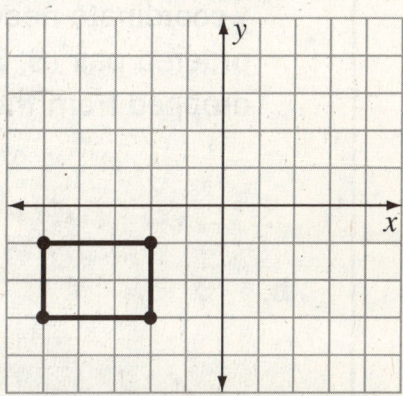

c. $A(-4, 3), B(-1, 4), C(3, 3), D(0, 2)$

The figure formed is a parallelogram.

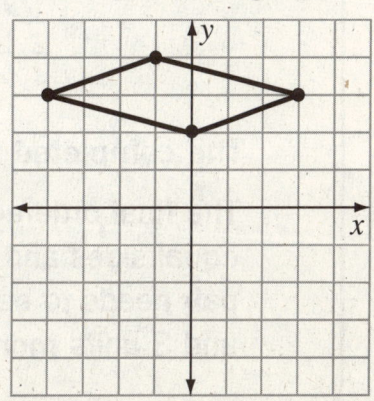

Additional Lesson F • **Math Course 1 Lesson Plan**   **A15**

Example 2 State the missing coordinate of a given geometric figure based on its properties

When complete, the graphs below will form geometric shapes. Determine the remaining coordinates of the figure based on its geometric type and then complete the drawing. Explain how you determined the final ordered pair.

a.

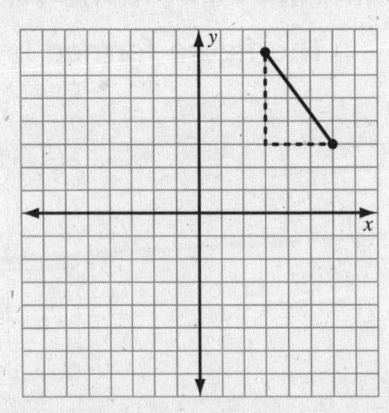

The completed figure will form a right triangle.

The final ordered pair is (3, 3). Because a right triangle must contain one right angle, the x-coordinate needs to be in line with the 3 from the ordered pair (3, 7) and the y-coordinate needs to be in line with the 3 from the ordered pair (6, 3). The intersection of the two lines dropped from the given ordered pairs meet at (3, 3).

b.

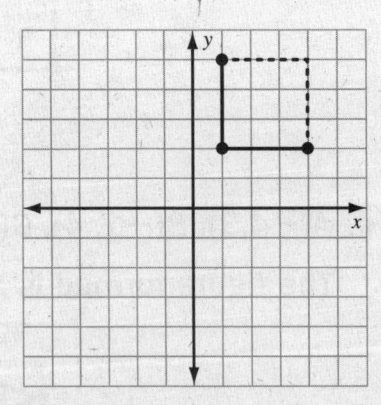

The completed figure will form a square.

The final ordered pair is (4, 5). Because a square has four equal sides and the opposite sides are parallel, the ordered pair needs to be in line with (4, 2) for the x-coordinate (4) and 3 units more for the y-coordinate (2 + 3).

Your Notes

✓ **Checkpoint** Complete the following exercises.

1. Plot the given ordered pairs on the graph paper. Connect them to form a geometric figure. Name the type of figure that has been formed.

   a. A(−2, 2), B(−6, 2), C(−6, 5), D(−2, 5)

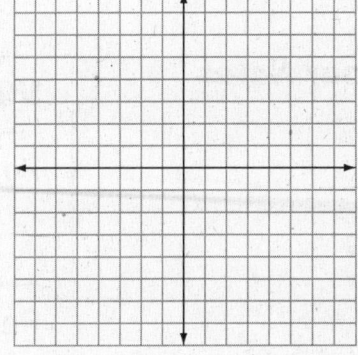

   b. A(−4, −3), B(−1, −6), C(−4, −6),

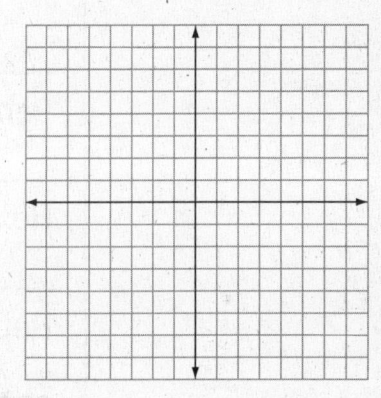

2. Based on the figure drawn, what would be the coordinates of point D? Explain how you determined your answer.

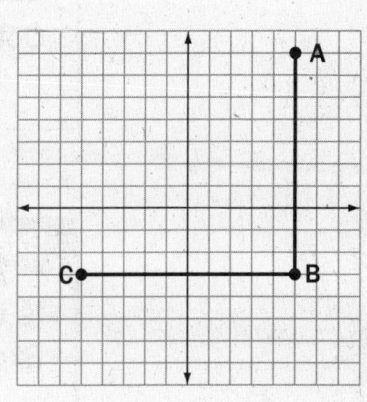

3. Determine what the new coordinates would be for a second rectangle, if you were to *fold* the graph on the *y*-axis. The new rectangle would be in the first quadrant.

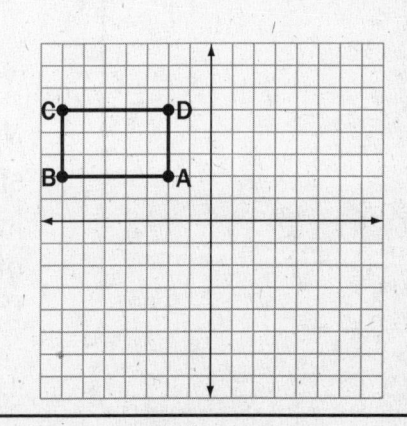

ADDITIONAL LESSON G

Polygons and Angles

Goal • Find angle measures in polygons.

Your Notes

VOCABULARY

Polygon:

Regular polygon:

Pentagon:

Hexagon:

Heptagon:

Octagon:

Example 1 — Identifying Figures

Is this figure a *polygon*, a *regular polygon*, or *not a polygon*? Explain.

a.

Not a polygon. The sides of the figure intersect at places other than just at the endpoints.

b.

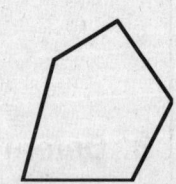

The figure is a polygon, but it is not regular. Its angles have different measures.

Example 2 — Angle Measures in a Polygon

Sum of angle measures in an *n*-gon: $(n - 2) \cdot 180°$

Measure of one angle in a regular *n*-gon: $\dfrac{(n - 2) \cdot 180°}{n}$

You can use *n*-gon, where *n* is the number of sides, to identify any polygon if you haven't learned it's name. A 13-gon is a 13-sided polygon.

Example 3 — Finding an Angle Measure

Find the measure of one angle in a regular hexagon.

A regular hexagon has 6 sides, so $n = 6$.

$\dfrac{(n - 2) \cdot 180°}{n} = \dfrac{(6 - 2) \cdot 180°}{6}$ Substitute.

$\qquad\qquad\quad = \dfrac{720°}{6}$ Simplify numerator.

$\qquad\qquad\quad = 120°$ Divide.

Answer: The measure of one angle in a regular hexagon is 120°.

Your Notes

✓ **Checkpoint** Complete the following exercises.

1. Find the sum of the angle measures in a heptagon.

2. Find the measure of one angle in a regular 12-gon.

ADDITIONAL LESSON H

Sketching Solids

Goal • Sketch solids.

Example 1 Sketching a Prism

Sketch a hexagonal prism.

1. Sketch two congruent hexagons.

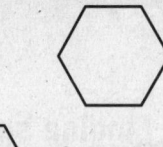

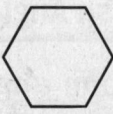

2. Connect the corresponding vertices using line segments.

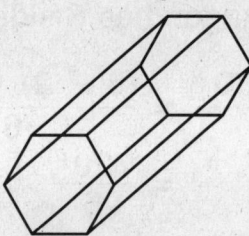

3. Make any "hidden" lines dashed.

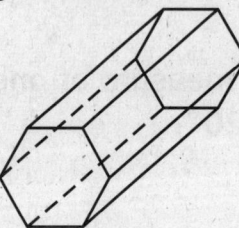

In Example 1, notice that six of the faces appear to be parallelograms even though they are actually rectangles. The parallelograms give the illusion of depth.

Your Notes

✓ **Checkpoint** Complete the following exercises.

Sketch the solid.

1. Rectangular prism

2. Pentagonal prism

A20 Math Course 1 Lesson Plan • Additional Lesson H

Example 2 — Sketching a Pyramid

Sketch a triangular pyramid.

1. Sketch a triangle for the base and draw a dot directly above the triangle.

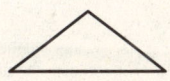

2. Connect the vertices of the triangle to the dot.

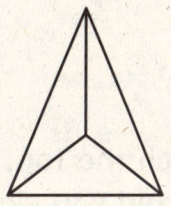

3. Make any "hidden" lines dashed.

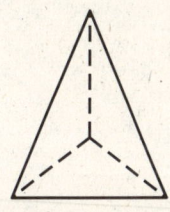

Example 3 — Sketching Three Views of a Solid

Sketch the top, side, and front views of the cylinder.

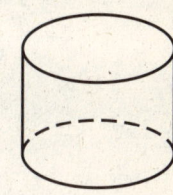

Solution

The top view of a cylinder is a circle.

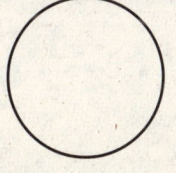

The side view of a cylinder is a rectangle.

The front view of a cylinder is a rectangle.

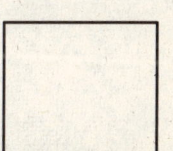

Additional Lesson H • **Math Course 1 Lesson Plan**

Your Notes

✓ **Checkpoint** Complete the following exercises.

3. Sketch a pentagonal pyramid.

4. Sketch the top, side, and front views of the pentagonal pyramid you sketched in Exercise 3.

ADDITIONAL LESSON I

Vertex-Edge Graphs, Circuits, Networks, and Routing

Goal • Apply the characteristics of vertex-edge graphs to circuits and networks. Include using subscripts to name the ordinal postion of a vertex.

Your Notes

VOCABULARY

Graph

Vertex

Edge

Adjacent Vertices

Adjacent Edges

Degree of a vertex

Path

Circuit

Ordinal

Subscript

Route

Network

Example 1 — Determine if a graph is a circuit by using the degree of each vertex

If a graph has any odd vertices, then it cannot be a circuit (starting and ending at the same point and traveling over each edge only once). If a graph has more than two odd vertices, then it cannot have a path.

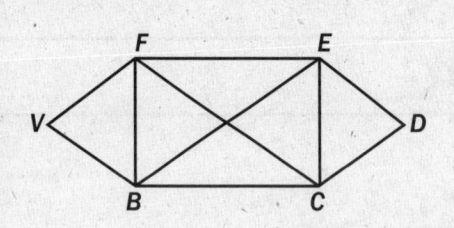

Degree of each vertex

A = 2
B = 4
C = 4
D = 2
E = 4
F = 4

Since all of the vertices are even, the figure can be traced starting at one vertex returning to the same vertex without tracing over one edge more than once.

Your Notes

✓ **Checkpoint** Complete the following exercises.

Find the degree of each vertex and determine if the graph is a circuit. Trace the graph and show that it forms a circuit or a path.

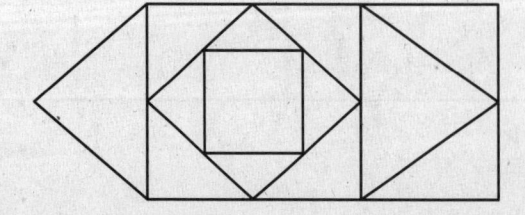

1.

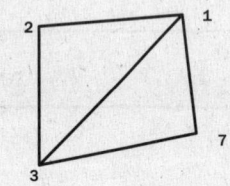

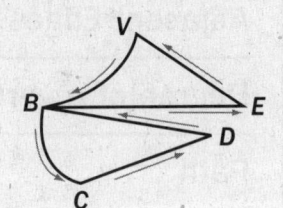

2. Place appropriate letters on this graph using subscript notation. Find the degree of each vertex and determine if the graph is a circuit. Trace the graph and show that it forms a circuit or a path.

A24 Math Course 1 Lesson Plan • Additional Lesson I

Example 2 — Determine if a network presents the best route basing the solution on the number of vertices and edges

The following network shows several cities and the paths connecting them. The vertices represent cities and the edges indicate nonstop airline routes between them.

Drawing 1

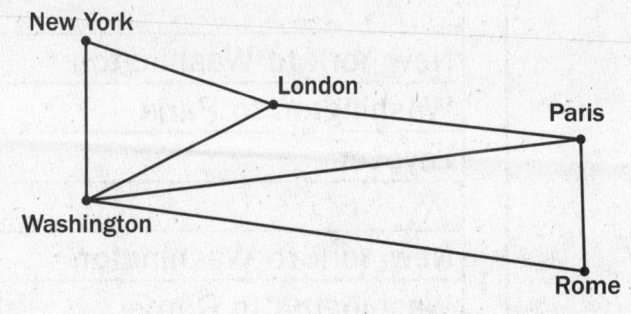

(Network with vertices: New York, London, Washington, Paris, Rome)

An alternate method is to mark the graph using subscripts.

Drawing 2

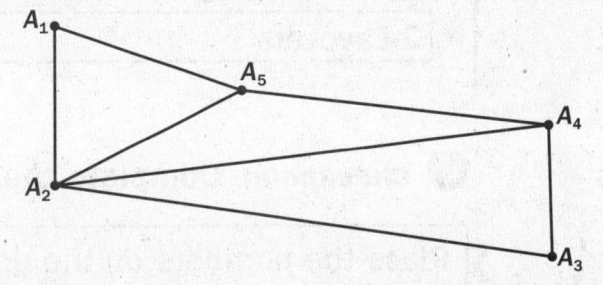

(Network with vertices: A_1, A_5, A_2, A_4, A_3)

Another alternate method is to mark the graph using the first letter of each city.

Drawing 3

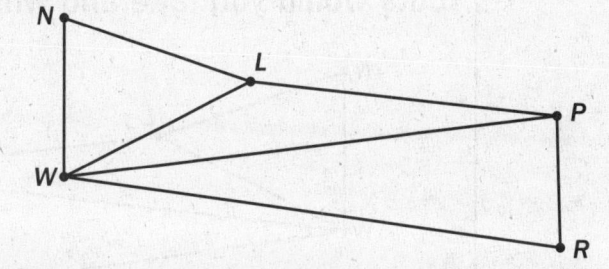

(Network with vertices: N, L, W, P, R)

According to this particular airlines network, there are direct flights between New York and London, between Washington and London, between Washington and Paris, and between Washington and Rome. There are no direct flights between New York and Paris and New York and Rome.

There are several paths that describe a trip from New York to Paris, using drawing 2; $A_1A_5A_4$, $A_1A_2A_4$, $A_1A_2A_5A_4$, and $A_1A_2A_3A_4$ or using drawing 3; NLP, NWP NWLP, and NWRP. The path that seems the most direct is NLP however, depending on cost, layover time and availability (see chart 1) one of the other paths may be a better choice. The consideration of these values determines a routing problem.

(continued)

Example 2 (continued)

Chart 1: The prices and times are listed below.

New York to London	$1414.00	6 hr. 50 min.
London to Paris	$147.00	1 hr. 15 min.
Layover		2 hr. 25 min.
New York to Washington	$142.00	1 hr. 15 min.
Washington to Paris	$1370.00	6 hr. 57 min.
Layover		2 hr. 47 min.
New York to Washington	$142.00	1 hr. 15 min.
Washington to Rome	$2321.00	11 hr. 20 min.
Rome to Paris	$393.00	2 hr. 10 min.
2 Layovers		4 hr. 25 min.

Your Notes

✓ **Checkpoint** Complete the following exercise.

Place the numbers on the graph and compare the different routes with respect to total cost and total time of each trip. Use the chart above for the total prices and time. Which route would you take and why?

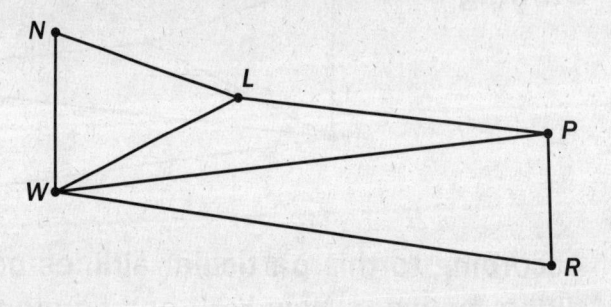

A26 Math Course 1 Lesson Plan • Additional Lesson I

ADDITIONAL LESSON J

Introduction to Recursive Functions for Sequences

Goal • Evaluate problems using basic recursive formulas.

Your Notes

VOCABULARY

Sequence

Recursive

Recursive formula

Term notation

Example 1 Write terms of sequences

a. Write the first 6 terms of the sequence 1, 4, 7, . . . where $t_n = t_{n-1} + 3$, that is, any term is determined by adding 3 to the previous term.

$t_4 = t_3 + 3$ $t_4 = 7 + 3 = 10$
$t_5 = t_4 + 3$ $t_5 = 10 + 3 = 13$
$t_6 = t_5 + 3$ $t_6 = 13 + 3 = 16$

Thus the first 6 terms are 1, 4, 7, 10, 13, 16

b. Write the first 5 terms of the sequence 1, 2, 5, . . . where $t_n = (t_{n-1})^2 + 1$, that is, 1 is added to the previous term squared.

$t_4 = (t_3)^2 + 1$ $t_4 = 5^2 + 1 = 25 + 1 = 26$
$t_5 = (t_4)^2 + 1$ $t_5 = 26^2 + 1 = 676 + 1 = 677$

Thus the first 5 terms are 1, 2, 5, 26, 677

Your Notes

✓ **Checkpoint** Complete the following exercises.

1. Write the first 6 terms of the sequence 1, 5, . . . where $t_n = t_{n-1} + 4$

2. The *Fibonacci numbers* are shown below. Use the Fibonacci numbers to answer the following questions.

   1, 1, 2, 3, 5, 8, 13, 21, 34, 55, 89 . . .

   a. Copy and complete: After the first two numbers, each number is the _____ of the _____ previous numbers.

   b. Write the next three numbers in the pattern.

Example 2 **Write a rule for the *n*th term of a sequence**

Find the *n*th term, that is, the formula or rule that is used to determine the next term in the sequence 1, 3, 7, 15, 31, 63 . . .

Examine each term. How do you get the second term from the first? How do you get the third term from the second? And so on.

$1 \times 2 + 1 = 3$

$3 \times 2 + 1 = 7$

$7 \times 2 + 1 = 15$

$15 \times 2 + 1 = 31$

$31 \times 2 + 1 = 63$

the previous term is multiplied by 2 and 1 is added to it.

The *n*th term $t_n = 2(t_{n-1}) + 1$

Your Notes

✓ **Checkpoint** Complete the following exercise.

1. Find the *n*th term, that is, the formula for determining the next term for the sequence 1, 6, 11, 16, 21, 26 . . .

ADDITIONAL LESSON K

Histograms

Goal • Make and interpret histograms.

Your Notes

VOCABULARY

Frequency table:

Frequency:

Histogram:

Example 1 — Making a Frequency Table

Auction The sellers on an Internet auction site tracked how many people viewed the auction each day. The data are listed below. Make a frequency table of the data.

15, 28, 36, 16, 18, 27, 40, 39, 25, 19, 36, 19, 42, 39, 27, 30, 49, 6, 27, 38, 0, 42, 37, 26, 17, 16, 25, 31, 29, 8, 10, 28, 34, 16, 9, 40, 32

Solution

1. Choose intervals of equal size that cover all the data values, which range from 0 to 49. In the table, each interval covers 10 whole numbers. The first interval is 0–9 and the last interval is 40–49.

2. Make a tally mark next to the interval containing a given number of viewers of the auction.

3. Write the frequency for each interval by totaling the number of tally marks for the interval.

Viewers	Tally	Frequency
0–9	IIII	4
10–19	JHT IIII	9
20–29	JHT IIII	9
30–39	JHT JHT	10
40–49	JHT	5

A30 Math Course 1 Lesson Plan • Additional Lesson K

Example 2 Making a Histogram

Phone Calls A business kept track of how many phone solicitors called them. The table shows the number of phone calls received each day. Make a histogram of the data.

Phone Calls	Tally	Frequency
0–4	||||| |||	8
5–9		0
10–14	||||| ||||| ||	12
15–19	||||| ||||| ||||| |||	18
20–24	||||| ||||	9

Solution

1. Draw and label the horizontal and vertical axes. List each interval from the frequency table on the horizontal axis. The greatest frequency is 18. So, start the vertical axis at 0 and end it at 20, using increments of 2.

2. Draw a bar for each interval. The bars should have the same width.

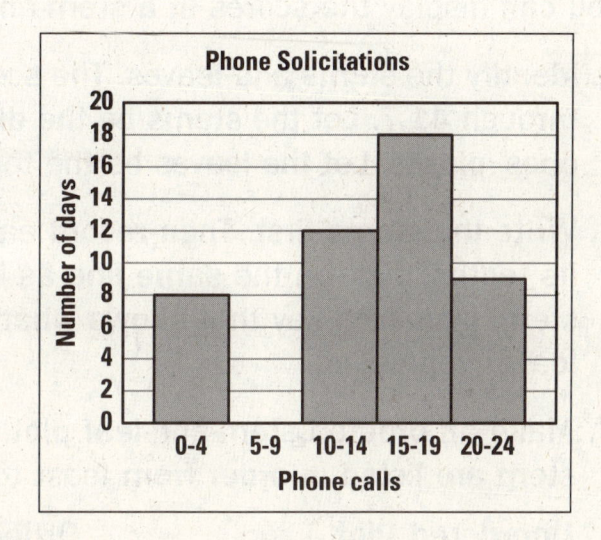

Phone Solicitations

(histogram: Number of days vs Phone calls; 0–4: 8, 5–9: 0, 10–14: 12, 15–19: 18, 20–24: 9)

Include horizontal grid lines.

Bars that are next to each other should not have a gap between them.

Make sure that your histogram includes all of the intervals in the table, even the intervals that have a frequency of 0.

ADDITIONAL LESSON L

Stem-and-Leaf Plots

Goal • Make and interpret stem-and-leaf plots.

Your Notes

VOCABULARY

Stem-and-leaf plot:

Example 1 — Making a Stem-and-Leaf Plot

Snowboarding The scores of the top 15 finishers of a snowboard half pipe competition are shown below. How can the data be displayed to show the distribution of the scores?

38.4, 40.6, 37.8, 38.9, 41.7, 39.2, 37.1, 41.4
40.5, 38.8, 40.9, 39.3, 41.2, 38.3, 37.1

Solution

You can display the scores in a stem-and-leaf plot.

1. Identify the stems and leaves. The scores range from 37.1 through 41.7. Let the stems be the digits in the tens' and ones' places. Let the leaves be the tenths' digits.

2. Write the stems first. Then record each score by writing its tenths' digit on the same line as its corresponding stem. Include a key that shows what the stems and leaves represent.

3. Make an ordered stem-and-leaf plot. The leaves for each stem are listed in order from least to greatest.

Unordered Plot

37	8 1 1
38	4 9 8 3
39	2 3
40	6 5 9
41	7 4 2

Key: 38 | 4 = 38.4

Ordered Plot

37	1 1 8
38	3 4 8 9
39	2 3
40	5 6 9
41	2 4 7

Key: 38 | 4 = 38.4

Your Notes

✓ **Checkpoint** Complete the following exercise.

> Make an ordered stem-and-leaf plot of the data.
>
> 1. Baseball pitch speeds (mi/h): 86, 83, 74, 95, 89, 97, 68, 88, 72, 97, 94, 85, 70, 89, 80, 93, 91, 84

Example 2 Interpreting a Stem-and-Leaf Plot

In a stem-and-leaf plot, a stem can be one or more digits. A leaf is usually a single digit.

Movies The stem-and-leaf plot below shows the ages of people in a movie theater. Use the stem-and-leaf plot to describe the data. What interval includes the most ages?

```
0 | 5 6 7 7 8 8 8 9 9
1 | 0 0 0 1 1 2 2 2 3 3 4 5 6
2 | 0 2 8 9
3 | 3 7
4 | 8
5 | 1
```
Key: 2 | 0 = 20

Solution

The oldest person is 51 years old and the youngest person is 5 years old. So the range of ages is 46 years. Most of the ages are in the 10–19 interval.

Example 3   **Making a Double Stem-and-Leaf Plot**

Swimming The data below show the number of laps swum during practice by swimmers on two different swim teams. Overall, which team swam more laps?

    Dolphins: 19, 25, 31, 26, 17, 25, 26, 18, 23, 19, 25, 24

    Sharks: 18, 25, 9, 15, 30, 24, 17, 18, 22, 16, 28, 19

Solution

You can use a double stem-and-leaf plot to compare the number of laps swum.

Dolphins		Sharks
	0	9
9 9 8 7	1	5 6 7 8 8 9
6 6 5 5 5 4 3	2	2 4 5 8
1	3	0

Key: 1 | 3 | 0 represents 31 and 30.

Answer: The dolphins swim team swam more laps because it had more swimmers swim a number of laps in the twenties.

Your Notes

✓ **Checkpoint** Complete the following exercise.

2. Make an ordered double stem-and-leaf plot to compare the times, in minutes, that two friends spent online in the last week.

    Omar: 35, 26, 30, 48, 55, 13, 38
    Joseph: 46, 15, 68, 0, 44, 49, 32

3. In general, who spent the most time online in the last week, Omar or Joseph?

ADDITIONAL LESSON M

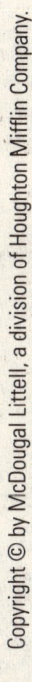

Misleading Data Displays

Goal • Determine if the data displayed is giving a misleading impression.

Your Notes

VOCABULARY
Data
Display
Scale
Interval
Range
Misleading Displays

Additional Lesson M • Math Course 1 Lesson Plan

Example 1 — Analyze a graph to determine how an incorrect conclusion may be drawn

The graph on the left displays the number of calories burned walking **down** a set of stairs while the graph on the right displays the number of calories burned walking **up** a set of stairs.

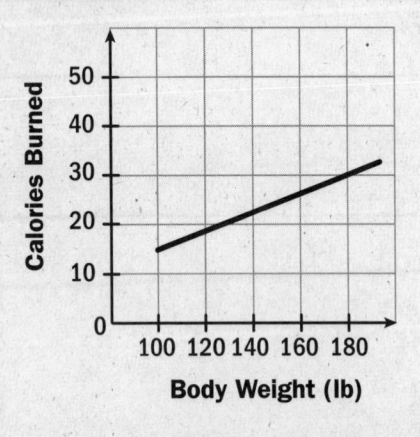

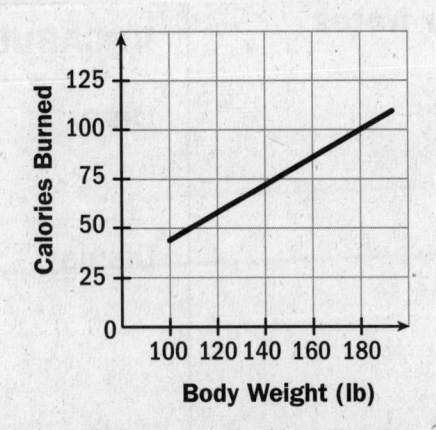

The two graphs appear to be very similar therefore implying that walking up or down the stairs burn the same amount of calories. This is an incorrect conclusion since the scales on the vertical axis are different. The choice of interval affects the slope of the lines.

Example 2 — Analyze a set of data to determine if the display is appropriate

The following data indicates the number of families with zero, one, two, or three pets.

From the display, the number having zero, one, two or three pets is difficult to determine. The upper level on the scale used for the vertical axis is too large and the size of the intervals is also too large to make an accurate estimate.

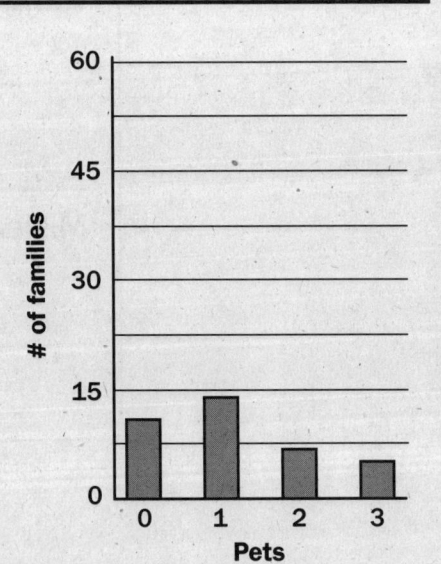

Your Notes

✓ **Checkpoint** Complete the following exercises.

1. The table and the circle graph show the same data about student participation in a school district's sports program. Explain how the graph could be misleading.

Grade Level	Participation
–	440 students
9	172 students
10	412 students
11	433 students
12	444 students

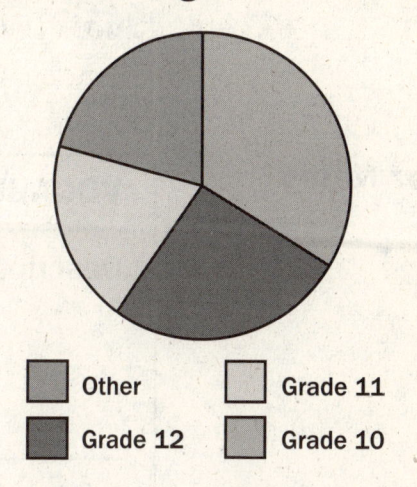

Other Grade 11
Grade 12 Grade 10

2. The scores of a student's last 10 math tests are given below. Explain how the display could be misleading.

Test Scores: 90, 62, 65, 75, 83, 80, 61, 82, 85, 68

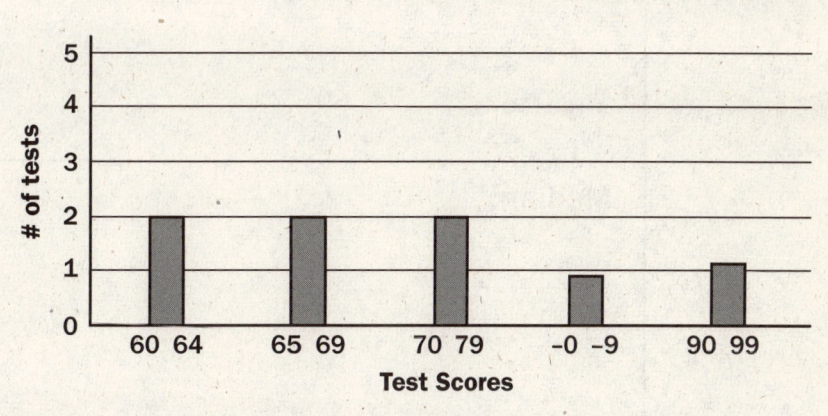

# of tests vs. Test Scores

Range	# of tests
60–64	2
65–69	2
70–79	2
–0 – –9	1
90–99	1

Additional Lesson M • **Math Course 1 Lesson Plan**

ADDITIONAL LESSON N

Designing and Conducting an Investigation

Goal • Use statistical methods to analyze and communicate data.

Your Notes

VOCABULARY

Descriptive Statistics:

Inferential Statistics:

Sample:

Mean:

Median:

continued

VOCABULARY *continued*

Mode:

Standard Deviation:

Formula for Standard Deviation:

Example 1 — Analyze data to determine how an incorrect conclusion may be drawn

In a particular factory, two machines package popcorn kernels into 1.25-pound containers. To test the packaging process, a quality control worker weighs a random sample of 20 containers from each machine. Find the mean, median, and mode. Use the results to make conclusions about the machines. The weight of the 20 containers from the two machines is listed below.

Container #	Machine #1	Machine #2
1	1.250	1.254
2	1.252	1.245
3	1.248	1.253
4	1.252	1.250
5	1.251	1.261
6	1.256	1.253
7	1.253	1.254
8	1.248	1.244
9	1.246	1.250
10	1.257	1.252
11	1.250	1.260
12	1.251	1.257
13	1.250	1.248
14	1.255	1.242
15	1.251	1.253
16	1.253	1.243
17	1.249	1.260
18	1.249	1.248
19	1.245	1.251
20	1.251	1.259
Mean	1.25085	1.25185
Median	1.251	1.2525
Mode	1.251 (4 times)	1.253 (3 times)
Standard Deviation	.00304	.00575

The means are almost equal, therefore no conclusion can be drawn from that data. However, the standard deviation of machine #1 (.00304) is less then the standard deviation of machine #2 (.00575). Machine #1 has less variability and will produce closer to the desired weight more often than machine #2.

Your Notes

✓ **Checkpoint** Complete the following exercise.

Design your own survey of interest to you or use the following data.

Mr. Smith commutes to Chicago daily. There are two possible routes, Hwy 90 or Hwy 290. One route is a diagonal line and the other is "L" shaped, however, both routes start at the same point in the suburbs and ends at the same point in Chicago. One week he traveled Hwy 90 and the other Hwy 290. The times for the trips are listed below. Determine the mean, median, mode, and standard deviation to determine the route that is more consistent.

Minutes per trip

	M	T	W	Th	F
Route 290	40	56	76	42	53
Route 90	54	45	64	53	51

Additional Lesson N • Math Course 1 Lesson Plan

ADDITIONAL LESSON 0

Experimental vs. Observational Study

Goal • Differentiate between an experiment and an observational study.

Your Notes

VOCABULARY

Descriptive Statistics:

Inferential Statistics:

Population:

Sample:

    a) Simple Random:

    b) Systematic:

    c) Stratified:

    d) Convenience:

    e) Self-Selected:

continued

VOCABULARY continued

Biased Sample:

    a) Underrepresented:

    b) Overrepresented:

Parameter:

Statistic:

Example 1 — Classifying samples and determining if the sample is biased

1. The officials of the National Football League (NFL) want to know how the players feel about some proposed changes to the NFL rules. They decide to ask a sample of about 100 players. Classify the sample.

   a. The official choose the first 100 players that volunteer their opinions.

   Self-selected

   b. The officials randomly choose 3 players from each of the 32 teams in the NFL.

   Stratified

   c. The officials have a computer generate a list of 100 players from a database that includes all of the players in the NFL.

   Simple Random

continued

Example 1 (continued)

2. Administrators at your school want to know if more vegetarian items should be added to the lunch menu. Decide whether the sampling method could result in a biased sample. Explain your reasoning.

   a. Survey every 10th student waiting in line to purchase lunch.

   This method could result in a biased sample because it underrepresents the students who do not purchase lunch. Some of these students may not purchase lunch because there are not enough vegetarian items on the lunch menu.

   b. Survey every 25th student who enters the cafeteria during the lunch period.

   This method is not likely to result in a biased sample because a wide range of students will be surveyed.

Your Notes

✓ **Checkpoint** Complete the following exercises.

Identify the population and the sample.

1. A quality control inspector needs to estimate the number of defective computers in a group of 250 computers. He tests 25 randomly chosen computers.

2. The manager of the human resources department at a company wants to know if any of the company's 281 employees would take advantage of a reduced membership to a health club. The manager asks a sample of 70 randomly chosen employees.

continued

Checkpoint continued

In Exercises 3–5, classify the sample related to the following situation.

The principal of a school wants to know if the students at the school would like to have the morning announcements posted on the school's Web site.

3. Survey the first 30 students who enter the cafeteria during the lunch period.

4. Survey every 10th female student and every 10th male student who enters the cafeteria during the lunch period.

5. Survey every 20th student who enters the cafeteria during the lunch period.

In Exercises 6–8, classify the sample.

6. The manager of a movie theater wants to know how the movie viewers feel about the new stadium seating at the theater. She asks every 30th person who exits the theater each Saturday night for a month.

7. The manager of a credit union wants to know whether its members utilize the on-line services offered on their Web site. He decided to call members who have been randomly chosen from a database of all of the members of the credit union.

continued

✓ Checkpoint continued

8. The owner of a bakery wants to know if its customers are satisfied with its selection of baked goods. She asks the first 20 people who make a purchase on a Saturday morning.

Decide whether the sampling method could result in a biased sample. Explain your reasoning.

9. On the first day of school, all of the incoming freshmen attend an orientation program. The principal wants to learn the opinions of the freshmen regarding the orientation program. He decides to ask the first 25 freshmen that he sees.

10. The manager of an apartment building wants to know if the residents are satisfied with his service. He writes each apartment number on a piece of paper and places the pieces of paper in a hat. Then he randomly chooses 10 apartment numbers. He decides to ask the residents of the 10 apartments about his service.

11. The members of the school drama club want to know how much students are willing to pay for a ticket to one of their productions. They decide that each member of the drama club should ask 5 of his or her friends what they are willing to pay.

ADDITIONAL LESSON P

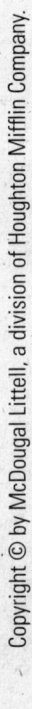

Inductive and Deductive Reasoning

Goal • Solve simple logic problems using inductive and deductive reasoning.

Your Notes

> **VOCABULARY**
>
> Inductive reasoning:
>
> Deductive reasoning:
>
> Law of Detachment:
>
> Law of Syllogism:

Example 1 Use the Law of Detachment

Use the Law of Detachment to make a valid conclusion in the true situation

If two angles have the same measure, then they are congruent. You know that $m\angle A = m\angle B$.

Solution

First, identify the hypothesis and the conclusion of the first statement. The hypothesis is "If two angles have the same measure." The conclusion is "then they are congruent."

Because $m\angle A = m\angle B$ satisfies the hypothesis of a true conditional statement, the conclusion is also true. So, $m\angle A \cong m\angle B$.

Additional Lesson P • Math Course 1 Lesson Plan   A47

Example 2   **Use the Law of Syllogism**

If possible, use the Law of Syllogism to write the conditional statement that follows from the pair of true statements.

a. If the electric power is off, then the refrigerator does not run.
   If the refrigerator does not run, then the food will spoil.

b. If $2x > 10$, then $2x > 7$.
   If $x > 5$, then $2x > 10$.

Solution

a. The conclusion of the first statement is the hypothesis of the second statement, so you can write the following statement.
   If the electric power is off, then the food will spoil.

b. Notice that the conclusion of the second statement is the hypothesis of the first statement.
   If $x > 5$, then $2x > 7$.

Your Notes

✓ **Checkpoint** Complete the following exercises for Examples 1 and 2.

1. If $\angle A$ is acute, then $0° < m\angle A < 90°$. Angle B is an acute angle. Using the Law of Detachment, what conclusion can you make?

2. If B is between A and C, then $AB + BC = AC$. E is between D and F. Using the Law of Detachment, what conclusion can you make?

3. If you study hard, you will pass all of your classes. If you pass all of your classes, you will graduate. Using the Law of Syllogism, what statement can you make?

4. If $x^2 > 9$, then $x^2 > 8$. If $x > 4$, then $x^2 > 9$. Using the Law of Syllogism, what statement can you make?

Example 3   **Use inductive and deductive reasoning**

What conclusion can you make about the sum of two even integers?

Solution

Step 1 Look for a pattern in several examples. Use inductive reasoning to make a conjecture.

$-2 + 4 = 2, -4 + 10 = 6, 6 + 8 = 14, 12 + 6 = 18, -20 + 14 = -6, -12 + 2 = -10, -6 + 2 = -4, -2 + (-6) = -8$

Conjecture: Even integer + Even integer = Even integer

Step 2 Let n and m be any integer. Use deductive reasoning to show the conjecture is true.

$2n$ and $2m$ are even integers because any integer multiplied by 2 is even.

$2n + 2m$ represents the sum of two even integers.

$2n + 2m$ can be written as $2(n + m)$.

The sum of two integers ($n + m$) is an integer and any integer multiplied by 2 is even.

The sum of two even integers is an even integer

Your Notes

✓ **Checkpoint** Complete the following exercise for Example 3.

5. What conclusion can you make about the sum of two odd integers? (Hint: An odd integer can be written as $2n + 1$, where n is any integer.)